Rethinking Nathaniel Hawthorne and Nature

Ecocritical Theory and Practice
Series Editor: Douglas A. Vakoch, METI

Advisory Board:
Sinan Akilli, Cappadocia University, Turkey; Bruce Allen, Seisen University, Japan; Zélia Bora, Federal University of Paraíba, Brazil; Izabel Brandão, Federal University of Alagoas, Brazil; Byron Caminero-Santangelo, University of Kansas, USA; Chia-ju Chang, Brooklyn College, The City College of New York, USA; H. Louise Davis, Miami University, USA; Simão Farias Almeida, Federal University of Roraima, Brazil; George Handley, Brigham Young University, USA; Steven Hartman, Mälardalen University, Sweden; Isabel Hoving, Leiden University, The Netherlands; Idom Thomas Inyabri, University of Calabar, Nigeria; Serenella Iovino, University of Turin, Italy; Daniela Kato, Kyoto Institute of Technology, Japan; Petr Kopecký, University of Ostrava, Czech Republic; Bei Liu, Shandong Normal University, People's Republic of China; Serpil Oppermann, Cappadocia University, Turkey; John Ryan, University of New England, Australia; Christian Schmitt-Kilb, University of Rostock, Germany; Joshua Schuster, Western University, Canada; Heike Schwarz, University of Augsburg, Germany; Murali Sivaramakrishnan, Pondicherry University, India; Scott Slovic, University of Idaho, USA; Heather Sullivan, Trinity University, USA; David Taylor, Stony Brook University, USA; J. Etienne Terblanche, North-West University, South Africa; Julia Tofantšuk, Tallinn University, Estonia; Cheng Xiangzhan, Shandong University, China; Hubert Zapf, University of Augsburg, Germany

Ecocritical Theory and Practice highlights innovative scholarship at the interface of literary/cultural studies and the environment, seeking to foster an ongoing dialogue between academics and environmental activists.

Recent Titles
Rethinking Nathaniel Hawthorne and Nature: Pastoral Experiments and Environmentality by Steven Petersheim
Ecocritical Concerns and the Australian Continent edited by Beate Neumeier and Helen Tiffin
The Poetics and Politics of Gardening in Hard Times edited by Naomi Milthorpe
Masculinity and Place in American Literature since 1950 by Vidya Ravi
The Way the Earth Writes: How the Great East Japan Earthquake Intervened in Conventional Literary Practice and Produced the Post 3.11 Novels by Koichi Haga
Ecomasculinities: Negotiating Male Gender Identity in U.S. Fiction by Rubén Cenamor and Stefan Brandt
Ecopoetics and the Global Landscape: Critical Essays by Isabel Sobral Campos
The Human-Animal Boundary: Exploring the Line in Philosophy and Fiction edited by Mario Wenning and Nandita Batra
Towards the River's Mouth (Verso la foce), Gianni Celati, A Critical Edition edited, translated, and introduced by Patrick Barron
Gender and Environment in Science Fiction edited by Bridgitte Barclay and Christy Tidwell
Ecological Crisis and Cultural Representation in Latin America: Ecocritical Perspectives on Art, Film, and Literature edited by Mark Anderson and Zélia M. Bora
Confronting Climate Crises through Education: Reading Our Way Forward by Rebecca Young
Environment and Pedagogy in Higher Education edited by Lucie Viakinnou-Brinson

Rethinking Nathaniel Hawthorne and Nature

Pastoral Experiments and Environmentality

Steven Petersheim

LEXINGTON BOOKS
Lanham • Boulder • New York • London

Published by Lexington Books
An imprint of The Rowman & Littlefield Publishing Group, Inc.
4501 Forbes Boulevard, Suite 200, Lanham, Maryland 20706
www.rowman.com

6 Tinworth Street, London SE11 5AL, United Kingdom

Copyright © 2020 by The Rowman & Littlefield Publishing Group, Inc.

All rights reserved. No part of this book may be reproduced in any form or by any electronic or mechanical means, including information storage and retrieval systems, without written permission from the publisher, except by a reviewer who may quote passages in a review.

British Library Cataloguing in Publication Information Available

Library of Congress Control Number: 2019956800

ISBN 978-1-4985-8117-2 (cloth)
ISBN 978-1-4985-8119-6 (pbk.)
ISBN 978-1-4985-8118-9 (electronic)

Contents

Acknowledgments		vii
Introduction: The Nature of Hawthorne's Pastoral Romances		ix
1	Investigating Hawthorne's Nonfiction Nature Writing	1
2	Observing the Laboratory of Nature in Hawthorne's Short Fiction	17
3	Reading Nature and the Human Body in *The Scarlet Letter*	45
4	Mapping Blood and Biology in *The House of the Seven Gables*	83
5	*Et in Arcadia Ego*: Adaptation and Natural Limits in *The Blithedale Romance*	119
6	Exploring the Ruins of the Human Animal in *The Marble Faun*	149
7	Postscript: Hawthorne's Unfinished Romances	177
Bibliography		185
Index		195
About the Author		209

Acknowledgments

I am grateful for all those who helped me through the various stages of progress on this book over the years. My colleagues and students at Indiana University East have consistently supported and encouraged me in this project. My department chair Margaret Thomas Evans deserves special recognition for her strong support of my research, providing the means to present portions of this book at conferences from the American Literature Association Conference in Boston to MLA conferences in Austin and Salt Lake City. The Faculty Research Support Fund at Indiana University East also provided me with the time and resources to complete the current form of this work. The outstanding work ethic and research sleuthing, not to mention editing skills, of my research assistant Caleb Warner have been invaluable resources to me as well during the later phase of this project.

I would also like to thank Hawthorne scholars, Americanists, and ecocritics who have supported the idea of this project along the way. Two scholars of environmental literature, Christoph Irmscher and Tom Hillard, expressed support for my project of connecting ecocriticism with the figure of Nathaniel Hawthorne. Monika Elbert and Richard Kopley, past presidents of the Nathaniel Hawthorne Society, also heard and read some of my ideas and offered helpful suggestions along the way. The roots of this project, however, go back to my time as a graduate student at Baylor University, where two generous Americanists—Joe Fulton and Sarah Gilbreath Ford—gave me excellent advice on an early version of these ideas in my dissertation. And I still treasure the camaraderie of fellow graduate students Jeffrey Bilbro and Bethany (Bear) Hebbard as they gave their invaluable feedback on early drafts in the quiet beauty of the balcony in the Bill Daniel Student Center. It was during this time that Jeff persuaded me to give Wendell Berry a closer read and Bethany introduced me to the delights of George McDonald's fantasy writing.

My deepest thanks, however, goes to my greatest supporter and encourager, my wife Elizabeth. She never flinched in her constant support and belief in me and my work, and I would not have been able to complete it without her help. Each of our four children has also been told tales of Hawthorne and his children, and Hawthorne's *Wonder Book for Girls and Boys* sits in a prominent place on the bookshelf in our home.

The librarians at the Phillips Library in Salem also contributed to this work, pulling numerous treasures from their archives to help me investigate Hawthorne's work and sources more thoroughly. Lastly, I'd like to thank Doug Vakoch, the series editor of the Ecocritical Theory and Practice series at Lexington Books, for his strong commitment to this project. And thanks to Lindsey Porambo Falk, Michael Gibson, Mikayla Mislak, and other editorial staff for working with me through the peer review process and manuscript preparation process. You have all been immensely helpful, and I am grateful!

Introduction
The Nature of Hawthorne's Pastoral Romances

Nathaniel Hawthorne is not usually counted among the nature writers of nineteenth-century America. American nature writers of this era generally follow a well-worn path, one along which Hawthorne is rarely mentioned unless as a deviation from the many around him who investigated questions of humans and nature afresh in the nineteenth century. Transcendentalist naturalists such as Henry David Thoreau might be found seeking out the secrets of the universe in the shape of a leaf, the growth of his beans, or observations of animal habitats and activities. Margaret Fuller could be found traipsing around the country in places as varied as the woods of Brook Farm and the lecture halls of Boston, discovering rhythms of nature that substantiated her feminist message. And, of course, the chief Transcendentalist guru Ralph Waldo Emerson was gaining followers with nature for his tutor as he spun out philosophical essays that encouraged the reformist direction of world shakers like himself.

Outside of the Transcendentalist community, renowned poets such as William Cullen Bryant and Henry Wadsworth Longfellow exulted in nature—the forest as "God's first temples" and the prairies as "the gardens of the Desert" or nature itself as our "fond mother."[1] Today we also remember famous women poets, conveniently forgotten for a century or more, who contributed much to this celebratory and investigatory attitude toward the natural world. A prime example can be found in Lydia Huntley Sigourney, whose poems celebrate the forests and mountains, "Ontario's billow" and "strong Niagara's thunders," and the "everlasting rivers" and the "ancient caves" of the North American continent.[2] And in Lydia Maria Child, whom Carolyn Karcher boldly hails as "First Woman in the Republic," we find a woman writer who defies patriarchal assumptions to posit that intermarriage between Europeans and Native Americans could produce and "exemplify the harmony with nature" that Europeans could have experienced.³ But unlike these and many other writers around him, Hawthorne stayed cooped up at a writing desk in his mother's attic pondering the dark secrets of the human heart. At least, so goes the myth of Hawthorne.

Like so many other myths, the notion of Hawthorne as a romantic genius developed in isolation from the world around him is based more on fable than on fact. Hawthorne's notebooks, letters, and travel sketches, along with numerous accounts of his friends and associates, reveal a writer in tune with his surroundings. Now that these letters and notebooks are readily available, Hawthorne scholars and nineteenth-century literary scholars in general have increasingly understood the image of a removed Hawthorne as a fictitious legend rather than an accurate representation. It bears mentioning that Hawthorne himself contributes to this romantic image of himself as a secluded author. In her consideration of the myths surrounding Hawthorne, Millicent Bell reveals that he was not an "owl" of the night, as he described himself to fellow writer Henry Wadsworth Longfellow, but was instead "a habitual daytime stroller about town and in the countryside, and he had regularly passed summer weeks in the deliberate exploration of New England, visiting rural communities, recording assiduously his encounters and observations."⁴ In her collection of essays titled *Hawthorne and the Real*, Bell is joined by other scholars of nineteenth-century American literature who likewise demonstrate Hawthorne's engagement with the world around himself.

Despite this recent critical attention to Hawthorne's actual lived experiences, the long tradition of viewing Hawthorne as an isolated romantic author whose brooding personality led him to obsess constantly and exclusively over the dark secrets of the human heart is not easily undone. As Edwin Haviland Miller has noted, biographers have routinely been fascinated with Hawthorne's claims to seclusion, but Miller himself takes for granted the veracity of Hawthorne's facetious account of "his lonely meditations and self-imposed isolation."⁵ Recent biographers have typically been more knowledgeable about Hawthorne's engagement with his social environment, but what casual readers of Hawthorne often think they know about him suggests that this older image of Hawthorne persists in the popular mind despite being repeatedly discounted by scholars such as Millicent Bell.

Most readers are not accustomed to thinking of Nathaniel Hawthorne as a nature writer in any sense. It is often assumed that Hawthorne was indifferent or even averse to the natural environment around him. Even before Frederick Crews popularized Hawthorne's dark "psychological themes" as a sign of his obsession with "the sins of the fathers" that overrode any other considerations in Hawthorne's writing, any depictions of nature in Hawthorne's writing had come to be read as little more than background material for his scenes of human drama.⁶ In *American Renaissance* (1941), F.O. Matthiessen posited

Hawthorne's love of solitude and seclusion as *the* defining characteristic of his writing processes and then proceeded to declare that nature was not very useful to such a mind: "[Hawthorne] did not share Thoreau's unswerving confidence that man could find himself by studying nature; indeed, in no respect is his difference from all the transcendental writers more fundamental than in this. Hawthorne visited nature in order to return, refreshed, to the world of men."[7] Matthiessen's text received widespread attention as a tour de force of New Criticism during its heyday, with Hawthorne as a prime example.

Similarly, Richard Brodhead received little challenge four decades later when he expanded on this conception of Hawthorne with the declaration that "Hawthorne is *not* a nature author but the diviner, behind appearances, of the hidden guilt Calvinism called 'Innate Depravity.'"[8] Brodhead's claim was made at a time when it was still largely presumed that writings that explore the psyche are by definition uninterested in really exploring anything outside of the human mind. Hawthorne does indeed have a strong fascination with the darker side of nature, and he has often been excluded from the study of literature and the environment for just that reason. There is growing attention, however, to the ways that darker views of nature illustrate the complexity of nature in a way that more idealized views tend to misrepresent. Eric Wilson, for example, considers the ecocritical implications of darker visions of nature in the nineteenth century. But like those before him, Wilson mentions Hawthorne only to dismiss him with a brief statement that relies upon old stereotypes: "Though Hawthorne is an astute critic of the excesses of modern science, he remains much more interested in the human heart—primarily its Calvinistic struggles with sin—than in relationships between humans and nature."[9] Wilson is by no means alone in his dismissal.

Hawthorne was not always presumed, however, to be uninterested in the natural environment. While Herman Melville was perhaps first to lay out Hawthorne's obsession with conceptions of human sin that stem from "appeals to that Calvinistic sense of Innate Depravity and Original Sin," Melville also characterizes Hawthorne directly as a writer whose work joins that of other "painters of Nature."[10] For Melville, Hawthorne's texts are not about either sin *or* nature but about both sin *and* nature. Similarly Transcendentalist and feminist Margaret Fuller, in her review of Hawthorne's second collection of short stories, pointedly praises Hawthorne for maintaining "[t]he same gentle and sincere companionship with nature" that she identifies as a hallmark of his earlier collection.[11]

Since Hawthorne's contemporaries associated him with the nature writers, we ought at least to consider the possibility. Such consideration is particularly important today in an age of growing environmental crisis when any insight into the relationship between humans and nature may help us make healthier and more responsible choices as inhabitants of the earth and its ecosystems.

In Lawrence Buell's groundbreaking work of environmental criticism, *The Environmental Imagination*, Thoreau is characterized an early icon of environmental consciousness and his writings "as a barometer of the pulsations, limitations, and promise of green thinking in America."[12] Indeed Thoreau has become the major nineteenth-century American figure with whom environmental literature is most strongly associated. And in Thoreau's friend Nathaniel Hawthorne we find an exemplar of nineteenth-century fiction that deliberately explores the relationship between humans and nature.

While countless critics have examined Hawthorne's use of allegory, surprisingly few have more than incidentally considered how nature and allegory work together in Hawthorne's writing. F.O. Matthiessen does so, of course, in his consideration of Spenser's influence on Hawthorne, noting that Hawthorne mixes allegory and pastoral in much the same way that Spenser does. Yvor Winters' essay on Hawthorne in a collection of essays titled *In Defense of Reason* and Michael Colacurcio's *The Province of Piety* advance almost contradictory accounts of Hawthorne's use of allegory, with Winters assuming a mechanical use (much as Matthiessen does) and Colacurcio carefully analyzing literary elements of Hawthorne's tales that artfully complicate initial assumptions about how allegorical tellings engage with one's world. Their accounts diverge so sharply that the only thing they seem to share is the verdict that Hawthorne did indeed use some form of allegory in his treatment of the natural world.

Literary scholars who *have* noted Hawthorne's treatment of the natural world are by no means united in their observations of the import of his work. Melissa Pennell, for example, simply adopts the common assumption that Hawthorne shares his darkest Puritan characters' deep suspicions of the natural world. Hawthorne scholar Nina Baym, however, offers a more incisive analysis of his treatment of nature, noting that the forest and the town in *The Scarlet Letter* are both good and evil rather than being simplistically aligned in a strict one-on-one relationship.[13] To date Darrell Abel's *The Moral Picturesque* remains probably the most thorough study of Hawthorne's treatment of nature. Abel pays close attention to the mixed threads of Puritan and Transcendentalist thought in Hawthorne's treatment of nature and concludes that Hawthorne draws out of those variant strains of thought their shared belief that nature "bear[s] the ambiguous imprints of its divine origin."[14] David Van Leer similarly traces how the main characters in *The Scarlet Letter* "all evince both Puritan and Transcendentalist traits."[15] Despite divergent viewpoints on Hawthorne's conceptions of nature, most scholars are in agreement that Hawthorne did weave together a variety of philosophical attitudes toward nature in his writing.

In her study of Hawthorne's attention to human and animal species while in Europe, Jennifer Mason traces Hawthorne's interest in animals as companion species. She also addresses a key concern of mine: "our long history of treating Hawthorne as an odd man out among a group of writers passionately interested in the nonhuman world—that is, as the only one of the great architects of the American Renaissance that held the rearguard and not the vanguard of American thinking about nature."[16] The time is now ripe for exploring the ecological concerns of Hawthorne's fiction and nonfiction alike. Indeed, my turn to Hawthorne's writing about nature represents a response to Lawrence Buell's call in *The Future of Environmental Criticism* for ecocritics to take note of the environmental "evocations" embedded in fiction as well as poetry and nonfiction.[17]

Cheryl Glotfelty, one of the earliest to use the term *ecocriticism*, describes it in terms that especially apply to Hawthorne's nature-oriented stories: "Ecocriticism takes as its subject the interconnections between nature and culture, specifically the cultural artifacts of language and literature. As a critical stance, it has one foot in literature and the other on land; as a theoretical discourse, it negotiates between the human and the nonhuman."[18] Rather than giving only passing attention to nature, ecocritics consider the interplay between human and nonhuman nature and explore the ways such concerns are represented in literature. By situating humans as members of a larger sphere, whether conceived of as a biosphere (sphere of the living) or ecosphere (sphere of the earth, its components and processes), ecocritics negotiate between the concerns of nature and culture and encourage the acceptance of our status as members of this larger sphere of nature. We are not the sum of all existence or the sole meaning of existence. The combination of these concerns makes Hawthorne's writing particularly suitable as a subject for ecocritical study.

Seeing nature and representing it in writing are more complex processes than they seem at first glance. Scholars who study literature and the environment today generally acknowledge that *nature* (the physical world outside of ourselves) and *culture* (the constructed world built by and upon our perceptions) cannot be wrenched apart. Karla Armbruster and Kathleen Wallace, among others, have compellingly argued that when we speak of "nature," we are already speaking about "culture" because we are always describing human perceptions as well as the physical environment that exists outside of ourselves. Therefore, if we are to make sense of the interaction between humans and our environment, we must acknowledge the outer world and inner world "as interwoven rather than as separate sides of a dualistic construct."[19] If we read Hawthorne's work anew in light of this sense of interwovenness, his focus on human perceptions in natural settings reveals a mind surprisingly alert to the difficulties of representing the natural world in a way that accurately displays the complex relationships between human and nonhuman nature.

A FRESH GLIMPSE OF NATURE

Given Hawthorne's time and place, he would have been extremely unaware or simply insensitive to his cultural milieu if he had *not* paid any attention to the natural world in his writing. At the beginning of the nineteenth century, the United States was a fledgling nation, still a bit wobbly on its feet yet serving as a proving ground for new ideas about government and social organization. The concept of natural law played a key role in the democratic experience of young America. Arguments for natural rights propagated by philosophers such as John Locke in seventeenth-century England and Thomas Paine in eighteenth-century America had served as the basis of argument for independence in the US Declaration of Independence and as the basis of the social contract spelled out by the Constitution and the attached Bill of Rights. These ideas routinely found their way into the writings of romance writers whose publications proliferated the American scene before Hawthorne, including poets such as William Cullen Bryant and fiction writers such as Washington Irving, James Fenimore Cooper, and Catharine Maria Sedgwick. Many of these writers were known for taking the elements of European romanticism and resituating them on the American continent where nature was less overcast by human civilization. Landscape painters such as Thomas Cole romanticized the American landscape by creating on overview perspective of the landscape rather than emphasizing the minute details. Such an approach—if handled poorly—may mute the details and idealize the landscape almost beyond recognition, but, on the other hand, it may suggest the natural scenery as an aggregate of the constituent parts of nature in any landscape setting. Romantic literature often attempted the same big picture approach to nature that was embraced by landscape artists like Thomas Cole.

In Concord especially, Hawthorne could not ignore nature. While Hawthorne's association with the Transcendentalists in the Concord community and elsewhere expanded his thinking about the environment, his choice of fiction as his primary mode of publication suggests that he is not walking lockstep with them. Buell at first considered the realist essay more attuned to environmental discourse than fiction, but later acknowledged that "realism scarcely exhausts what deserves to be said about texts as environmental representations.... Indeed, an individual text must be thought of as environmentally embedded at every stage from its germination to its reception. At each stage, how environmentality gets encoded and expressed is always both partial and greater than one first notices."[20] Buell also calls into question his earlier method of considering less apparently environmentally situated texts as "a subspecies of 'environmental text,' the first stipulation of which was that the nonhuman environment must be envisaged not merely as a framing device but as an active presence, suggesting human history's implication in natural history." Instead, he now advocates that we examine texts without explicitly environmental statements for potential elements of "environmentality."[21] I contend not only that Hawthorne's writing bears the characteristics of environmentality but also that it does in fact address the environment in many cases as an active presence whose history affects and is affected by human history. As such, natural history and human history can often be seen working side by side.

For Hawthorne, nature is a reality that is often veiled, often disguised, and only occasionally actually seen by humans. And it is better to register one's awareness of this cultural wrapping than to represent nature as a reality untouched by humans. The irony of discussing nature is that what one produces is always a representation of nature rather than the thing itself. In *The Scarlet Letter* (1850), Hawthorne cautions that assumptions about nature are often based not so much on nature as upon "long hereditary habit, which has become like nature."[22] Likewise, in *The House of the Seven Gables* (1851), he suggests that what often passes for nature is actually "custom so immemorial that it looks like nature."[23] Arguments based on nature, Hawthorne suggests, are often actually arguments for socially constructed versions of nature that shape nature into the image of the beholder. In *The Blithedale Romance* (1852), Hawthorne develops this idea through a narrator whose limited perspective is routinely described in terms of the visual and who can only occasionally observe nature in its reality: "There was, at such moments, a novelty, an unwonted aspect, on the face of Nature, as if she had been taken by surprise and seen at unawares, with no opportunity to put off her real look, and assume the mask with which she mysteriously hides herself from mortals."[24] But living in nature is not the only way to catch such glimpses, for the narrator catches fleeting glimpses of nature in the city as well: "Bewitching to my fancy are all those nooks and crannies, where Nature, like a stray partridge, hides her head among the long-established haunts of men! It is likewise to be remarked, as a general rule, that there is far more of the picturesque, more truth to native and characteristic tendencies, and vastly greater suggestiveness in the back view of a residence, whether in town or country, than in its front. . . . Realities keep in the rear."[25] Hawthorne intimates that even though nature is only rarely and partially seen even by those who make a study of it, nature is indeed a reality with which humans must grapple in coming to terms with the human condition. And it is a rousing reality, much like a "stray partridge" that can sometimes be "seen at unawares," whether in the woods or fields or in the "nooks and crannies" where nature intermittently shows itself in its true form.

Despite Hawthorne's delight in the natural world, it is also true that his observations of delusional human understandings of nature do often weigh heavily on his fiction. The darker aspects of nature featured in his stories of fearful Puritans like Young Goodman Brown are not entirely absent from his notebooks either. He braces against the harsher weather of the natural world, for example, and eventually leaves his sometime home in the Berkshires because of the cold winters. But his displeasure at the harshness of nature does not make him fear it: "How inhospitable Nature is during a rain!" he exclaims in one notebook passage, contrasting the hot sunny days when nature still provides a respite under the shady trees with the lack of respite for humans and birds on rainy days. "And what becomes of birds in such a soaking rain as this? Is hope and an instinctive faith so mixed up in their nature that they can be cheered by the thought that the sunshine will return? or do they think, as I almost do, that there is to be no sunshine any more?"[26] The changes and events of nature clearly work on Hawthorne's mind and mood, making him reflective enough to compose thought-provoking contemplations on the interrelationships shared by members of the natural world.

Rather than writing self-assured philosophical treatises on nature in the manner of Emerson, then, Hawthorne contemplates nature as a fascinating yet opaque reality in his notebooks and his fiction. And he becomes adept at adapting the conventions of pastoral romance to his development of American romance. Hawthorne was well aware of the long tradition of pastoral literature that preceded him, having read pastorals repeatedly since his childhood. Before the European settlement of America, the pastoral ideal had long been associated with an idyllic past when humans were in perfect harmony with nature—whether in the Garden of Eden narrative of the Hebrew Bible, in the Golden Age of Arcadia that proved so productive for Greek pastoral, or in classical works or Renaissance pastoral romances. While the birth of pastoral in Western literature can be traced at least back to Theocritus's ancient Greek bucolic poetry, Virgil's *Eclogues* (37 BCE) are often considered the first developed pastoral. In English, pastoral makes its debut with the publication of Edmund Spenser's *Shepheardes Calendar* (1579). And it is such pastoral romances that were a ubiquitous presence in Hawthorne's early reading. Since childhood Hawthorne had read the "fairyland" pastoral romances of Shakespeare, Spenser, Milton, and others. His entrance exams for Bowdoin College required him to read Greek and Latin works, including Virgil's *Eclogues*.[27] Later adaptations of the pastoral in works such as Miguel de Cervantes's satirical *Don Quixote* (1605–1615) and Daniel Defoe's novel *Robinson Crusoe* (1719) provided examples of ways to reshape the pastoral to changing contexts while retaining a strong focus on the relations between humans and nature. Hawthorne's reading of these works as well as British Gothic novels and the romantic poetry of Wordsworth and Coleridge give further shape to the natural world in his literary imagination. His own modifications of pastoral romance within the American context would provide him with a point of entry into the conversations about what it meant to be an American close to nature in a way no longer thought possible in an old and long-established European civilization.

PASTORAL, ROMANCE, AND SCIENCE

Both *pastoral* and *romance* have been subjected to intense criticism over the last century, especially as the constructedness of these seemingly natural forms has become inescapably apparent. In the most general sense, *pastoral* denotes a country setting. Pastoral literature is not, however, simply literature set in the country. Deriving from the Latin *pastoralis*, the term has to do with the "tending of livestock" and poetic creativity in natural spaces as much as with the country setting itself.[28] Typically, the pastoral setting inspires the poet to consider relations between humans and nature, nature and civilization, city and country, and nature and art. According to the *Oxford English Dictionary*, the genre of romance denotes "a fictitious narrative, usually in prose, in which the settings or the events depicted are remote from everyday life, or in which sensational or exciting events or adventures form the central theme." Closely related to this understanding of "romance," the term can also be used simply to refer to "the character or quality that makes something appeal strongly to the imagination, and sets it apart from the mundane; an air, feeling, or sense of wonder, mystery, and remoteness from everyday life; redolence or suggestion of . . . adventure, heroism, chivalry, etc."[29] When romance and pastoral come together, the result is often an imaginative scene in which the relationship between humans and nature is worked out as an adventure at a remove from contemporary society.

Since the publication of Raymond Williams' *The Country and the City* (1975), pastoral has frequently been subject to criticism as an overidealization of nature that closes its eyes to the less attractive features of the natural world. And certainly the kind of pastoral poems that Williams most harshly critiques deserve this judgment. Such poems usually served as copies of other poems rather than legitimate attempts to represent nature as it is, developing into highly stylized pastoral as a simulation that falsifies more than it reveals about the relationship between humans and nature. However, pastorals do not always work that way—neither before nor after the neoclassical era. What they do have in common in romances (fictional accounts set first to poetry, then to prose) are the following elements: visitors from the city/ court who have become estranged from nature, have become corrupted by too much civilization, and must spend time in the country to get back in tune with nature before returning revitalized to the city or court. Even Williams does not altogether dismiss the value of pastoral. Instead, he argues that the pastoral became a vapid reflection of what it once was. "Neo-pastoral as a court entertainment is one thing," Williams declares, "Neo-pastoral in its new location, the country-house and its estate, is quite another."[30] But when pastoral had descended to the level that it no longer contained the elements of counter-pastoral that Williams found so productive in earlier pastorals that depicted harsh realities attendant upon shepherds tending their sheep, Williams found it distastefully decorous. It was no longer actively involved in the search for truth that Williams identifies as a key characteristic of earlier pastoral works.

Hawthorne was not unaware of critiques of pastoral writing that were arising even in the nineteenth century. "Blair's Rhetoric," one of the required texts at Bowdoin College when he was a student, may have contributed to Hawthorne's understanding of the pastoral.[31] In lecture thirty-nine, immediately following a lecture titled "The Nature of Poetry, Its Origin and Progress, Versification," Blair lambasts "the dull and insipid" pastorals of Alexander Pope and writers like him, but asserts that these writers' lack of innovation rather than any constraints coming from the form itself may be to blame: "In this lies the difficulty of pastoral writing . . . [T]he pastoral is most meagre in subject and least diversified in strain. Yet this defect is not to be ascribed solely to barrenness of subjects. It is in great measure the fault of the poet. For human nature and human passions are much the same in every situation and rank of life. What a variety of objects within the rural sphere do the passions present!"[32] Always a student of human nature and passions, Hawthorne may well have been inspired by Blair's treatment of the pastoral to examine the rural environment with a philosophical eye. It is significant that Hawthorne wrote pastoral prose rather than pastoral poetry, allowing him to cast off trite expressions about nature that marked too much of the poetry of his time.

In the twentieth century, Raymond Williams was joining earlier writers such as William Empson and Leo Marx, both of whom posited some varieties of pastoral as more authentic than others. "The essential trick of the old pastoral, which was felt to imply a beautiful relation between rich and poor," Empson claims in *Some Versions of Pastoral* (1935), "was to make simple people express strong feelings (felt as the most universal subject, something fundamentally true about everybody) in learned and fashionable language (so that you wrote about the best subject in the best way)."[33] In this world the apparent conventionalities of pastoral originally served as a form of cultural critique rather than necessitating the stance of political quietism later associated with pastoral. Distinguishing between realistic and heroic pastorals, Empson proceeds to classify seven "versions" of pastoral into these two categories. According to Empson, heroic pastorals typically create an "absurdly artificial" picture of life cloaking political motives in falsified aesthetic representations of reality, while realistic pastorals serve as "as a natural expression for a sense of social injustice."[34]

In *The Machine in the Garden* (1964), Marx differentiates between sentimental and complex pastoral. As Marx describes it, sentimental pastorals offer popular but vapid concepts of nature as a sentimentalized retreat from the city. Complex pastoral, on the other hand, is an imaginative form of pastoral that depends upon "the real" as a counterforce to "the idyllic."[35] Drawing attention to a distinctively American version of the pastoral, Marx traces in some detail the potential of Shakespeare's *The Tempest* as new world pastoral, a potential Hawthorne makes use of in *The Blithedale Romance*, which begins in the midst of a snowstorm he refers to as a tempest. As Marx and others have compellingly demonstrated, the apparently unadulterated landscape of young America invited the reawakening of the pastoral impulse in literature. Buell extends upon Marx's claims to suggest that American pastoral is typically a realistic art in which "the mimetic level is earthier and a literal referent more specified than in, say, an eclogue by Virgil or Spenser."[36] Buell finds this earthy kind of art conducive to ecocritical inquiries.

Through much of the twentieth century, critical discussions of the pastoral frequently followed Williams in considering Renaissance pastoral a dynamic form of art superior to the more limpid pastorals of the late seventeenth and eighteenth centuries. Hawthorne seems to have reached a similar conclusion himself, developing his artistic prowess by returning most often to the texts of Spenser, Shakespeare, and Milton, all of whom he had read repeatedly since childhood. According to his sister Elizabeth, Hawthorne "studied" the work of Shakespeare and Milton and others and bought his first copy of Spenser's *Faerie Queene* "[a]s soon as he was old enough to buy books for himself."[37] In England he bought an impressive new copy of *The Faerie Queene*, which he read aloud to his family during long evenings together in that country.[38] According to Hawthorne's son Julian, his father has more in common with the Renaissance writers than with any other writers, living or dead. Listing Shakespeare, Milton, Bunyan, Spenser, Sidney, and others as writers whose works had been part of the now-burned Hawthorne library, Julian offers this observation: "The great English writers [of the Renaissance] saw the phantasmagory of Creation more nearly from his own point of view than others did."[39] Discussing Hawthorne's writing methods and sources further, Julian claims that "nature was always [Hawthorne's] groundwork and quarry."[40] Like the Renaissance pastoralists who took their art of writing seriously, Hawthorne composed with an eye to representing the human condition within a changing world where nature and spirit whispered mysteriously at the edges of human knowledge.

In the writings of Spenser, Shakespeare, and Milton, pastoral is rarely simplistic or totalizing. In his introduction to Shakespeare's *Cymbeline*, Martin Butler distinguishes between "soft pastoral," the pleasant vision of life invoked by comedy, and "hard pastoral," which often threatens (whether or not it produces) a tragic end. Describing the princes hidden in the woods, Butler points out that "their life is far from savage, but their landscape is an austere life contrasting with court comforts, the 'hard pastoral' of the mountains rather than a 'soft pastoral' of the fields."[41] What is important to notice here is that the pastoral itself, even at the height of its usage in Renaissance literature, does not fall neatly within a single generic category. Most directly, the standard distinction between the good countryside and the bad court may be exposed as a false dichotomy since there is good and bad both in nature and "good" and "bad" in civilization. The dark side of the natural world can be seen in bears or savages that eat (or threaten) people, and the good of human civilization can be seen in (restored) courts that protect the people from external threats. Paradise Lost another example of such mixture of forms, as Milton combines hard pastoral and soft pastoral in what Jeffrey Theis has called a "sylvan pastoral," which "provides a focal point for Adam and Eve as they learn the importance of interacting with and defining tangled, complex topographies in a way that renders seemingly profuse and unbounded spaces into known places."[42] Renaissance pastoral thus can be said to avoid the easy generalizations that mark the later development of pastoral in eighteenth-century poetry. Rather than offering a simplistic or an easily decoded view of life, its narrative structure can yield to both comedy and tragedy. By combining Renaissance pastoral with other conceptions of the natural world (such as the Gothic), Hawthorne creates literary art that is not simply derivative. He is looking for new representations that can reveal the deeper truths of reality.

Like his English predecessors of the Renaissance, Hawthorne employed pastoral as a mode of social critique that allowed him to comment on society from a distance. Like them, he reshaped the dichotomies of art and nature, nature and grace, idealism and realism to reflect and challenge his own society's cultural norms. While Hawthorne positions humans as artist figures in the natural world, he draws back from overly blithe expectations of achieving perfect harmony either with the natural world or within human society. And yet he does not suppose an essential antagonism between nature and society. Instead, the tensions created by humans coming to terms with their environment allow for self-critique and thoughtful, if sometimes uneasy, deliberations on alternative ways of viewing the world. In pastoral romance, Hawthorne finds an approach to nature that is adaptable to the particularity of the American situation. With its roots firmly planted in Renaissance humanism, Hawthorne's pastoral mode of composition seeks to find what the natural world can teach us about what it means to be human. Drawing from Renaissance pastoral to shape his artistic investigations of nature, Hawthorne places the contemporary fashion of Transcendentalist idealism under the scope—especially in *The Blithedale Romance*. Although Hawthorne registers his skepticism of the Transcendentalist belief in nature's unmediated efficacy, he also shares some of their key convictions. Like Emerson, Hawthorne embraces the idea of spiritualized nature. Like Emerson, Hawthorne celebrates the natural world in ways that are foreign to his sterner Puritan characters. Hawthorne is wary, however, of Emerson's Transcendentalist faith in humans' ability to interpret the natural world so adequately as to make complete sense of the human condition.

Hawthorne's near contemporary British models were also important to his choice of prose fiction as the shape of his pastoral romance, with authors such as Sir Walter Scott most obviously leading the way. Taking Samuel Johnson's definitions as his starting point, Scott quibbles with the notion that romance needs to include "love and chivalry" but agrees that romance depends upon "wild adventures." For Scott, however, the difference between the romance and the novel is this: the romance is "a fictitious narrative in prose or verse; the interest of which turns upon marvellous and uncommon incidents," and the novel is "a fictitious narrative, differing from the Romance, because the events are accommodated to the ordinary train of human events, and the modern state of society."[43] However, Scott argues that "[t]he progress of Romance, in fact, keeps pace with that of society. . . . Romance and real history have the same common origin."[44] Nonetheless, there is no gainsaying the fact that the mixture of fiction and history that constitutes romance makes for a special kind of composition. Scott acknowledges the tendency of romancers "to exaggerate, until the thread of truth can scarce be discerned in the web of fable which involves it; and we are compelled to renounce all hope of deriving serious or authentic information from the materials upon which the compounders have been so long at work."[45] Despite his recognition of the distortions created by poorly-composed romances, Scott finds the genre's popularity so strong that it is "worthy of [Miguel de Cervantes'] satire" in *Don Quixote*. "But the existence of an Arcadia," Scott continues, "a pastoral region, in which a certain fantastic sort of personages, desperately in love, and thinking of nothing else but their mistresses, played upon pipes, and wrote sonnets from morning to night, yet were supposed all the while to be tending their flocks, was too monstrously absurd to be long credited or tolerated."[46] Such a golden age was too far removed from what most people could imagine to be true to serve for Scott as a productive basis for writing. Hawthorne too limited himself only to references to Arcadia, or the "Fairyland," as he tended to call it. His actual settings were grounded in historical times and places that could be documented.

For Hawthorne, romance is a genre well suited to acquaint the reader with the truth of the actual world through the power of an imagination actively experimenting with the natural world. The prefaces of Hawthorne's romances trace his evolving sense of the viability and suitability of this genre for his writing. By Hawthorne's own admission, his use of romance stems partly from its very plasticity, its willingness to bend the rules of literary decorum in its attempts to seek out the truth of the human condition in the tensions between human understandings of the natural environment. But like the pastoral before it, the romance has been attacked by critics, some of whom claim that its highly representational qualities should exclude it from the canon of environmental literature. Appearing just as ecocriticism and green studies began to gain attention within the American and British academies, Jerome McGann's *The Romantic Ideology* (1983) characterizes literary romanticism as an ideology blind to the "uncritical absorption in Romanticism's own self-representations."[47] Such an understanding of romanticism is of course at odds with ecocriticism's emphasis on the nonhuman environment as a reality that needs to be recognized and valued in order to come to terms with the environmental crises of the twenty-first century. Indeed, if romanticism can be wholly equated with the rhetorical and aesthetic appropriation of nature for ideological ends, there would be little reason to pay attention to most nineteenth-century writers.

Indeed, the relationship between romanticism and ideology can be construed quite differently. In the case of more complex romances, romanticism satirizes or at least interrogates ideology perhaps as often as it appears. In his study of nineteenth-century British nature poets, Jonathan Bate proposes that romanticism can and should often be understood as "a theory of ecosystems and unalienated labour" rather than an ideological "theory of imagination and symbol."[48] Karl Kroeber also takes issue with critics like McGann, calling into question the assumption that romantic writing about the natural environment serves merely as an indication of psychological displacements. Responding to McGann's skepticism of romantic intuitions of transcendence, Kroeber claims, "An ecologically oriented criticism directs itself to understanding persistent romantic struggles to articulate meaningful human relations within the conditions of a natural world in which transcendence is not an issue."[49] Kroeber's position delineates a space in which romanticism can be considered as something other than a mere mask serving to disguise an ideological bent. Bowing to McGann's demands for rejecting transcendence, however, Kroeber's approach severely constricts our ability to consider the manner in which romanticism may bear relevance to current environmental discourse. It is certainly true that transcendence *as an ideology* hampers the work of those committed to seeking out the implications of physical reality. Transcendence that allows room for the immanence of the natural world, however, is not inherently opposed to the aims of ecocriticism. For transcendence can be understood as something imbricated in and thus intimately concerned with physical reality.

In romance, Hawthorne adopts a self-consciously representative genre rather than using the nonfiction form of the essay sometimes facilely associated with things *as they really are*. In his short stories and book-length romances, Hawthorne wraps his observations of nature in the stories of Americans who serendipitously experience nature in its true form, if only for a moment. Hawthorne continually redefines romance but what remains uniform throughout his writing is his sense that romance allows the observer use of the imagination to help make sense of the actual world in general and of the American landscape in particular. As Edwin Eigner noted half a century ago, "Many writers of romances require not only strange circumstances and abnormal psychology to portray their visions, but exotic scenery, as well. But their imaginary landscapes provide a way to reality, not an escape from it."[50] For Hawthorne, certainly, fiction is not a separation from real life, but a way of helping us use our imagination in an attempt to understand the deeper realities behind surface appearances.

Hawthorne is interested in nature not only as story material. His romances and notebooks alike engage with a surprising number of scientific developments of his era. During his college days, a number of Hawthorne's required textbooks focused on scientific study of the natural world. Geography, chemistry, and mineralogy figured among his required courses.[51] During the second year of Hawthorne's college career, the mineralogy textbook was updated and expanded to include a section on geology, an area of study that the professor writing the book notes has been "rapidly increasing in the United States."[52] Professor Cleaveland, a nineteenth-century instructor at Bowdoin during Hawthorne's years as a student there, had collected many of the most recent geological reports for the updated version of the textbook he wrote and used at Bowdoin, *An Elementary Treatise on Mineralogy and Geology* (1822). Westward expansion and the concomitant study of landforms previously unmapped and uncategorized by European systems captured the excitement of geologists, visual artists, and writers alike. As Rebecca Bedell points out in her study of Thomas Cole and other landscape painters of nineteenth-century America, geology rather than biology was the science of discovery during the beginning of this transitional state of American society.[53] Thus, it is little surprise that Hawthorne's scientific comments focus at first on geological observations. In the introduction of a short story, he calls the White Mountains "the laboratory of Nature."[54] In a brief notebook entry where he describes an outing with a number of other literati in the Berkshire Mountains, Hawthorne describes his spelunking experience by pointing out the geological structure of a cave they visited: "The walls present a specimen of how Nature packs the stone, crowding huge masses, as it were, into chinks and fissures, and here we see it in the perpendicular or horizontal layers, as Nature laid it."[55] Recent advances in the field of geology, along with American sites being closely examined for the first time by Europeans and European Americans, made it an expansive and imaginative area of study for antebellum Americans.

In nineteenth-century Europe, however, biology was the dominant area of scientific study for those thinking about changes in our knowledge of the natural world. Having published or sent to press all of his stories and all four of his major romances before Darwin's *On the Origin of Species* was published, Hawthorne is nonetheless tuned in to some of the questions and findings that inform Darwin's revolutionary text. With varying degrees of enthusiasm and skepticism, he incoporates into his fiction nineteenth-century scientific terms (e.g. adaptation, transmutation, development, constitution, physiognomy, and race) referring to emerging evolutionary theory as well as quasi-scientific inquiries into phrenology and what is now known as scientific racism. The British title of his last romance, published shortly after *On the Origin of Species*, is *The Transformation*, another term used in the nineteenth century to discuss changing species.

In his notebooks too, it is clear that Hawthorne is tuned in to discussions about the relationship between humans and other animals. About a year before his work on this last romance was drawing to a close, Hawthorne describes a conversation in which he and Mr. Powers, an American sculptor in Italy, discuss the relationship between humans and animals: "We talked, furthermore, about instinct and reason, and whether the brute creation have souls, and, if they have none, how justice is to be done them for their sufferings here; and Mr. Powers came finally to the conclusion that brutes suffer only in appearance, and that God enjoys for them all that they seem to enjoy, and that man is the only intelligent and sentient being."[56] Hawthorne does not directly express agreement or disagreement, but he seems skeptical of Powers' untested assumptions about the experiences of other members of the natural world. Hawthorne does suggest that almost the opposite could be true as well: "There might be beings inhabiting this earth, contemporaneously with us, and close beside us, but of whose existence and whereabouts we could have no perception, nor they of ours, because we are endowed with different sets of senses; for certainly it was in God's power to create beings who should communicate with nature by innumerable other senses than those few which we possess."[57] The secrets of nature, Hawthorne intimates, are wrapped up in the secrets of the supernatural, and by examining one to the exclusion of the other, we are apt to overlook very real possibilities. Hawthorne concludes this reflection with a comment that theorizing however long and hard without ample evidence seems foolhardy: "He has evidently thought much and earnestly about such matters, but is apt to let his idea crystallize into a theory, before he can have sufficient data for it."[58] Hawthorne typically cloaks his more speculative observations of human and nonhuman nature in the guise of narrative; in so doing, he avoids taking a decided stance on controversial issues but all too often slides into his famously ambiguous stances that offer little clarity for interacting productively with the developing issues of the day—even issues as consequential as slavery. Nonetheless, his fictive speculations provide the space for mental experimentation with the competing senses of reality current in the nineteenth century and often continuing into our era as well.

HAWTHORNE'S NATURE WRITING

Hawthorne's multifaceted adaptations of pastoral romance, along with his attention to emerging scientific theories as means to investigate nature, outline his contention that multiple lenses are needed to evaluate America's alignment with nature. In adapting Renaissance pastoral to the American scene, Hawthorne does not simply imitate the writers of the Renaissance. Instead, he adapts past versions of the pastoral to his own reshaping of the American idyll while grappling with American Transcendentalist notions of the natural world, Puritan allegories of Nature, and more recent Gothic and sentimental works of fiction. As a literary form that can incorporate a multiplicity of viewpoints, pastoral could be adjusted to the diversity of American experience and could enable an exploration of the so-called new world. By using inherited artistic forms as well as his lived experience of living close to the natural world, Hawthorne participates in nineteenth-century debates about nature by showing that ideas of natural law are all too often merely reflections of one's own solipsistic thinking.

Rather than simply obsessing on the apparent dichotomies between art and nature, country and city, nature and civilization, Hawthorne treats such contrasts as twin components of the wholeness of the universe. Noting the "productive tensions" in Hawthorne's work, Claudia Johnson has described the psychological effect of the contrasts that enliven his work.[59] Hawthorne's varying treatments of nature in his texts indicate his belief that the truth of nature, and of humans' relationship to the rest of the natural world, can be discovered in the heteroglossia created by the interplay between cultural inheritance, personal experience, and imaginative consideration of emerging scientific knowledge.

For Hawthorne, nineteenth-century American debates about nature were nothing new. They were the continuation of conversations started by the seventeenth-century Puritans whom Hawthorne criticizes for killing accused witches and persecuting Quakers and American Indians alike. In Hawthorne's nonfiction and the short fiction composed before his book-length romances, we see a writer paying close attention to the natural world in which history has been playing out and continues to play out. My first chapter takes passages from his notebooks and other nonfiction that exemplify Hawthorne's nature writing—whether observing the scenery of America and other countries or noticing the plants and animals with whom we share the space of our world. In my second chapter, I examine his short fiction as an artistic engagement with the laboratory of nature in stories that serve as eco-allegories or investigations of the relations between human and nonhuman nature. Hawthorne's meditations on nature in such works not only enable but encourage my investigations into the environmental quality of his work.

In the chapters that follow, I bring ecocriticism to bear on Hawthorne's book-length American romances by exploring his various approaches to understanding the environment and human responses to it. Nature, as viewed through a pastoral lens adapted to other literary forms, was a topic Hawthorne considered crucial to American identity. Drawing upon the pastoral literature of the Renaissance era as a corrective to more exclusivist American views of nature, Hawthorne obliquely critiques American exceptionalism even while investigating questions about humans and nature that are raised by the American experience—questions that continued to haunt and fascinate him and his contemporaries. Hawthorne's adaptation of traditional literary forms to enter nineteenth-century debates about nature illustrates his interest in the perpetual question of what it means to be human in general and in one's particular time and place.

In the third chapter, I offer a fresh reading of *The Scarlet Letter* (1850) as an attempt to open and read the Book of Nature and to discern the place of the human body within that book. When Hawthorne turns his energies to writing book-length romances, *The Scarlet Letter* becomes his first major effort to seek out Emerson's much-touted "original relation to the universe" in America, as represented in New England history from the seventeenth-century Puritans to the nineteenth-century Transcendentalists.[60] This romance contains Hawthorne's most famous description of romance as "a neutral territory, somewhere between the real world and fairy-land, where the Actual and the Imaginary may meet, and each imbue itself with the nature of the other."[61] What is often missed in this description is the doubleness of the phrases "real world" and "fairy-land." The real world is often taken to refer to material reality, but to a Platonic sensibility the ideal speaks of a reality that may reference but also supersede the material. In Emerson's famous essay *Nature*, material reality is presented primarily in such a Platonic mode. Hawthorne, on the other hand, does not communicate a purely Platonic sensibility; the differences between dreams and reality in his tales are sometimes ambiguous.

Hawthorne's "fairy-land" speaks of an imagined place, but this place is drawn from images of the natural world and refers to the woods near Walden often referred to as "Fairy Land" by the Hawthorne family and others in Concord.[62] During a recent trip to Concord, I was delighted to discover that a beautiful section of woods between Walden and the Town of Concord still bears the name "Fairyland," along with a "Fairyland Pond" that is often visited by school groups today.[63] In this sense, Hawthorne's notion of the Actual and the Imaginary as intertwined aspects of each other becomes more invested in the real world than in a mere flight of fantasy. Hawthorne's description of romance prepares us to open the Book of Nature, but this is followed in his introduction by a lengthy discussion of the animal nature of fellow workers at the Custom House that sets the stage for his consideration of the human body as a part of nature.

In the preface to *The House of the Seven Gables* (1851), Hawthorne extends his definition of romance by following Sir Walter Scott's lead in differentiating between the romance and the novel. For Hawthorne, the novel is constrained to "a very minute fidelity," while the romance is more open to the presentation of truth "under circumstances, to a great extent, of the writer's own choosing or creation."[64] It is the "truth of the human heart" that romances dramatize, and yet the romancer is free to "so manage his atmospherical medium as to bring out or mellow the lights and deepen and enrich the shadows of the picture."[65] Hawthorne suggests that the romancer ought to exercise judicious caution, however, in order "to mingle the Marvellous rather as a slight, delicate, and evanescent flavor."[66] Hawthorne's request at the end of the preface that "the book may be read strictly as a Romance, having a great deal more to do with the clouds overhead, than with any portion of the actual soil of the County of Essex" seems to disavow any connection to "the Actual" world as mere coincidence.[67] However, this disavowal is more than a little tongue-in-cheek, given the town of Salem's ready ability to point out the street and house that Hawthorne describes. Hawthorne's disavowal is also ironic given the way he shapes the preface to draw attention to "real estate" and to the name of a place associated with witchcraft trials of seventeenth-century Puritan aristocrats.[68] In a story where natural and supernatural may collude to right the wrongs perpetrated against the individuals who are displaced from the land they have called home, the relation between the Actual and the Imaginary is again at play. The land, like the people, may be wronged; and both may eventually find ways to resist those wrongs. In my chapter on *Seven Gables*, I draw attention to the way Maule's curse raises issues of blood that resonate with nineteenth-century Americans grappling with property rights in a world where politicians have justified injustices such as the Fugitive Slave Act and the now-notorious Indian removals from their ancestral lands.

By the time Hawthorne wrote *The Blithedale Romance* (1852), he had been reflecting for a number of years on the definition of romance. While he claims in the preface that his experience in the Brook Farm society "is altogether incidental to the main purpose of the romance," this time he does admit that he "has ventured to make free with his old, and affectionately remembered home, at BROOK FARM, as being certainly the most romantic episode of his own life,—essentially a daydream, and yet a fact,—and thus offering an available foothold between fiction and reality."[69] His stated intent to separate this book from his Brook Farm experience even as he admittedly draws upon it elicited readers' skepticism even when it was first published. In *Blithedale*, Hawthorne's definition of romance becomes more slippery: he characterizes romance as a combination of "fiction and reality" built upon what seems to be "a daydream" but is actually "a fact."[70] In this romance, we witness the disintegration and failure of a highly romanticized pastoral ideal. *The Blithedale Romance* represents both the satire of romance and the romance of satire. In my chapter on this romance, I focus on the natural limits discovered by the utopianists at Blithedale—limits on how they might adapt physically to the environment that are nowhere more evident than in the unavoidable presence of death and human self-interest that places us out of concord with the natural world.

In my chapter on *The Marble Faun*, I focus on Hawthorne's attempted retrieval of an affinity with nature. In this last completed book-length romance, Hawthorne links art and nature through the figure of a faun named Donatello. When this animal-human faun Donatello unconsciously compliments Miriam, she exclaims, "Nature and art are just at one, sometimes."[71] Through her voice, Hawthorne repeats the statement of Polixenes in *The Winter's Tale*, who describes the process of grafting branches a natural art, declaring, "The art itself is nature" (4.4.97).[72] Shakespeare's pastoral romance includes a seeming statue coming to life. Although the statue stays in the sculpture gallery in Hawthorne's *Marble Faun*, the statue comes to life in the shape of Donatello, who looks just like it and seems to be a faun just like it.

In the preface of *The Marble Faun* (written in 1859), Hawthorne claims only to have attempted to compose "a fanciful story" rather than any kind of "portraiture of Italian manners and character."[73] His claim notwithstanding, Hawthorne's book was used as a travel guide by tourists to Italy in the later years of the nineteenth century. Claiming himself "somewhat surprised to see the extent to which he had introduced descriptions of various Italian objects" as he was revising the book in a "complete change of scene" in England, Hawthorne declares that his only reason for choosing Italy as "the site of his Romance" is that it provides him with "a sort of poetic or fairy precinct, where actualities would not be so terribly insisted upon, as they are, and must needs be, in America."[74] Hawthorne's contrasts between English and Italian scenery suggest that writing romance is a recursive process that goes back and forth not only between the Actual and the Imaginary but also between immediacy and memory—the visual image and the mental image. When Hawthorne claims that he finds Italy a more suitable location for romance because "there is no shadow, no antiquity, no mystery, no picturesque and gloomy wrong, nor anything but a commonplace prosperity, in broad and simple daylight," in America he should again be read with a degree of skepticism.[75] His preface was written on October 15, 1859, the day before John Brown's raid on Harper's Ferry at a time when Hawthorne and many of his fellow Americans were already well aware of the looming shadow of approaching the approaching Civil War. As early as 1854, while in England, Hawthorne had written to his college roommate Horatio Bridge, noting that from across the ocean "it looks to me as if there were an actual fissure between the North and the South, which may widen and deepen into a gulf."[76] As Larry Reynolds has noted in his study of Hawthorne's political makeup, Hawthorne's declaration of the lack of "gloomy wrong" should be considered "somewhat ironic, given his concern that America itself was bitterly divided over slavery and was on the precipice of civil war."[77] The ironic undertones of this preface only add to the irony of this and earlier prefaces, collapsing distinctions between nature and culture, gloom and beauty, as well as between the Actual and the Imaginary.

Hawthorne's narratives often undermine the narrator's voice when it is most adamant, suggesting the need to pay attention to more than one voice. For underneath the rhetoric of freedom and equality in nineteenth-century America lurk the troubling realities of slavery and the so-called Indian removals. Most of the "absent" Native Americans and "Black Scipios" are safely located in the past of Hawthorne's stories. Toni Morrison has famously called attention to the "dark, abiding, signing Africanist presence" in American literature, even in works that seem to be largely absent of nonwhite races.[78] In Hawthorne's writing, the mark of this absent Africanist presence is placed alongside the mark of a removed Native American presence. This is perhaps most obvious in *The House of the Seven Gables*, where "Black Scipio" appears repeatedly to serve as a butler, once reproaching a visitor for "look[ing] so black at me" and yet another time "show[ing] the whites of his eyes."[79] Yet the black servant is only a brief memory of the past for nineteenth-century New Englanders. In this same text, all we find left of American Indians is the missing "Indian deed," which when finally found displays "the hieroglyphics of several Indian sagamores."[80]

With all their claims and disclaimers, then, Hawthorne's prefaces articulate a complex ever-changing form of pastoral romance—a much-nuanced type of nature writing. Given the variety of views and voices in Hawthorne's romances, his writing is particularly suited to Mikhail Bakhtin's concepts of dialogic tensions and his identification of the heteroglossia of speech types in nineteenth-century prose fiction.[81] These concepts are especially well suited for texts about nineteenth-century America, a democratic country that ostensibly hears the voices of all people, including those who are not members of an aristocratic class. Hawthorne's romances and short stories often work as a heterogeny of voices, including questions the narrator asks or attempts to answer, manuscripts within the texts, frame stories, prefaces that seem to be in the author's words at times and in a fictive narrator's at other times, unreliable narrators who tell the story in first person, and occasional speeches of minor characters unaccompanied by any narrative interpretations of those speeches.

It is my hope that a closer look at Hawthorne's nature writing will allow for a reassessment of his work, especially by those who are accustomed to thinking of him in terms of the romantic genius or solitary figure developed in isolation from the world around him. In light of this aim, my work includes extensive quotes from his actual nature writing that bear a closer look by contemporary readers of Hawthorne, given what we may think we know about him as a dark Romantic. While he is not a Transcendentalist, his friendship with them and other nature writers suggests an often-overlooked development in Hawthorne's writing that I am holding up for reexamination. As will be evident in the chapters that follow, other Hawthorne scholars have already been doing some of this work albeit not so directly in the field of environmental studies.

In my study, it also became increasing evident that Hawthorne's religious sensibilities played a greater part than one might suspect of the man who wrote "Sunday at Home" about his preference for staying outside the church. A later nineteenth-century writer, Emily Dickinson, similarly avoided the organized forms of religion available to her and yet shows a strong spiritual sensibility in her writing. Her poem "Some keep the Sabbath going to Church" may provide a voice for Hawthorne in saying, "I keep it, staying at Home."[82] But it is clear in many of the passages I analyze in the following pages that Hawthorne's attitude toward the natural environment involves his contemplation of possible overlapping spiritual and physical realities. While not determining his thought, then, religious and spiritual questions of the soul influence Hawthorne's emerging environmental ethos.

And finally, nineteenth-century events weighed heavily on Hawthorne's mind as he was writing. Scientific findings in fields of geology and biology especially were revolutionizing many peoples' thinking about the status of religion during Hawthorne's time. Hawthorne's interests in the layers of the mountains and the transmutations of humans and other animals, which will be discussed in the following pages, demonstrate that he was listening to the conversations that challenged many traditional interpretations of the Bible.

And as other Hawthorne scholars have recently noted, the shadow of the Civil War weighed heavily on Hawthorne and seemed to challenge his own assumptions about the world as well as those of many other people around him. And so I believe it is most concordant with Hawthorne's milieu and composing practices to read his famous ambiguity as an attempt to experiment with differing possibilities on how to conceptualize humans' place in this world.

NOTES

1. William Cullen Bryant's poem "A Forest Hymn" begins with the sentence, "The groves were God's first temples." Bryant begins his poem "The Prairies" with the lines "These are the gardens of the Desert, these / The unshorn fields, boundless and beautiful." Henry Wadsworth Longfellow's poem titled "Nature" begins with the analogy of nature "[a]s a fond mother."

2. These references are all taken from one of Sigourney's most-frequently anthologized poems titled "Indian Names."

3. Carolyn L. Karcher, *The First Woman in the Republic: A Cultural Biography of Lydia Maria Child* (Durham: Duke University Press, 1994), 110. Karcher also notes that Child collapses the supposed distinction between nature and culture through her characters: "Just as Brown, the standard-bearer of culture, discloses affinities with nature, so Hobomok, that prince of nature, discloses affinities with culture" (28).

4. Millicent Bell, "Hawthorne and the Real," in *Hawthorne and the Real: Bicentennial Essays*, ed. Millicent Bell (Columbus: Ohio State University Press, 2005), 3.

5. Edward Haviland Miller, *Salem Is My Dwelling Place: A Life of Nathaniel Hawthorne* (Iowa City: University of Iowa Press, 1992), 16.

6. Frederick Crews, *The Sins of the Fathers: Hawthorne's Psychological Themes* (Berkeley: University of California Press, 1989).

7. F.O. Matthiessen, *American Renaissance: Art and Expression in the Age of Emerson and Whitman* (New York: Oxford University Press, 1968), 238.

8. Richard H. Brodhead, *The School of Hawthorne* (New York: Oxford University Press, 1986), 26.

9. Eric Wilson, *Romantic Turbulence: Chaos, Ecology, and American Space* (New York: St. Martin's Press, 2000), xiv.

10. Herman Melville, "Hawthorne and His Mosses," review of *Mosses from an Old Manse,* by Nathaniel Hawthorne, in *Nathaniel Hawthorne: The Contemporary Reviews*, ed. John L. Idol, Jr. and Buford Jones (New York: Cambridge University Press, 1994), 107, 112.

11. Margaret Fuller, review of *Mosses from an Old Manse,* by Nathaniel Hawthorne, in *Nathaniel Hawthorne: The Contemporary Reviews*, 73.

12. Lawrence Buell, *The Environmental Imagination: Thoreau, Nature Writing, and the Formation of American Culture* (Cambridge, MA: Belknap Press, 1995), 25.

13. Nina Baym, *The Scarlet Letter: A Reading* (Boston: Twayne, 1986), 44.

14. Darrel Abel, *The Moral Picturesque: Studies in Hawthorne's Fiction* (West Lafayette, IN: Purdue University Press, 1988), 42.

15. David Van Leer, "Hester's Labyrinth: Transcendental Rhetoric in Puritan Boston," in *New Essays on The Scarlet Letter*, ed. Michael Colacurcio (New York: Cambridge University Press, 1985), 62.

16. Jennifer Mason, *Civilized Creatures: Urban Animals, Sentimental Culture, and American Literature, 1850-1900* (Baltimore: Johns Hopkins University Press, 2005), 23.

17. Lawrence Buell, *The Future of Environmental Criticism* (Malden, PA: Blackwell, 2005), 55. More recently, Buell has expanded upon the notion of environmental literature to include both poetry and fiction as well as nonfiction, noting that that "[t]he strategy of converting subjective place-evocation into a shareable representation of environmentality without bounds is not the property of any one genre or style."

18. Cheryl Glotfelty, introduction to "Literary Studies in an Age of Environmental Crisis," in *The Ecocriticism Reader: Landmarks in Literary Ecology*, ed. Cheryl Glotfelty and Harold Fromm (Athens: University of Georgia Press, 1996), xix.

19. Karla Armbruster and Kathleen R. Wallace, eds. *Beyond Nature Writing: Expanding the Boundaries of Ecocriticism* (Charlottesville: University of Virginia Press, 2001), 4.

20. Buell, *The Future of Environmental Criticism*, 44.

21. Buell, *The Future of Environmental Criticism*, 25.

22. Nathaniel Hawthorne, *The Complete Works of Nathaniel Hawthorne,* vol. 5, *The Scarlet Letter and The Blithedale Romance,* with Introductory Notes by George Parsons Lathrop. Riverside Edition (Boston: Houghton Mifflin, 1883), 200. Unless otherwise identified, all references to Hawthorne's work are to the 1882–1883 *Riverside Edition.*

23. Hawthorne, *The Complete Works of Nathaniel Hawthorne*, vol. 3, *The House of the Seven Gables and The Snow-Image and Other Twice-Told Tales,* with Introductory Notes by George Parsons Lathrop. Riverside Edition (Boston: Houghton Mifflin, 1883), 36.

24. Hawthorne, *Complete Works*, vol. 5, 394.

25. Hawthorne, *Complete Works*, vol. 5, 489–90.

26. Hawthorne, *The Complete Works of Nathaniel Hawthorne*, vol. 9, *Passages from the American Note-Books of Nathaniel Hawthorne,* with Introductory Notes by George Parsons Lathrop. Riverside Edition (Boston: Houghton Mifflin, 1883), 314–15.

27. Bowdoin College, *Laws of Bowdoin College* (Hallowell, ME: Goodale, 1817), 3.

28. "pastoral, n. and adj." *OED Online.* March 2018. Oxford University Press.

29. "romance, n. and adj." *OED Online.* March 2018. Oxford University Press.

30. Raymond Williams, *The Country and the City* (New York: Oxford University Press, 1973), 22.

31. Bowdoin College, *Laws of Bowdoin College*, 29.

32. Hugh Blair, *An Abridgement of Lectures on Rhetoric* (Boston: Thomas & Andrews, 1803), 194–95.

33. William Empson, *Some Versions of Pastoral* (New York: New Directions, 1974), 11.

34. Empson, *Some Versions of Pastoral*, 13, 16.

35. Leo Marx, *The Machine in the Garden: Technology and the Pastoral Ideal in America* (New York: Oxford University Press, 2000), 5, 25.

36. Lawrence Buell, "American Pastoral Ideology Reappraised," *American Literary History* 1 (1989): 5.

37. Randall Stewart, "Recollections of Hawthorne by His Sister Elizabeth," *American Literature* 16, no. 4 (1945): 319.

38. Julian Hawthorne, *Hawthorne Reading: An Essay* (Cleveland: Rowfant Club, 1902), 65. Hawthorne's son Julian recalls the "handsome illustrated copy of 'The Faerie Queene,'" which Hawthorne got while they were in England and says that, "at evening, for many weeks, he read it to us aloud: the first of the series of great readings that we had from him, though long before he had thus roamed through the English classics with his wife."

39. Hawthorne, *Hawthorne Reading*, 79.

40. Hawthorne, *Hawthorne Reading*, 100.

41. Martin Butler, introduction to *Cymbeline*, by William Shakespeare (New York: Cambridge University Press, 2005), 12.

42. Jeffrey S. Theis, *Writing the Forest in Early Modern England: A Sylvan Pastoral Nation* (Pittsburgh, PA: Duquesne University Press, 2009), 232–33.

43. Sir Walter Scott, "Essay on Romance," in *The Miscellaneous Prose Works of Sir Walter Scott*, vol. 6 (Edinburgh: Robert Cadell, 1834), 100.

44. Scott, "Essay on Romance," 104.

45. Scott, "Essay on Romance," 107.

46. Scott, "Essay on Romance," 161.

47. Jerome J. McGann, *The Romantic Ideology: A Critical Investigation* (Chicago: The University of Chicago Press, 1983), 1.

48. Jonathan Bate, *Romantic Ecology: Wordsworth and the Environmental Tradition* (London: Routledge, 1991), 10.

49. Karl Kroeber, *Ecological Literary Criticism: Romantic Imagining and the Biology of Mind* (New York: Columbia University Press, 1994), 38.

50. Edwin M. Eigner, "The Bad Tradition and the Romance of Man," in *Robert Louis Stevenson and the Romantic Tradition*, ed. Edwin M. Eigner (Princeton: Princeton University Press, 1966), 17.

51. Bowdoin College, *Laws of Bowdoin College*, 29.

52. Parker Cleaveland, *An Elementary Treatise on Mineralogy and Geology, Designed for the Use of Pupils, – For Persons, Attending Lectures on these Subjects, – and as a Companion for Travellers in the United States of America*, vol. 1, 2nd ed. (Boston: Cummings and Hilliard, 1822), vi.

53. Rebecca Bedell, *The Anatomy of Nature: Geology and American Landscape Painting, 1825-1875* (Princeton: Princeton University Press, 2001), 4–5.

54. Hawthorne, *The Complete Works of Nathaniel Hawthorne*, vol. 1, *Twice-Told Tales*, with Introductory Notes by George Parsons Lathrop. Riverside Edition (Boston: Houghton Mifflin, 1882), 178.

55. Hawthorne, *Complete Works*, vol. 9, 197.

56. Hawthorne, *The Complete Works of Nathaniel Hawthorne*, vol. 10, *Passages from the French and Italian Note-books*, with Introductory Notes by George Parsons Lathrop. Riverside Edition. (Boston: Houghton Mifflin, 1883), 376.

57. Hawthorne, *Complete Works*, vol. 10, 376.

58. Hawthorne, *Complete Works*, vol. 10, 377.

59. Claudia D. Johnson, *The Productive Tensions of Hawthorne's Art* (Tuscaloosa: University of Alabama Press, 1981), 8. Johnson uses the term "productive tensions" primarily to investigate the interplay of psychological drama and artistic technique in Hawthorne's work, but "productive tension" is also a helpful way to characterize his treatment of apparent oppositions between humans and the rest of the natural world.

60. Ralph Waldo Emerson, *Nature and Selected Essays*, ed. Larzer Ziff (New York: Penguin, 2003), 35.

61. Hawthorne, *Complete Works*, vol. 5, 55.

62. Rose Hawthorne Lathrop, *Memories of Hawthorne* (Boston: Houghton Mifflin, 1897), 211.

63. See "Fairyland Pond," The Walden Woods Project, The Thoreau Institute at Walden Woods, www.walden.org/property/fairyland-pond.

64. Hawthorne, *Complete Works*, vol. 3, 13.

65. Hawthorne, *Complete Works*, vol. 3, 13.

66. Hawthorne, *Complete Works*, vol. 3, 13.

67. Hawthorne, *Complete Works*, vol. 3, 16.

68. Hawthorne, *Complete Works*, vol. 3, 16.

69. Hawthorne, *Complete Works*, vol. 3, 321.

70. Hawthorne, *Complete Works*, vol. 3, 322.

71. Hawthorne, *Complete Works*, vol. 6, 29.

72. William Shakespeare, *The Winter's Tale*, ed. Stephen Orgel (New York: Oxford University Press, 2008), 173.

73. Hawthorne, *The Complete Works of Nathaniel Hawthorne*, vol. 6, *The Marble Faun, or, The Romance of Monte Beni*, with Introductory Notes by George Parsons Lathrop, Riverside Edition (Boston: Houghton Mifflin, 1883), 15.

74. Hawthorne, *Complete Works*, vol. 6, 15.

75. Hawthorne, *Complete Works*, vol. 6, 15.

76. Hawthorne, *The Centenary Edition of the Works of Nathaniel Hawthorne*, vol. 17, *The Letters, 1853-1856*, ed. William Charvat et al. (Columbus: Ohio State University Press, 1983), 294.

77. Larry Reynolds, *Devils and Rebels: The Making of Hawthorne's Damned Politics* (Ann Arbor: University of Michigan Press, 2008), 204.

78. Toni Morrison, *Playing in the Dark: Whiteness and the Literary Imagination* (Cambridge, MA: Harvard University Press, 1992), 5.

79. Hawthorne, *Complete Works*, vol. 3, 225, 230.

80. Hawthorne, *Complete Works*, vol. 3, 374–75.

81. Mikhail Bakhtin, *The Dialogic Imagination: Four Essays*, ed. Michael Holquist, trans. Caryl Emerson and Michael Holquist (Austin: University of Texas Press, 1981), 263. Bakhtin speaks of these ideas in terms of converging speeches:

"Authorial speech, the speeches of narrators, inserted genres, the speech of characters are merely those fundamental compositional unities with whose help heteroglossia [*raznorečie*] can enter the novel; each of them permits a multiplicity of social voices and a wide variety of their links and interrelationships (always more or less dialogized)."

82. Dickinson's poem "Some Keep the Sabbath Going to Church" is traditionally numbered 236.

Chapter 1

Investigating Hawthorne's Nonfiction Nature Writing

> Nature cannot be exactly reproduced on canvas or in print; and the artist's only resource is to substitute something that may stand instead of and suggest the truth.
>
> —Nathaniel Hawthorne, *English Notebooks*[1]

To understand the development of Hawthorne's environmental sensibility, it is important to take at least a brief inventory of the physical places that drew his attention. This includes the Maine forests and farms along Sebago Lake as well as the witch-haunted streets of his Salem childhood and the majestic pines and mighty Androscoggin River surrounding his rural Maine college as well as the Boston city lights that attracted his attention as a young man. After college, he was not relegated to his mother's attic as he liked to claim but was fond of traveling the New England and New York countryside where he saw the White Mountains, the landscape along the Erie Canal, Niagara Falls, and more. Upon his marriage, he moved to the Transcendentalist neighborhood of Concord, Massachusetts, and the nature-celebrating denizens of that place left their indelible imprint on him. After a brief return to Salem, Hawthorne moved to the Berkshires of Western Massachusetts, a place famous for the beauty of its natural scenery as well as its attraction for prominent literati such as Catharine Maria Sedgwick and Herman Melville. His move back to eastern Massachusetts and finally back to Concord immediately preceded his years abroad in the countrysides of England and Italy before his final return back to pastoral Concord on the eve of the Civil War.

Hawthorne's early travel sketches and the observations he jotted in his notebooks often reflect upon the relationship between human and nonhuman nature, and these reflections inform the shape of many of his fictional narratives that follow. Away from the witch-haunted streets of his childhood home in Salem, Hawthorne composed copious descriptions of the natural world that demonstrate his intimate, first-hand knowledge of the natural world in many places that he traveled and lived during the different seasons of his life. American and European mountains, lakes, forests, rivers, meadow, orchards, and gardens are frequently featured, often eliciting questions of the relationship between human and nonhuman nature. Hawthorne's fictional depictions of the natural world take on added significance when placed alongside his comments about the natural world in his notebooks. As I argue elsewhere, "The travel sketches that develop from Hawthorne's rambles are replete with reminders that nonhuman nature is a reality independent of human acknowledgement rather than being a mere projection of human consciousness, as some of his fictional characters seem to think. Most significantly, his stories of the White Mountains, the Erie Canal, and the celebrated landmark of Niagara Falls show that the natural landscape left its indelible imprint on his mind during the pre-Concord years."[2]

The pastoral settings of Hawthorne's Maine residences contributed significantly to his personal knowledge of the "wild" American landscape. Bowdoin College, for example, was situated in a pastoral setting of rural Maine. In a dedicatory preface to Horatio Bridge, an old college friend, Hawthorne describes their college days at Bowdoin: "While we were lads together at a country college,—gathering blue-berries, in study-hours, under those tall academic pines; or watching the great logs, as they tumbled along the current of the Androscoggin; or shooting pigeons and gray squirrels in the woods; or bat-fowling in the summer twilight; or catching trouts in that shadowy little stream which, I suppose, is still wandering river-ward through the forest,— though you and I will never cast a line in it again."[3] During Hawthorne's years at Bowdoin, the college buildings were situated in a small clearing surrounded by miles of forest on three sides and a river on the other. A faculty member during Hawthorne's time there describes the setting in pastoral terms: "The level earth, through whose slippery carpet of scanty herbage and withered pine leaves shot up, in their season, the frequent blueberry and wintergreen; the air charged with resinous odors; the blackened tree-trunks which told of former fires; the subdued and sombre light; the tinkling cowbells and the gentle rustle of the breeze in the branches above."[4]

For Hawthorne, the natural world is rarely mere background material even before he meets the Transcendentalists and responds to their enthusiastic embrace of nature as a teacher. His early travel writings—most of them during or following his college years—show his growing awareness of nature as an active presence with a reality that exists apart from any romantic descriptions he might hear or compose. Although Hawthorne typically composes his narratives in a romantic mode, he brings frequent attention to the way his mode represents physical reality. At Fort Ticonderoga, Hawthorne's traveling narrator's romanticized images of battles past are displaced by the stark reality of the present world: "Tall trees have grown upon its ramparts, since the last garrison marched out, to return no more, or only at some dreamer's summons, gliding from the twilight past to vanish among realities."[5] In Hawthorne's telling, the realities of the trees growing in and around the abandoned fort proclaimed the longevity of the natural world as opposed to the temporal wars—and dreams—of humans. While dreamers like Hawthorne might remember the past, the presence of the natural world attests to a reality not to be undone by our dreams or imagined histories of the past. Drawing attention to the limits of his own style of writing, Hawthorne shows his awareness that romanticism may not always adequately address the human condition. The fact that he employs romanticism nonetheless suggests that despite its shortcomings he is convinced that romance does have a role to play in understanding the human condition.

Although the woods and ocean near Salem may have crowded with ghosts and witches in Hawthorne's imagination, his travels through the New England and New York countryside gave him more uplifting experiences in the natural world. But it is during his time with the Transcendentalists that his thinking about humans and nature develop most fully. Concord especially held out its pastoral charms for Hawthorne and his family. Hawthorne's notebooks also trace his travels abroad, mostly in England and Italy. And contemplations on nature continue to fill his notebooks, giving him much material that he later shapes into his last two published books—*The Marble Faun*, a romance set in Italy, and *Our Old Home*, a collection of travel sketches from his time in England. Understanding the extent of Hawthorne's nature writing is impossible without becoming familiar with the copious notebooks that he filled while traveling about the American landscape as well as the landscapes of England and Italy. In these writings, we see a writer attending to nature in a manner that might not be as intense as that of his Transcendentalist friend Thoreau but that nonetheless takes the natural world seriously as a reality in its own right.

WRITING NATURE IN CONCORD

When Hawthorne first moves with his bride Sophia Peabody to the Transcendentalist neighborhood of Concord in 1842, he frequently compares their newlywed life in this pastoral setting to Adam and Eve in the Garden of Eden. In Concord, Hawthorne becomes a well-known friend of Transcendentalists and becomes more acquainted with their writing, including Emerson's famous essay *Nature*. Hawthorne no doubt has this essay in mind when he writes of his experience as a gardener and a frequenter of the hillsides and woods of Concord: "It is as if the original relation between man and Nature were restored in my case, and as if I were to look exclusively to her for the support of my Eve and myself,—to trust to her for food and clothing, and all things needful, with the full assurance that she would not fail me."[6] Here he expresses his feelings of unity with nature, a unity that includes religious undertones when he compares his wife Sophia to Eve. Hawthorne also recalls going boating on the Lily Pond and experiencing such a oneness with nature that he wishes for more. God, humans, and nature are in harmony in Concord, if only for a season.

In 1849, before the publication of Hawthorne's first major book-length romance, Emerson sent him a presentation copy of the second edition of *Nature*.[7] Originally published several years before Hawthorne's arrival in Concord, Emerson's *Nature* called for a return to nature by contrasting European corruption and loss of nature with the promise of rediscovering nature on the huge, largely uncivilized continent of America. America was newness incarnate. "The foregoing generations beheld God and nature face to face; we, through their eyes. Why should not we also enjoy an original relation to the universe?" Emerson queries.[8] Many of Emerson's fellow Transcendentalists put his ideas about nature to the test in works such as Thoreau's famous literary text *Walden; or, Life in the Woods* and Fuller's *Summer on the Lakes, in 1843*. While Thoreau's study of Walden Pond and Walden Woods and its vicinity was more empirically driven than Emerson's visionary proclamations, Thoreau does claim a kind of "original relation" with nature as a result of his experiment in Walden Woods. "Every morning," he writes, "was a cheerful invitation to make my life of equal simplicity, and I may say innocence, with Nature herself."[9] Thoreau later claimed that his childhood pastime of fishing had already given him an intimate "acquaintance with Nature" and that his life at Walden had made him like "[f]ishermen, hunters, woodchoppers, and others, spending their lives in the fields and woods" who are by their lifestyles "a part of Nature themselves" and thus "are often in a more favorable mood for observing her, in the intervals of their pursuits, than philosophers or poets even, who approach her with expectation."[10] Obtaining that original relation to nature, for Thoreau, is a process and a lifestyle, not simple observation by itself.

Margaret Fuller's work is less bound by the form of the essay that Emerson adopts as the medium of environmentally inclined writing, but her study is similarly undergirded with the question of how to become intimate enough with nature to have an original relation that might lead to accurate interpretations of nature. "I would beat with the living heart of the world," writes Fuller, "and understand all the moods, even the fancies or fantasies, of nature. I dare to trust to the interpreting spirit to bring me out all right at last—to establish truth through error."[11] While Hawthorne similarly investigates nature for the secrets of existence, he is less optimistic about being able to achieve unity with nature or to interpret it unambiguously. Like the Transcendentalists, Hawthorne values nature as a teacher. Unlike the Transcendentalists—especially Emerson—he does not expect nature to be easily understood or to signify only beauty and benevolence.

Hawthorne's writing also represents a response to Emerson's declaration of America as a place of "new lands, new men, new thoughts" and his call for "our own works and laws and worship" to be developed through intimate relationships to the natural world rather than in opposition to it.[12] In the preface of *Mosses from an Old Manse*, Hawthorne's last collection of short stories to be written before transitioning to book-length romances, Hawthorne mentions that "the Old Manse" where he is living with his wife in Concord is the very place where Emerson wrote his famous essay.[13] This acknowledgment suggests Hawthorne's debt to Emerson even before Emerson gave Hawthorne a second-edition copy of *Nature*. Hawthorne addresses Emerson's questions with a mixture of fascination and skepticism. He is quick to articulate his wariness of Emerson's influence, for example, when characterizing him as "a beacon burning on a hill-top." The light cast by Emerson, he notes, "revealed objects unseen before,—mountains, gleaming lakes, glimpses of a creation among the chaos, but, also, as was unavoidable, it attracted bats and owls and the whole host of night birds, which flapped their dusky wings against the gazer's eyes, and sometimes were mistaken for fowls of angelic feather. Such delusions always hover nigh whenever a beacon-fire of truth is kindled."[14] Much as John Winthrop's vaunted Puritan city upon a hill had attracted less desirable elements of Puritanism as well as its soon-to-be-dashed hopes for a pure New World community, so Emerson's Transcendentalist beacon on a hill was not as pure and true as Emerson's followers might have hoped.

Leo Marx's groundbreaking book *The Machine in the Garden* bears a title inspired by Hawthorne's record of a reverie in Walden Woods, a contemplation on nature interrupted by the sound of an approaching steam engine. Analyzing the intrusion of the locomotive into the pastoral scene Hawthorne is describing, Marx notes that this interruption "forc[es] him to acknowledge the existence of a reality alien to the pastoral dream. What begins as a conventional tribute to the pleasures of withdrawal from the world—a simple pleasure fantasy—is transformed by the interruption of the machine into a far more complex state of mind," Marx claims.[15] While this disjunction is clearly emblematized by the approach of the train near Walden Woods, Marx overlooks another arrival Hawthorne announces in the notebook passage in question—most likely because it was not included in the earlier passages from Hawthorne's notebooks, whose publication had been supervised by Sophia Hawthorne. Perhaps this earlier arrival and Hawthorne's discussion of it offended Sophia's Transcendentalist leanings. For it is a mosquito rather than the train that initiates Hawthorne's sense of unease with "pleasant views" about nature, and the mosquito's entry changes Hawthorne's contemplations of the placidity of nature by demonstrating the dynamism within the natural order. The sound of the mosquito interrupts Hawthorne's reverie: "And hark, terrible to the ear, here is the minute but intense hum of a musquito [*sic*]. Instinct prevails over all the nonsense of sentiment; we crush him at once, and there is his grim and grisly corpse, the ugliest object in nature. This incident had disturbed our tranquility," Hawthorne declares. Noting further that this incident serves to decenter humans from their presumed position of superiority in the web of nature, Hawthorne states: "In truth, the whole insect tribe, so far as we can judge, are made more for themselves, and less for man, than any other portion of creation."[16] This dynamism of nature connects humans to the natural world, foregrounding humans as a part of nature and its processes rather than having an entirely separate existence. Despite this significant omission, Marx's influential now-classic text does acutely recognize in Hawthorne a writer concerned with the way the industrial revolution unbalances our relationship with the natural world, potentially disturbing the equilibrium of humans with the environment as humans use and abuse nature and simultaneously become estranged from it.

Following Marx, John Gatta has recently drawn attention to Hawthorne's descriptions of the Old Manse, his home in the pastoral setting of Concord. Delineating Hawthorne's descriptions of the vegetables of his garden, the fruits of the orchard, and the act of gardening outside his home as a contemplation on nature and what it teaches us, Gatta convincingly presents Hawthorne's notebook descriptions of life at the Old Manse as "a form of environmental literature."[17] Gatta argues that gardening is especially important in Hawthorne's contemplation of nature as a work of divine creativity: "To be sure, the gardener invests a modicum of labor in his domestic plot—and to that extent, according to Hawthorne, qualifies as a cocreator with God of his own biotic environment."[18] Gatta considers the Old Manse writings as Hawthorne's "green phase," and Buell similarly characterizes "the Old Manse" as "[t]he first canonical work outside the transcendentalist ranks that celebrated Concord as a place of notable bucolic philosophers and literati."[19]

It is in Concord—his American Eden—that Hawthorne finds gardens and orchards a rich site of connection between human and nonhuman nature, as well as between the present, past, and future. He takes great pleasure in his gardens and his own gardening efforts, reflecting on growing things to which he contributes and valuing the good of existence they represent even apart from what they do for humanity:

[T]he greatest interest of these vegetables does not seem to consist in their being articles of food. It is rather that we love to see something born into the world; and when a great squash or melon is produced, it is a large and tangible existence, which the imagination can seize hold of and rejoice in. I love, also, to see my own works contributing to the life and well-being of animate nature. It is pleasant to have the bees come and suck honey out of my squash-blossoms, though, when they have laden themselves, they fly off to some unknown hive, which will give me back nothing in return for what my garden has given them. But there is much more honey in the world, and so I am content.[20]

Hawthorne's contemplation on gardening celebrates the living world outside of its utility for humans and delights in his contributions to its health and growth. By interacting with the rest of the natural world as a member of that world rather than as an aloof utilitarian and by participating in the birth of new substances into the world, Hawthorne suggests, he is able to experience a sense of wholeness that comes from living out his part in nature. When contemplating the old orchard standing nearby, Hawthorne similarly exults in the tangible connection between himself and nature and the previous occupant of the house: "The same trees offer their fruit to me, as freely as they did to him,—their old branches, like withered hands and arms, holding out apples of the same flavor as they held out to Dr. Ripley in his lifetime. Thus the trees, as living existences, form a peculiar link between the dead and us."[21] Planted things—whether gardens or orchards—provide continuity between generations of humans while foregrounding the ongoing relationship between human and nonhuman nature.

Hawthorne's delight in nature is also evident in a scintillating meditation on springtime called "Buds and Bird Voices." In this brief nature essay, Hawthorne takes great pleasure in the knowledge that each spring "the old paradisiacal economy of life is again in force."[22] "Thank Providence for Spring!" Hawthorne writes, "The earth—and man himself, by sympathy with his birthplace—would be far other than we find them if life toiled wearily onward without this periodical infusion of the primal spirit."[23] Nature writings like this one, famous in Hawthorne's own day but less well known today, placed him in the public mind as a nature writer of sorts before his book-length romances were published. Herman Melville called this essay "a delicious thing" in the same book review that famously declared a "great power of blackness" in the dark side of Hawthorne's writing. Hawthorne's darkness was hardly recognized before Melville pointed it out because, as Melville puts it: "He seems to be deemed a pleasant writer, with a pleasant style," a writer with plenteous "Indian-summer sunlight on the hither side of [his] soul."[24] But Melville points out the dark side of Hawthorne's soul too, concluding with a bit of advice for readers who only see the sunny side of Hawthorne: "You may be witched by his sunlight,—transported by the bright gildings in the skies he builds over you; but there is the blackness of darkness beyond; and even his bright gildings but fringe and play upon the edges of thunder-clouds."[25]

Nearing the conclusion of his first season in Concord, Hawthorne determines that "on the whole, my first independent experiment of agriculture is quite a successful one."[26] Contrasting his congenial interaction with the natural world through gardening with the feeling of animosity provoked by his hard labor of Brook Farm, Hawthorne reflects upon a particularly beautiful day:

> This is a glorious day,—bright, very warm, yet with an unspeakable gentleness both in its warmth and brightness. On such days, it is impossible not to love Nature, for she evidently loves us. At other seasons she does not give me this impression, or only at very rare intervals; but in these happy autumnal days, when she has perfected the harvests, and accomplished every necessary thing that she had to do, she overflows with a blessed superfluity of love. It is good to be alive now. Thank God for breath,—yes, for mere breath! when it is made up of such a heavenly breeze as this. . . . There is a pervading blessing diffused over all the world. I look out of the window and think, "Oh perfect day! Oh beautiful world! Oh good God!"[27]

These contemplations on nature again suggest that time spent in nature somehow provides human connection with the spiritual world as well as with the natural world—that embedded in the reality of the physical world is the sign and revelation of a spiritual world.

Despite his sense of uneasiness about the way industrializing society is encroaching upon the natural environment, Hawthorne at first celebrated nature as something grander and ultimately more powerful than humans. Following a beautiful afternoon at Walden Pond, Hawthorne begins describing the beauty of nature he sees there but pauses to declare that "it is in vain for me to attempt to describe these autumnal brilliancies, or to convey the impression which they make on me. . . . Luckily, there is no need of such a record; for Nature renews the scene, year after year."[28] Words are not adequate to the task of describing the scene. Only being in nature can do so. But Hawthorne continues to try. On one of the shores of the pond, Hawthorne observes the huts of Irish railroad workers and compares their homes to ant-hills, which he characterizes as "something in which Nature has a larger share than man."[29] While his attitude toward the Irish workers is difficult to ascertain, his conclusion about nature is clear. Anthills stand as material evidence that nature includes more than human civilization, that nature is not only about humans.

WRITING NATURE ABROAD

During his time abroad, Hawthorne's growing sense of environmental consciousness becomes even more apparent. At first, he continues to assume that nature is stronger than humans and that the triumph of nature is to be celebrated as an inevitable and pleasant outcome. At the ruins of an old Scottish palace, for example, Hawthorne pauses to reflect on the reemergence of natural growth in this regal building once stamping human civilization atop nature: "Grass and weeds, indeed, have found soil enough to flourish in. . . . It was very mournful, very beautiful, very delightful, too, to see how Nature takes back the palace, now that kings have done with it, and adopts it as part of her great garden."[30] Hawthorne's movement from "mournful" to "beautiful" to "delightful" suggests a progression from a mostly human-centered point of view to an increasing regard for the larger biosphere as he continues to contemplate the significance of the scene he is observing.

But it is also during his time abroad that Hawthorne emphasizes the environmental destruction occasionally hinted upon in Hawthorne's American notebooks. In a travel sketch titled "Pilgrimage to Old Boston," drawn directly from his travels through the English landscape, Hawthorne contrasts the beauty of the physical environment with the ugliness of the factories now dotting the English landscape:

> We saw, along the wayside, the never-failing green fields, hedges, and other monotonous features of an ordinary English landscape. There were little factory villages, too, or larger towns, with their tall chimneys, and their pennons of black smoke, their ugliness of brick-work, and their heaps of refuse matter from the furnace, which seems to be the only kind of stuff which Nature cannot take back to herself and resolve into the elements, when man has thrown it aside. These hillocks of waste and effete mineral always disfigure the neighborhood of iron-mongering towns, and, even after a considerable antiquity, are hardly made decent with a little grass.[31]

Hawthorne's passage jolts the reader from the hypnotic greenery of "an ordinary English landscape" to the unsightly "hillocks of waste and effete mineral" in these "iron-mongering towns"—a disturbing sight not easily forgotten. This passage does not simply celebrate the beauty of nature, like some of Hawthorne's earlier notebook entries. Instead, it sounds a prescient cautionary note about the increased human destruction of the environment being caused by an industrializing society.

This particular travel sketch is notable for its variegated descriptions of the English landscape, sometimes in comparison with the wilder scenes of the American landscape. Hawthorne also creates a vivid contrast between the "very striking" scenes of "the show-districts, such as the Lake country, or Derbyshire" and the pleasant but less striking scenes in much of the country with its "long and gradual ascents, bleak, windy, and desolate, conveying the very impression which the reader gets from many passages of Miss Brontë's novels, and still more from those of her two sisters."[32] But desolate as the moors may be, Hawthorne is again strangely fascinated by the English landscape when he travels more rapidly through the countryside by train: "The old highways and foot-paths were as natural as brooks and rivulets, and adapted themselves by an inevitable impulse to the physiognomy of the country; and, furthermore, every object within view of them had some subtile [*sic*] reference to their curves and undulations; but the line of a railway is perfectly artificial, and puts all precedent things at sixes-and-sevens."[33]

In Sheffield, however, contrasts within nature are again apparent even away from a view of the landscape. The city of Sheffield, Hawthorne declares, must be "smokier than all England . . . unless Newcastle be the exception," a smokiness that gives the city an appearance of "sulphurous vapor" that disappears as they enter a forest "of young and thriving plantations, which will require a century or two of slow English growth to give them much breadth of shade."[34] Nature and civilization here seem to be vying for the upper hand rather than achieving the harmony Hawthorne expects to see. At the ruins of an old Roman arch above the Lincoln Cathedral, Hawthorne again finds something poetic but very real in the crumbling old human-built edifice being overtaken by nature: "It is a rude and massive structure, and seems as stalwart now as it could have been two thousand years ago; and though Time has gnawed it externally, he has made what amends he could by crowning its rough and broken summit with grass and weeds, and planting tufts of yellow flowers on the projections up and down the sides."[35] The contrasts Hawthorne describes in the variegated greenery and bleak moors of the countryside and the ugliness wrought by the instruments of industrialization further demonstrate Hawthorne's awareness of the ways that human activity is changing the world. And these changes are ominous, hinting of results that may not ultimately be beneficial to humans or the environment.

His journeys through the English countryside appear to convince Hawthorne of the value and perhaps even the necessity of slowing down to absorb nature's presence and processes more deliberately. Taking a steamer up the River Witham, Hawthorne remarks that traveling slowly "allowed us time enough and to spare for the objects along the shore" even though the landscape was "one unvaried level over the whole thirty miles of our voyage."[36] The interspersing of natural scenery and human habitations gives him plenty to contemplate:

> The landscape was tame, to the last degree, but had an English character that was abundantly worth our looking at. A green luxuriance of early grass; old, high-roofed farm-houses, surrounded by their stone barns and ricks of hay and grain; ancient villages, with the square, gray tower of a church seen afar over the level country, amid the cluster of red roofs; here and there a shadowy grove of venerable trees, surrounding what was perhaps an Elizabethan hall. . . . The river retains its canal-like aspect all along; and only in the latter part of its course does it become more than wide enough for the little steamer to turn itself round.[37]

The English greenery, rivers, and people appear capable of existing in harmony with each other. This seeming peaceful coexistence of humans and nature is almost tranquilizing, but that tranquillity is about to be tested.

As he does earlier in the iconic scene of the train—and mosquito!—breaking into his reveries at Walden Pond, Hawthorne interrupts his description of this lovely scene with an event that sharply disturbs any placidity that has settled over the observer (and reader). "The only memorable incident of our voyage," Hawthorne writes, "happened when a mother-duck was leading her little fleet of five ducklings across the river, just as our steamer went swaggering by."[38] By characterizing the passage of the ship as "swaggering" and paying attention to the mother duck and her ducklings, Hawthorne offers a critique of the way that human progress can threaten natural processes. Commenting that he rushed up to witness "the catastrophe" since he recognized immediately that they "could not possibly avert it," Hawthorne shows his sympathy for the little animals being displaced by human action: "The poor ducklings had uttered their baby-quacks, and striven with all their tiny might to escape; four of them, I believe, were washed aside and thrown off unhurt from the steamer's prow; but the fifth must have gone under the whole length of the keel, and never could have come up alive."[39] This haunting image is designed to clearly elicit reader's sympathy for the little animals who share the earth and its water with humans whose control over nature causes violence sometimes even when that is not their purpose. This event clearly demonstrates the ways that human creations can disturb the processes of nature.

Hawthorne's sense of companionship with the animals—other members of the biosphere—again comes into play when he finally reaches Old Boston. He feels himself almost at home, commenting on the life of the people "very cheerful in the morning sun . . . in the day's primal freshness," and he wishes himself a jackdaw so that he could fly with the birds in the impressive bell tower of St. Botolph's Church where they "evidently have pleasant homes in their hereditary nests among its topmost windows, and live delightful lives, flitting and cawing about its pinnacles and flying buttresses."[40] These birds have converted human edifices to their own purposes, finding a way to live in harmony with the humans around them much more successfully than the poor ducks who got plowed over by the steamboat. Hawthorne's observations of the jackdaws and ducks suggest that there are ways for human and nonhuman nature to adapt themselves to each other rather than obliterating each other, but that some cases call for human caution if animals are not to be displaced—perhaps violently.

One difference from American landscapes that Hawthorne notices in England is that "[o]n the rudest surface of English earth, there is seen the effect of centuries of civilization, so that you do not quite get at naked Nature anywhere."[41] Further, as a result of the famous poems of the Lake Poets, the nature in that beautiful region of England is something rarely seen with one's own eyes: "Every point of beauty is so well known, and has been described so much, that one must needs look through other people's eyes, and feels as if he were looking at a picture rather than a reality."[42] In his reverie of the famous Lake Country that so inspired the British Romantic poets, Hawthorne questions attempts to create picturesque natural settings, querying whether "people of real taste should help Nature out, and beautify her, or perhaps rather *prettify* her so much as they do,—opening vistas, showing one thing, hiding another, making a scene picturesque, whether or no. I cannot rid myself of the feeling that there is something false—a kind of humbug—in all this."[43] Nonetheless, he ends this lengthy reflection by admitting that "it is good to think of Wordsworth, in quiet, past days, walking in his home-shadow of trees which he knew, and training flowers, and trimming shrubs, and chanting in an undertone his own verses up and down the winding walks."[44] This vacillation between love of nature and regret for human representations of nature as often "a kind of humbug" even while he himself represents nature in his writing belies an inescapable tension between even the most direct representations of nature and the actual experience of being in nature.

When comparing literary art to visual art in Europe, Hawthorne expands upon his earlier claim that nature is hard to recognize in its true form. "Nature cannot be exactly reproduced on canvas or in print," Hawthorne observes, concluding that, like painters, literary artists can only "substitute something that may stand instead of and suggest the truth."[45] The reproduction of images in paint or ink makes literature and visual art a *re-presentation* of natural images and processes rather than actually giving us nature itself. Further problematizing representations of the natural world, Hawthorne suggests that Nature remains shrouded to casual observers:

> But, in truth, I doubt if anybody ever does really see a mountain, who goes for the set and sole purpose of seeing it. Nature will not let herself be seen in such cases. You must patiently bide her time; and by and by, at some unforeseen moment, she will quietly and suddenly unveil herself, and for a brief space allow you to look right into the heart of her mystery. But if you call out to her peremptorily, "Nature! unveil yourself this very moment!" she only draws her veil the closer; and you may look with all your eyes, and imagine you see all that she can show, and yet see nothing.[46]

With these words, Hawthorne explicitly draws attention to the subjectivity and limited capacity of human perception in observing nature. For Hawthorne, nature must be encountered by patient observation and alertness to its surprising sights rather than by simply glancing at it or hastily demanding to know all its secrets. Thus, Hawthorne's statements about the difficulty of seeing nature and his more obscure observations of nature demonstrate not his lack of interest but his determination to let the environment manifest itself to him on its own terms.

In Italy as in England, Hawthorne again composes extensive descriptions of natural scenery in all its seeming harmony and discord. While Hawthorne prefers American fruits to the majority of the Italian ones he has in abundance and whose beauty he finds much more remarkable than their taste, he does acknowledge his great fondness for the wide variety of figs and grapes in Italy.[47] Here in Italy, Hawthorne again reflects on the ways mosquitoes pose a challenge for anthropocentric views of the world. He calls Italian mosquitoes "horribly pungent little satanic particles" and revels in squashing them, noting with surprise his own feelings of spiteful vengeance on the mosquitoes but declaring that "it is impossible not to impute a certain malice and intellectual venom to these diabolical insects."[48] However, he immediately questions his misattribution of malice and intellect, speculating that perhaps "our health, at this season of the year, requires that we should be kept in a state of irritation, and so the mosquitoes are Nature's prophylactic remedy for some disease; or whether we are made for the mosquitoes, not they for us. It is possible, just possible," he adds, "that the infinitesimal doses of poison which they infuse into us are a homoeopathic safeguard against pestilence; but medicine never was administered in a more disagreeable way."[49] So, even though the displeasure we experience when a mosquito draws blood from us argues against the idea that mosquitoes exist for the good of humans, it is possible that they do us and the world more good than we know. Even if mosquitoes do serve a function by inoculating us against terrible diseases, however, their method of inoculation suggests that something other than human comfort is at work in the processes of nature. And it is also quite possible that they may in fact not be made for humans at all. In this latter suggestion, Hawthorne gives the shadowy outlines of an eco-consciousness that displaces humans from the center they are accustomed to command within the natural world.

Yet this is not the first time Hawthorne would at least hint of the displacement of anthropocentric views of the world. While living in Concord, he had similarly lamented that the squash-bug was killing the vegetables but not the weeds of his garden: "Perhaps, if we could penetrate Nature's secrets, we should find that what we call weeds are more essential to the well-being of the world than the most precious fruit or grain. This may be doubted, however, for there is an unmistakable analogy between these wicked weeds and the bad habits and sinful propensities which have overrun the moral world; and we may as well imagine that there is good in one as in the other."[50] Weeds serve as analogies of the threat to the well-being of people as well as being actual threats to the well-being of his garden plants. Thus, for Hawthorne, nature serves as our teacher as well as reminding us of the existence of nonhuman reality.

In 1858 Italy, Hawthorne does not find nature only in the actual outdoors. For Rome is a land of art as well as a land of nature. And here Hawthorne composes numerous contemplations on artwork and artifacts depicting nature. Visiting the art studio of a Swiss man named Mueller, Hawthorne characterizes the elderly gentleman's artwork as highly "faithful transcripts of whatever Nature has most beautiful to show, and which she shows only to those who love her deeply and patiently. They are wonderful pictures, compressing plains, seas, and mountains, with miles and miles of distance, into the space of a foot or two without crowding anything or leaving out a feature, and diffusing the free, blue atmosphere throughout."[51] At the Museum of Natural History, Hawthorne finds "a very good collection of almost everything that Nature has made,—or exquisite copies of what she has made,—stones, shells, vegetables, insects, fishes, animals, man; the greatest wonders of the museum being some models in wax of all parts of the human frame."[52] Thus, artistic representations and collections of nature as well as actual natural scenery piqued Hawthorne's imagination and contributed to his own artistic modes of representing the natural world in his writing.

These numerous samples of Hawthorne's nonfiction nature writing, taken together, demonstrate an intensity of interest in the natural world that places Hawthorne well within the terrain of nineteenth-century nature writers. Nature is not mere background, but instead is an essential part of human existence and experience and must be explored thoroughly if one is to make sense of the human condition. The natural environment serve as a teacher and home for humans, and humans are intimately related to nature through their status as natural beings. Thus, understanding the purpose of human existence includes a recognition of a nonhuman reality that includes other members of the biosphere who are related to and affected by humans. Hawthorne's passages of nature writing in his noteboooks demonstrate the persistence of his interest in nonhuman nature and its relation to human existence and activity. Furthermore, these passages provide important insight into the thoughts that were on Hawthorne's mind as he composed his romances before and after his time abroad. The relationship between humans and nature is disturbed in an industrializing culture, and Hawthorne's writing increasingly hints that the outcome looks grim for both humans and nonhuman nature. The nature writings of Hawthorne's notebooks thus call for a thoroughgoing reconsideration of how Hawthorne's fiction engaged nineteenth-century American discussions about nature.

NOTES

1. Hawthorne, *The Complete Works of Nathaniel Hawthorne*, vol. 8, *Our Old Home, and English Note-Books, vol. 2,* with Introductory Notes by George Parsons Lathrop. Riverside Edition. (Boston: Houghton Mifflin, 1883), 478.

2. Steven Petersheim, "Hawthorne and Natural Landscapes," in *Nathaniel Hawthorne in Context*, ed. Monika Elbert (New York: Cambridge University Press, 2018), 378.

3. Hawthorne, *Complete Works*, vol. 3, 386–87.

4. Cleaveland, *An Elementary Treatise on Mineralogy and Geology, Designed for the Use of Pupils, – For Persons, Attending Lectures on these Subjects, – and as a Companion for Travellers in the United States of America*, 2–3.

5. Hawthorne, *Complete Works*, vol. 3, 597.

6. Hawthorne, *Complete Works*, vol. 9, 300–01.

7. Ralph Waldo Emerson, *The Journals and Miscellaneous Notebooks of Ralph Waldo Emerson*, vol. 11. 1848–1851, ed. A.W. Plumstead, William H. Gilman, and Ruth H. Bennett (Cambridge, MA: Belknap Press, 1975), 156.

8. Emerson, *Nature and Selected Essays*, 35.

9. Henry David Thoreau, *Walden* (Princeton: Princeton University Press, 2004), 88.

10. Thoreau, *Walden*, 210.

11. Margaret Fuller, *Summer on the Lakes, in 1843* (Urbana: University of Illinois Press, 1991), 82.

12. Emerson, *Nature and Selected Essays*, 35.

13. Hawthorne, *The Complete Works of Nathaniel Hawthorne*, vol. 2, *Mosses from an Old Manse*, with Introductory Notes by George Parsons Lathrop. Riverside Edition (Boston: Houghton Mifflin, 1882), 13.

14. Hawthorne, *Complete Works*, vol. 2, 42.

15. Marx, *The Machine in the Garden: Technology and the Pastoral Ideal in America*, 14–15.

16. Hawthorne, *The Centenary Edition of the Works of Nathaniel Hawthorne*, vol. 8, *The American Notebooks*, ed. William Charvat et al. (Columbus: Ohio State University Press, 1983), 248.

17. John Gatta, *Making Nature Sacred: Literature, Religion, and Environment in America from the Puritans to the Present* (New York: Oxford University Press, 2004), 99.

18. Gatta, *Making Nature Sacred*, 104.

19. Gatta, *Making Nature Sacred*, 323.

20. Hawthorne, *Complete Works*, vol. 9, 299.

21. Hawthorne, *Complete Works*, vol. 9, 295.

22. Hawthorne, *Complete Works*, vol. 2, 170.

23. Hawthorne, *Complete Works*, vol. 2, 180.

24. Melville, "Hawthorne and His Mosses," 106–108.

25. Melville, "Hawthorne and His Mosses," 106–108.

26. Hawthorne, *Complete Works*, vol. 9, 857.

27. Hawthorne, *Complete Works*, vol. 9, 857.

28. Hawthorne, *Complete Works*, vol. 9, 359–60.

29. Hawthorne, *Complete Works*, vol. 9, 360.

30. Hawthorne, *Complete Works*, vol. 8, 493.

31. Hawthorne, *The Complete Works of Nathaniel Hawthorne*, vol. 7, *Our Old Home, and English Note-Books, vol. 1*, with Introductory Notes by George Parsons Lathrop. Riverside Edition (Boston: Houghton Mifflin, 1883), 169.

32. Hawthorne, *Complete Works,* vol. 7, 170.
33. Hawthorne, *Complete Works,* vol. 7, 171. Charlotte Bronte was being celebrated by the literati at this time, publishing her novel *The Professor* in 1857, the same year her biography was written by Elizabeth Gaskell. Most of her fame stemmed from her 1847 novel *Jane Eyre,* however, which is indeed famous for its bleak scenery. In her sisters' works too, desolate heaths of the English countryside help to set the mood—*Wuthering Heights* by Emily Bronte and *Agnes Grey* by Anne Bronte. All three of their most famous novels were published in the same year, 1847.
34. Hawthorne, *Complete Works,* vol. 7, 172.
35. Hawthorne, *Complete Works,* vol. 7, 181.
36. Hawthorne, *Complete Works,* vol. 7, 185.
37. Hawthorne, *Complete Works,* vol. 7, 185–86.
38. Hawthorne, *Complete Works,* vol. 7, 186.
39. Hawthorne, *Complete Works,* vol. 7, 186.
40. Hawthorne, *Complete Works,* vol. 7, 188–89.
41. Hawthorne, *Complete Works,* vol. 8, 8.
42. Hawthorne, *Complete Works,* vol. 8, 9.
43. Hawthorne, *Complete Works,* vol. 8, 28.
44. Hawthorne, *Complete Works,* vol. 8, 28.
45. Hawthorne, *Complete Works,* vol. 8, 478.
46. Hawthorne, *Complete Works,* vol. 8, 254–55.
47. Hawthorne, *Complete Works,* vol. 10, 421–22.
48. Hawthorne, *Complete Works,* vol. 10, 422.
49. Hawthorne, *Complete Works,* vol. 10, 422.
50. Hawthorne, *Complete Works,* vol. 9, 353.
51. Hawthorne, *Complete Works,* vol. 10, 180.
52. Hawthorne, *Complete Works,* vol. 10, 303.

Chapter 2

Observing the Laboratory of Nature in Hawthorne's Short Fiction

> Oh, you are ungrateful to our mother earth! . . . Come what may, I never will forget her! Neither will it satisfy me to have her exist merely in idea. I want her great, round, solid self to endure interminably, and still to be peopled with the kindly race of man, whom I uphold to be much better than he thinks himself.
>
> —Nathaniel Hawthorne, "The Hall of Fantasy"[1]

"It is as if the original relation between Man and Nature were restored in my case," Nathaniel Hawthorne wrote in his notebook in August 1842, a few months after relocating to the Transcendentalist community in Concord, Massachusetts, with his new bride Sophia. "My business is merely to live and to enjoy; and whatever is essential to life and enjoyment will come as naturally as the dew from heaven."[2] Hawthorne's assertion that his primary "business" is "to live and to enjoy" presages the thought of Henry David Thoreau, whom he came to know well in Concord. Thoreau would later write about his business in life in *Walden*, "I went to the woods because I wanted to live deliberately . . . to live deep and suck out all the marrow of life."[3] Like Thoreau, Hawthorne took on Emerson's query in *Nature*: "Why should not we . . . enjoy an original relation to the universe?"[4] Like the Transcendentalists, Hawthorne desires an "original relation" between humans and nature even though he does not wholly embrace their unquestioning adulation of nature, considering the overlapping realities of human and nonhuman nature as enigmas only partially apprehended by humans.

The persistent references to *nature* and *human nature* in Hawthorne's fiction denote an ongoing inquiry into the cross-pollination between human culture and nonhuman nature. Hawthorne accepted the common belief of his time that because the American landscape was less developed by human action than the European civilization from which they came, the patterns of nature were more clearly seen on the American continent. Hawthorne's short stories that attend to the natural environment seem to concur with this Transcendentalist assumption, investigating the human condition in the light of his newfound intimacy with the natural environment. Quite often, Hawthorne interpolates the historical and cultural development of the United States with images of the American landscape. The nature imagery in Hawthorne's work implicitly calls humans to understand and live in accord with a world in which culture and nature are intertwined realities. As Hawthorne put it in a letter to a friend, addressing the cultural form of poetry alongside the vegetables of his garden: "I do not agree with you that poetry ought not to be brought into common life. If flowers of Eden can be made to grow among my cabbages and squashes, it will please me so much the better; those excellent vegetables will be just as good to eat, and the flowers no less delightful to see and smell."[5] Cultural forms or stories (such as poetry or Eden) and biological nature (vegetables) are hard to separate, and Hawthorne considers such separation neither necessary nor desirable. Culture is more "pleasing" and "delightful" when infused with the natural world. The garden itself is not a pristine image but already mingles human action with environmental processes to yield its vegetables and other cultivated plants. As such, it represents the overlap between nature and culture that Hawthorne found inextricable even as he searched for pure forms of nature.

Hawthorne's time in the Transcendentalist community of Concord resulted in an outpouring of fiction, culminating in the publication of the collection of tales titled *Mosses from an Old Manse* in 1846. Not surprisingly, given his frequent rambles through the woods and scenery of Concord, frequently in the company of his Transcendentalist neighbors, the natural environment is foregrounded in numerous selections of this work. In "The Old Manse," the introductory sketch of his new book, Hawthorne associates his stories with the river, the garden, the orchard, and "the sunshine glimmering through the willow branches" as well as the tree-lined path leading to "the dear Old Manse" itself.[6] *Mosses from an Old Manse* does not, however, represent the first example of Hawthorne's environmentally aware writing. In his earlier collection of tales and in his nonfiction notebook entries and letters, he recounts his experiences on a family farm and a rural college in Maine as well as his rambles through the New England countryside as a young man and his romantic tales of historical and nineteenth-century settings and characters. In his earliest tales, many of which were written during his travels through the New England and New York countrysides, the natural world is a fertile site for the workings of his literary imagination; here reality and romance grow side by side. Alfred Weber, Beth L. Lueck, and Dennis Berthold trace

Hawthorne's travels through the New England and New York countryside in 1832, aptly concluding that the White Mountains and Niagara Falls were the two features of the landscape that left the most lasting impressions on him.[7] In Hawthorne's Concord tales, humans who ignore or defy their connection to natural processes do so to their own detriment since the natural environment exists as a reality to which humans are bound by their existence as biological beings. Even in tales that insist upon the reality of the natural world, Hawthorne displays a growing sense of awareness that human culture shapes every human observer's perception of the natural world, making any fiction or nonfiction description of the natural environment a kind of cultural artifact.

It is no secret that Hawthorne's writing bears the imprint of a romanticized view of Nature—sometimes idealized and often with dark undertones. Even a cursory study of Hawthorne's short fiction reveals vacillating approaches and responses to the natural environment: Nature is alternately loved, feared, ignored, trampled, and respected by his characters. But Hawthorne's fiction in the 1830s and 1840s indicate his growing sense of the complexity of the relation between human imbrication in the natural world and his artistic development as a writer delving into the secrets of human nature. What is most often overlooked by today's readers is his deep awareness of the material world as a reality not fully recognized by his Puritan and non-Puritan characters alike. Quite often, Nature is feared or ignored by the figures of his fiction, but some of his characters acknowledge and even celebrate the natural world. The many instances of the environmental evocations in Hawthorne's early writings indicate in Hawthorne an environmentally attuned sensibility whose scope has been largely neglected.

ENVIRONMENTAL AND CULTURAL LANDSCAPES OF NEW ENGLAND

The White Mountains of New Hampshire, which Hawthorne describes as "Earth's undecaying monuments," gave him material for some of his finest early fiction.[8] The stories Hawthorne sets in the White Mountains foreground the natural environment with the narrator's explicit acknowledgment of a nonhuman reality that antedates human knowledge of these "old crystal hills, whose mysterious brilliancy had gleamed upon our distant wanderings before we thought of visiting them."[9] Sometimes these mountains serve as the site of secrets about the natural world that produce speculative whispers in the human community, and at other times the mountains erupt with vital processes that involve humans within the larger scope of reality represented by the earth and its creatures. In "The Ambitious Guest," for example, Hawthorne describes the constant threats of inhospitable weather, a reality that cannot merely be wished away, in the Notch of the White Mountains "where the wind was sharp throughout the year, and pitilessly cold in the winter."[10] The stern reality of nature is intensified by the constant threat of destruction faced by a family living at the foot of a mountain that "towered above their heads, so steep, that the stones would often rumble down its sides and startle them at midnight."[11] The family is forced to come face to face with the uncontrollable power of nature in a way they might have escaped if the father had attained his desire for "a good farm" somewhere "round the White Mountains; but not where they could tumble on our heads."[12] An unnamed "Ambitious Guest" who has stopped for the night and regaled the family with his aspirations for immortal fame shares the doom of the family living under the shadow of the mountain whose processes they have not fully understood and to which they have not fully acclimated when the processes of nature come alive in a crushing rockslide that kills the family and their guest. Simply put, the processes of nature in this instance at least show themselves to be stronger and longer lasting than human activity. As shaped by Hawthorne, this story serves as an exemplar of the danger of pursuing human ambitions without due attention to the processes of the natural world in which humans live.

Hawthorne's emphasis on the power of nature over humans suggests an untraditional attitude toward the natural environment, a kind of reversal which Christopher Johnson describes succinctly in his study of the literature produced by writers entranced by the White Mountains:

> Hawthorne was reversing the relationship between humanity and nature that had been predominant in American culture. Humanity's mission, dating from the colonial period, had been to modify nature by clearing the forests, planting trees, damming rivers, and constructing roads and towns. But through the metaphor of the avalanche that buried the Willey family, the author is saying that, in reality, nature is the awesome force that acts on humanity, and to imagine otherwise reveals a deeply flawed and hubristic view of the relationship between humanity and the natural world.[13]

Hawthorne's story is based on actual account of a major rockslide in the Notch of the White Mountains that occurred on August 28, 1826. The Willey family was caught in its path while rushing to a shelter they had prepared for such an event. Ironically, the whole family was killed while their house remained untouched. Hawthorne visited this area four years after the event, experiencing the inhospitable weather he describes in his story. In a letter dated September 16, 1832, Hawthorne writes to his mother about his arrival at "Ethan Crawford's house," a hotel also called the Notch House, about three miles from the Willey disaster. When he traveled to nearby Mt. Washington, he experienced the inclement weather he describes in his story: "The other particulars . . . how it snowed all the way, and how, when I got up the mountains on one side, the wind carried me a great distance off my feet and almost blew me down the other, and how the thermometer stood at twelve degrees below the freezing point, I shall have time enough to tell you when I return."[14]

In a study of the social implications of this story and its effect on Hawthorne's story, John Sears finds that the widespread publicity of the Willey family's fate in the face of this natural disaster made it "not just news, but a cultural event," an event that "Hawthorne's audience was trained to ask, what did the destruction of the Willeys indicate?"[15] Because he is focused upon the public response to questions of Providence in the face of this natural disaster, Sears passes over the environmental implications of Hawthorne's tale. Ian Marshall, on the other hand, reduces this "cautionary tale" to a lesson teaching us that "we should be careful about where we choose to settle and attentive to transitory environmental cues."[16] Hawthorne's story does allude to the collusion of natural and divine forces, describing the event in apocalyptic biblical terminology: "The foundations of the earth seemed to be shaken, as if this awful sound were the peal of the last trump."[17] Marshall offers a poignant suggestion, however, when he identifies another possible theme of the story: "the trickster nature of nature . . . beyond our control, and constantly capable of surprising us."[18] Hawthorne's tale suggests that there are forces greater than humans at work here, whether the awful forces of providence or the awful forces of nature or some combination of the two. Humans who fail to fully recognize the potency of natural reality risk falling victim to its processes. In the face of these processes, humans are forced to acknowledge an economy of life and being that repositions humans not as the solitary center of the natural world but as one member in it. American landscape artist Thomas Cole was also impressed enough by the Notch of the White Mountains to draw upon this setting as the basis for one of his famous paintings (see figure 2.1).

Hawthorne's interest in human interaction with the mountains is again evident in "The Great Carbuncle," another early story set in the White Mountains. Originally subtitled "A Mystery of the White Mountains," the natural setting is again foregrounded by drawing on regional Native American legends which Hawthorne regretfully calls "both too wild and too beautiful, to be adequately wrought up, in prose." This story gives the account of an unlikely assortment of people pursuing a legendary gem in a "remote and solitary region" where "a vast extent of wilderness lay between them and the nearest settlement."[19] Those individuals who refuse to observe or reflect upon the patterns of nature are the ones most doomed to failure in this story. The Cynic pronounces the foolishness of the doctor's effort to find the miraculous carbuncle of fabulous brilliance, crying out, "Why, you blockhead, there is no such thing, in *rerum natura*."[20] During his college years, Hawthorne would have become familiar with the Latin phrase *rerum natura*, the nature of things, in John Locke's

Figure 2.1 The Notch of the White Mountains (Crawford Notch) by Thomas Cole, 1839. Public Domain.

famous essay *On Human Understanding*, which was required reading for all Bowdoin students during Hawthorne's college years.[21] Locke writes that *"the certainty"* given by our senses "is as great as . . . *our condition needs*" but appeals to the value of the senses against anyone who "will be so sceptical as to distrust his senses, and to affirm that all . . . is but the series and deluding appearances of a long dream, whereof there is no reality." Instead, Locke asserts, we can be certain that things exist outside ourselves, "in *rerum natura.*"[22] The uncertainty in Hawthorne's story arises not from the question of whether any reality exists outside of ourselves (a question that will haunt some of Hawthorne's later tales) but instead from the question of whether a certain gem actually exists or is merely a legendary fabrication built upon vain fancies.

While most of those seeking the gem have little understanding of or sympathy for the natural environment, Matthew and Hannah, a naïve young couple of newlyweds are actually more environmentally attuned than their fellow seekers. They have already learned how to live in harmony with nature in their rural cottage, and they continue to live in harmony with nature during and after their ascent into the White Mountains. Johnson similarly observes that "[t]hey take on the characteristics of the deer of the forests, and in washing themselves in the river, they perform an ablution that leaves them morally and spiritually cleansed. Because they are grounded in the world of nature, they live by authentic values that will guide them to a destiny that is far different from those of the other fortune seekers."[23] When the young couple sees the carbuncle, revealed as a gigantic rock formation too great for them to retrieve, they are not disillusioned but return to their cottage at the foot of the mountains, grateful for the opportunity to have seen the gem in its natural splendor. Many of their counterparts, on the other hand, are debilitated by the process as they seek not companionship with nature but triumph over it. The Seeker is killed in his attempt to retract the whole side of the great rock, situated as it is in a cliff beside the mountain lake. The Cynic is literally blinded by his refusal to see the great shining light of the gargantuan gem. The rest of the party of seekers never sees it. The Merchant, like the Seeker and the Cynic, is given no name, but his attempts to benefit commercially from his experience ironically reduces him to poverty. The other two named characters, Lord de Vere and Dr. Cacaphodel, are the only ones not harmed by their attempts. Lord de Vere simply returns to his ancestral homes across the sea with a story of his adventures in America, and Dr. Cacaphodel finds some satisfaction from what he learns about the world through this experience even though he never obtains the carbuncle. A scientist and professor, the good doctor approaches the mountain with an air of inquiry, calling it "the laboratory of Nature."[24] Failing in his effort to find the fabled carbuncle, he instead conducts experiments on a unique granite stone he finds in the White Mountains and publishes the results in a folio that may gain at least a small readership. This story, when paired with Hawthorne's later stories of scientist figures, suggests that when scientists approach nature with an air of inquiry rather than one of mastery, they may expect better results even if they do not experience the natural world in the same way that lovers do.

These stories of the White Mountains serve as eco-allegories that bear witness to the vitality of natural processes at work in the mountains. In both situations, the mountains seem worthy of respect even though many of its visitors and some of its residents fail to respect its processes. And this lack of proper respect leads to the demise of many people. The self-inherent reality of the natural environment revealed by these stories offers a challenge to anthropocentric views of the world by causing humans to physically bump up against these realities. Besides the physical landscape of New England, the historical and cultural landscape also gave Hawthorne plenty of writing material.

Most readers of Hawthorne have acquired a customary approach of commenting on the moral and historical development of the American nation in Hawthorne's work. Yet even the most historically minded of these tales are frequently not without their environmental evocations. Reginald Cook, for example, offers a classic reading of "Young Goodman Brown": "In a literary epoch when the dominant field of action was the frontier settlement, the forest, and the fort, Hawthorne focussed [sic] on the world of moral imagination."[25] While Hawthorne certainly is interested in the moral imagination, his references to the natural world have in many cases been too quickly tossed aside as romantic fluff rather than receiving the careful scrutiny they deserve. Hawthorne's historical tales include numerous instances of characters who—trying to find their place within the natural world—project their own preconceptions, desires, wishes, or fears onto nature to such an extent that the environment seems little more than a projection of their psyches. In "My Kinsman Major Molineux," a story set in the Revolutionary era, the young country lad Robin finds nature a companion even in the heart of the unfamiliar city; for the moon accompanies him through the darkened streets on his journey in search of his kinsman. Max Autrey interprets this story as an allegory of "the change from an agrarian to an urban society being initiated in America at that time."[26] It is that, but it is also a story in which the environment figures into the human condition as natural phenomena—such as the moonlight and even the memories of natural rhythms of a country life on the farm—influence Robin's actions.

When he peers inside the church in the middle of the dark city, Robin sees the moonlight fall upon the open page of the Bible in the pulpit and cannot help but "shiver with a sensation of loneliness, stronger than he had ever felt in the remotest depths of his native woods" because he was now the only "breathing thing" in this place.[27] This vague longing for a "breathing" presence, while not explored further, suggests his recognition of kinship not only with Major Molineux but also with the larger community of "breathing things." The scene at the church also reminds Robin of his closeness to nature when he is in the company of family and friends with whom he is accustomed to attend worship beneath "the great old tree" just outside his farmer-preacher father's home.[28] On the farm, Robin would have gained familiarity with the natural rhythms of the earth, reliable rhythms that seem unaccountably disturbed in the heart of the city even in the light of the moon. Young Robin's increasingly belligerent attitudes toward the inhospitable city, oddly stirring with life in the middle of the night, parallels the exuberant chaos of Boston on the brink of the American Revolution. This excited dissonance reflects the uninitiated country boy's turmoil in this seemingly unnatural environment. Robin warms to the next "breathing thing" he sees, however, when an older gentleman in the street finally treats him as a fellow being and extends a hand rather than exacerbating his discomfort. In the end, he joins the raucous laughter of the crowd at the sight of his tarred and feathered Loyalist uncle, but we are not told whether he chooses to stay in the city, as the older gentleman urges him to do, or whether he proceeds in his stated desire to return to the countryside. The mixed emotions of Robin represent, of course, the movement from innocence to experience that is a feature of all coming-of-age stories, but it also suggests the difficulty of discerning how humans fit with the natural world.

In "Young Goodman Brown," Hawthorne presents readers with another uninitiated youth whose response to the natural world provides a strong contrast to young Robin's embrace of the natural world as a teacher. Young Goodman Brown, a colonial Puritan youth, is flummoxed in his attempts to read the natural environment. In accord with Puritan presumptions about nature, Brown sees the natural environment not as a place of vitality or even a neutral background but as a dynamic setting in which "[t]here may be a devilish Indian behind every tree" and a place where those not under the thumb of the Puritan leaders might secretly be engaging in hidden pleasures, gathering with "fiend-worshippers," or participating in "witch-meetings[s]."[29] Most readers notice that Brown's transition from the familiarity of the Puritan village to the unfamiliar forest parallels a movement from the world of external reality to the internal world of the mind. What is less often noted is that this transition illustrates the fact that Young Goodman Brown's conceptions of the natural world have been manipulated by Puritan constructions of the American wilderness. Young Goodman Brown responds to the unfamiliar natural environment with the interpretive tools at his disposal—Puritan teachings that make him distrust the wilderness as a place of evil. Paul Lindholdt draws attention to Puritan bioregionalism by noting their "intimate affiliations with locale" and points to "Young Goodman Brown" as an example of the effects of Puritan conceptions of nature: "Young Goodman Brown of Nathaniel Hawthorne's famous tale undergoes his ordeal because the belief system of his community suggested it, because community culture had sown the seeds of his malaise."[30] Brown's increasing cynicism at the end is exacerbated because he cannot decide how he should make distinctions between what he actually sees and what he dreams he sees. His deep suspicion of the natural world, despite his initial determination to know it, translates into deep suspicion of the human community as well when he realizes that Puritan teachings leave him vulnerable and unprepared for the world that is really out there.

While "My Kinsman Major Molineux" and "Young Goodman Brown" foreground the permeability of notions of authority in Puritan and Revolutionary era history, the characters' attitudes toward the "authority" of the natural environment greatly influence their ability or inability to recognize their ecological connection to the world. Both young Robin Molineux and Young Goodman Brown move from a position of naiveté to one of experience, but their differing attitudes toward the natural world result in radically different outcomes: the fearful Brown becomes deeply cynical while young Robin's response is left to the reader's conjecture but is more hopeful about both humans and the natural world. Religious considerations inform the way they read the natural world, but their readings present contrasting theological views of the natural environment. While Young Goodman Brown's orthodox Puritanism leads him to expect stark oppositions between the natural world and all that is sacred and familiar, Robin associates the sacred and the familiar *with* nature rather than *against* it—even to the point of wondering, "Had nature, in that deep hour, become a worshipper in the house which man had builded?"[31] Some scholars associate Robin with pantheism, noticing that Robin's attitude toward worship and nature are so closely aligned as to be almost identical. However, it seems more plausible to say that Robin thinks nature may teach him how to worship since he supposes nature may be a fellow worshipper.

Rather than seeking direction in nature, as Robin does, Young Goodman Brown observes nature with a suspicious attitude that rejects what Robin accepts without question. Such juxtaposing religious views of nature in Hawthorne's stories suggest that religion must respond to the reality of the natural world but that religious views of the natural world are by no means uniform, dependent as they are upon the attitudes, motivations, and preconceived ideas of religious individuals. Addressing the role of "nature" in subjective seeing—whether secular or sacred—William Cronon astutely observes: "Those who have no difficulty seeing God as the expression of our human dreams and desires nonetheless have trouble recognizing that in a secular age Nature can offer precisely the same sort of mirror."[32] Hawthorne remains open to the range of possible interpretations of the world, and the relationship between humans, nonhuman nature, and the divine remains for him a largely unresolvable enigma that he continues to puzzle over for the remainder of his life. What is clear is that religious perspectives in Hawthorne's stories shape how one reads the natural world. These readings result in views that often emphasize either antagonistic or harmonious human interactions with the natural world, views shaped by the human observer's fear and suspicion of the landscape or by the observer's perception of companionship with the elements of the natural environment. What Hawthorne hints in "Young Goodman Brown," he makes explicit in other Puritan stories written during this period: the harshest Puritans attempt to rule humans and nature alike, in part by carefully manipulating human perceptions of the natural world.

In "The May-pole of Merry-Mount," Hawthorne frames the conflict between the Puritans and the merry-makers as a time when "Jollity and gloom were contending for an empire" while those who loved nature and those who feared nature alternately frolicked and frowned.[33] The merry-making cavaliers, friends of the Native Americans and active participants in the pagan nature festival around the Maypole, are pitted against the Puritan leader John Endicott, a governor whom Hawthorne introduces as "the Puritan of Puritans" and "the severest Puritan of all."[34] While the "Votaries" of the Maypole took delight in the "wilder glee of the fresh forest" and danced a wild masque to celebrate "what life is made of," a group of concealed Puritan watchers led by Endicott "compared the masques to those devils and ruined souls, with whom their superstition peopled the black wilderness."[35] Here Hawthorne clearly characterizes as the Puritans' fear of the so-called black wilderness of the natural world as "superstition." Endicott and his followers interrupt the nature-celebrating festival of May Day and establish his rule over his British countrymen who would befriend Native Americans and celebrate the natural world. The fact that these Puritans are acting at the behest of Endicott suggests that "the severest" Puritan view is becoming the dominant one. Aside from provoking Endicott's indignation, the merry-makers at the Maypole are shortsighted in adopting a view of nature that ignores the unforgiving aspects of the landscape just as the Puritans under Endicott undermine its beauties. At least for the short term, ignoring the dangers of nature has more immediate and deadly consequences for old world settlers from England.

As Michael Colacurcio and others have demonstrated, Hawthorne was well aware of the contesting views of nature at Mount Wollaston, as set forth by Puritan historian William Bradford on the one hand and the "pagan" Anglican Thomas Morton on the other. In Hawthorne's story, neither the neo-pagans at the Maypole nor the harsh Puritans who distrusted nature are given much approval by the narrator. In Colacurcio's review of versions of this story that Hawthorne would have read in Bradford and elsewhere, he firmly establishes that Hawthorne is well aware of the long history of this story as a "Puritanic reduction masquerading as a perfect dichotomy" with the choice not only between "Puritan or Reveller, Gloom or Jollity" but also between "Grace or Nature" (*Province* 254). George Decker similarly frames the conflict between the two parties in Hawthorne's story as "a choice between two utopian communities, the one seeking to recreate Arcadia and the other Pentateuchal Israel in the North American wilderness."[36] However, the environment of the new world is only partially comprehended by both groups: "Nature anywhere [in "the vast American wilderness"] is double—cheerful and melancholy, light and dark—and therefore not to be comprehended truly by the single-minded, simplifying vision either of Puritan or Cavalier; but here, where the winters are long and the forests endless, the Puritan vision is *more* adequate to the facts."[37] Hawthorne's rejection of Puritan dichotomies demonstrates a more sanguine view of nature than is often credited to Hawthorne. Yet Hawthorne also casts a shadow over nature-loving idealists of the nineteenth century who saw nothing but beauty in the world around them.

In another Hawthorne story titled "Endicott and the Red Cross," Hawthorne's castigated "Puritan of Puritans" Endicott promulgates a view of the natural world that is much at odds with the celebration of nature associated with nineteenth-century romanticists. Endicott begins with a question: "Wherefore have we come hither to set up our own tombstones in a wilderness?"[38] Not satisfied simply by associating nature with death rather than life, Endicott answers his own question with the assertion that the Puritans' ultimate goal in this new world ought to be to establish mastery over the natural world, reshaping it to their political and religious purposes:

> A howling wilderness it is! The wolf and the bear meet us within halloo of our own dwellings. The savage lieth in wait for us in the dismal shadow of the woods. The stubborn roots of the trees break our ploughshares, when we would till the earth. Our children cry for bread, and we must dig in the sands of the seashore to satisfy them. Wherefore, I say again, have we sought out this country of a rugged soil and wintry sky? Was it not for the enjoyment of our civil rights? Was it not for liberty to worship God according to our conscience?[39]

To a severe Puritan like Endicott, nature is an entity to be overthrown by plowing and digging in order to establish a godly civilization in which civil rights and freedom of conscience are honored, at least for those who follow Endicott's Puritan ideals. In Endicott's rendition of the world, civilization is clearly superior to nature. Although Endicott frames his speech as an endorsement of freedom and religious devotion, his hostility toward the natural world as well as his hostility toward the "heretic" who speaks out from his position of punishment in the stocks is evident. Even his vaunted defiance of the British flag and the British king as a sign of the coming battle for American independence from British rule gives evidence of his desire to control everything in his sight and to eradicate any who limit his own power to rule. The natural world proffers one of the challenges to Endicott's absolute power, and so he shapes it as a "howling wilderness" to be eschewed or overthrown by his followers.

A Puritan governor in colonial Massachusetts was at once a political leader and a religious leader. As a religious leader bent on enforcing his power, Endicott condemns those who worship nature in the Maypole dance. As a political leader intent upon establishing his rule, he manipulates his Puritan followers' understanding of the natural environment as an enemy to be conquered. Hawthorne's presentation of Endicott as a villain who wishes to subjugate the Puritan population and all those around the Puritan community to his own whims implies a critique of Endicott's privileging of civilization, a critique underscored by Hawthorne's own repeated statements of preference for "wilderness" over civilization in his letters to and from his mother's family home in Maine. While in Salem for schooling before his college years, Hawthorne as a teenager repeatedly wrote family members in Maine, alternately longing to "savagize" and "run wild" once again with his younger sister, wishing for the days when he hunted and fished at the lake and in the woods, dreaming of "walking by the Sebago," and "sigh[ing] for the woods."[40] He also wistfully recalls working on "the very green" farm, gardening, and taking care of the goats.[41] Hawthorne used pastoral terminology to encourage his uncle's efforts to "make the 'Wilderness blossom like the rose'" by restoring his Maine fruit trees damaged by drought. And he used pastoral language again upon hearing that his mother was considering returning to Salem, urging her strongly to stay in Maine: "If you remain where you are, think how delightfully the time will pass, with all your children round you, shut out from the world, and nothing to disturb us. It will be a second Garden of Eden."[42] To the young Hawthorne, the wilderness offered a delightful alternative to the Puritan-shaded civilization of nineteenth-century Salem, in whose shadows he resided except during the years he spend at the family residence at Sebago Lake in Maine.

Hawthorne's Puritans are not, however, always suspicious of the natural world. This is most evident in "Roger Malvin's Burial," a frontier story that follows the life of a Puritan family outside the religious centers of Salem and Boston. This story refers to "Lovell's Fight," a battle between Native Americans and British-Americans, but complicates the opposition between these groups by suggesting that Puritans on the frontier share much in common with the Native Americans whose lands they have invaded. As James McIntosh notes, "one of the chief assumptions" established at the outset of Hawthorne's account is that, "the frontiersmen are made morally equivalent to the Indians."[43] Both Puritans and Indians exhibit "open bravery" and act "in accordance with civilized ideas of valor," and both sides boast deeds worthy of tales of "chivalry."[44] The narrator seems to tolerate the motive behind both groups' actions—Native Americans trying to save their homes from Puritans who built houses upon the lands Native American tribes had long inhabited and Puritans attempting to protect their loved ones from those who fought against them. Larry Reynolds has recently drawn attention to Hawthorne's pacifist leanings, however, and if we are to read this tale from the point of view of a pacifist, we quickly see Native Americans and Puritans both being subtly condemned for their savage warfare, and Hawthorne does not dwell on the battle but on the situation of the Puritan frontiersman after the battle.

Hawthorne's story is centered, however, upon the Puritan family living on the frontier after this deadly battle, a family that adapts to the natural environment by adopting at least some of "the customs of the Indians."[45] Hawthorne explicitly notes that the literal details of the natural environment—the "tangled and gloomy forest"—provide a stark contrast to an idealized natural world in some "dreamer's land of fantasy," but he adds that, nonetheless, "there was something in their way of life that Nature asserted as her own."[46] During Hawthorne's time in the woods of Raymond, Maine, where he lived as a young man with his mother and sisters, he gained first-hand knowledge of the southwestern region of Maine where Lovell's Flight occurred, and thus he is able to describe the landscape in some detail. The features of the landscape are "diversified by swells of land, resembling huge waves of a petrified sea," and he imagines the family building their cabin in "a wild and romantic spot" in one of the "hollows" of the hills.[47] The perspective is reversed as the trees are personified and exhibit either pity for the family so isolated from other humans or "fear that men were coming to lay the axe to their roots at last."[48] Moving from a perspective of the environment's effects on human settlement to recognition of humans' effects on the natural world, this story employs historical fiction as a type of environmental writing.

Although the figurative treatment of Nature in "Roger Malvin's Burial" does romanticize nature, the presence of such figurative language does not erase the natural environment. Instead, Hawthorne's personifications of Nature act as a force that shapes human life and action, with Nature being characterized as a motherly being that "seemed . . . as if she sympathized with mortal pain and sorrow" and as a life-form that mourns its own present and future desolation.[49] In his analysis of this story, James McIntosh notes, "Nature is by turns a figure for secret natural energies, a figure for maternal sympathy, and a figure for the howling wilderness" and concludes that Nature holds "power as a fictive presence" in this story.[50] While the personifications of Nature empower Hawthorne's fiction, these personifications suggest not merely an illusory presence but the real presence of a dynamic natural environment. The various personifications of Nature suggest diverse patterns within the natural world, patterns that cannot be disturbed without consequence but also patterns to which humans may adapt if they build a humble cottage rather than carving out yet another new city in the so-called wilderness. Like earlier examples of historical fiction, "Roger Malvin's Burial" registers Hawthorne's recognition of the literal reality underlying any personified presence of nature as well as his awareness of the way humans shape and are shaped by the natural environment.

Leo Marx also notices Hawthorne's environmentally-attuned fiction in a later short story titled "Ethan Brand." Marx reads this story as a commentary on the intrusion of factories that disturb the never-quite-achieved accomplishment of the American idyll. In Hawthorne's story, a lime kiln functions as an analogy for the factory, and as its "smoke and jets of flame issuing from the chinks and crevices of this door, which seemed to give admittance into the hill-side, it resembled nothing so much as the private entrance to the infernal regions, which the shepherds of the Delectable Mountains were accustomed to show to pilgrims."[51] By contrasting the pastoral scene of shepherds on "the Delectable Mountains"—a scene associated with John Bunyan's allegorical *Pilgrim's Progress*—with the smoke and fire of the factory, Hawthorne transplants old world literary tropes into the American soil.

In the notebook entries from which the tale of "Ethan Brand" is derived, Hawthorne conveys a double sense of excitement and horror as he describes the factories and mills planted in the midst of the beautiful natural scenery of the Berkshires. Marx notes that "[a]lthough the striking sight of factories in the wilderness does not appear in the tale," as it does in his notebook entries, "Hawthorne's feelings about it do. Ethan is destroyed by the fires of change associated with factories, and nothing confirms this fact as forcibly as the meretricious idyllic vision that follows his death."[52] By his death in the fires of the kiln, Ethan Brand supplies his followers with a material body which, when burned, crumbles into "special good lime," which may enrich the soil but only at a cost—dead humans and natural spaces "branded" by the disfiguring fires of industrial progress.[53] By transforming his anxieties about the impact of factories on the Berkshire Mountains into an allegory, as he does in "Ethan Brand," Hawthorne's details about the natural environment and the factory alike are muted, but his story nonetheless offers forceful implications for the human relationship to the environment. The workers in the lime kilns following the path started by Ethan Brand, a man in search of the Unpardonable Sin, may be participating in an unpardonable sin by causing at least some measure of irreparable damage to the environment.

"THE MATERIAL AND THE MORAL" IN CONCORD

When Hawthorne moved to Concord with his Transcendentalist bride Sophia Peabody after publishing his first collection of tales, his new relationship with the nature-loving Transcendentalists in Concord undoubtedly drew his attention once more to the human relation to the natural world. As his earlier stories demonstrate, Hawthorne's understanding of the significance of the natural world was already nuanced by this time. But his attention to nature took a more personal tone when he moved to the Old Manse, a setting where the river, trees, and garden ensconced him in the natural world. "It was here that Emerson wrote Nature," Hawthorne states in the introduction to *Mosses from an Old Manse*.[54] His stories and sketches from this period indicate that the Transcendentalists spurred Hawthorne to continue and intensify his engagement with the natural world even if he did not always share their views. As Darrel Abel has noted, Hawthorne celebrated the "continuously regenerative" system of the natural world in his Concord writings.[55] Such celebration is most apparent in the introductory sketch "The Old Manse." In this extended essay—a mixture of nature writing, social commentary, and stoking of the literary imagination—Hawthorne describes the processes and sanctity of the natural world in numerous ways as he is gardening, walking through the woods, going boating or fishing, lounging on the riverbank, or otherwise enjoying nature by himself or with Ellery Channing or other friends in Concord.

In "The Hall of Fantasy," which by its very title seems antagonistic to an environmental ethos of any kind, Hawthorne articulates a nuanced view of the relationship between humans and the natural environment. The narrator foregrounds the story's apparent disconnection from physical reality by speculating that the story's eponymous hall "give[s] the impression of a dream, which might be dissipated and shattered to fragments by merely stamping the foot upon the pavement."[56] But rather than "float[ing] above the world in some aesthetic ether," to use Cheryl Glotfelty's provocative metaphor, Hawthorne's story draws attention to the interconnections between the earth and its creatures and thereby participates in what Glotfelty describes as "an immensely complex global system, in which energy, matter, *and ideas* interact."[57] For the focus of this story is not so much about the tributes to human ingenuity that line the dreamlike hall as it is about the conversation elicited by the narrator's passage down the hallway in the company of his friend and guide. When his friend suggests that the earth might as well be destroyed, the narrator protests, noting that he "cannot bear to have her perish" and that he wishes the earth's "prolonged existence for her own dear sake."[58]

When his friend contends that the "moral enjoyments" of a future spiritual world will outweigh the "material enjoyments" of the present world, the narrator denounces his friend's "ungrateful[ness] to our Mother Earth" and chides him for lightly dismissing the unique experience of living in a place where "the material and the moral exist together." In this story, Hawthorne pays much more attention to the innate value of the earth than might be expected of a nineteenth-century writer of romance as profoundly fascinated as Hawthorne is by the moral quandaries of life. The bare outline of an environmental ethos can be found in the narrator's assertion that "the material and the moral exist together" in an inimitable way on planet earth.[59] "Come what may," the narrator continues, "I will never forget her! Neither will it satisfy me to have her exist merely in idea. I want her great, round, solid self to endure interminably."[60] While allowing for notions of human uniqueness within the natural world and accepting the possibility of a future state of existence, Hawthorne employs the narrative voice to construe human uniqueness as a mark of moral responsibility to the well-being of the rest of the world rather than a license for exploiting it. While Hawthorne's stories do not typically indicate a thoroughgoing ecocentric point of view, "The Hall of Fantasy" gestures strongly in that direction. This fictive sketch stands as a challenge to antagonistic and exploitative attitudes toward the earth and insist upon earth's value as an irreplaceable reality, an unparalleled site of existence.

Another story of this period that is "Earth's Holocaust," the tale of an apocalyptic world of sorts, one in which reformers thrust the emblems of Western cultural institutions into a great bonfire in the attempt to return to a natural state of being. A desperate bookworm who sees his books disappearing into the fire is chided with a series of questions: "Is not Nature better than a book? Is not the human heart deeper than any system of philosophy? Is not life replete with more instruction than past observers have found it possible to write down in maxims?"[61] As a half-hearted critique of American aspirations to establish an entirely new society according to natural laws rather than received ones, the tale is haunted by the words of the devil-like character who laughs into his sleeves that unless the human heart is destroyed, "It will be the old world yet!"[62] While intimating that human foibles and ill will are ineradicable, the narrator nonetheless promotes the efforts to adopt actions aligned with the processes of the natural world.

In "The New Adam and Eve," another story included in *Mosses*, Hawthorne writes a kind of new world tale in which the title characters wake to find themselves all alone not in a garden but in a postapocalyptic city emptied of people but still filled with their effects. As the couple gazes without understanding at the seemingly unnatural city, they try to make sense of their situation by remembering their attachment to each other and by investigating their surroundings. While "The New Adam and Eve" is often read as a kind of honeymoon tale, given the fact that Hawthorne had moved to Concord with his new bride not long before writing this story of two lovers all alone in the world, it is also a story that investigates the human connection to the natural world. Hawthorne's tale recognizes the human imbrication in the ecosphere, particularly in the kinship humans share with all biological life forms. When the bewildered couple first find themselves in the middle of the city, Eve sees "a small tuft of grass" growing on the sidewalk and "eagerly grasps it . . . sensible that this little herb awakens some response within her heart."[63] In an inversion of the biblical story of Adam and Eve, Hawthorne's Eve keeps Adam from being tempted by gold or books, reminding him of their natural identity. When they reach the edge of the city, they begin to feel much more at home. Here they encounter the vibrancy of nonhuman nature as they move together "across green fields and along the margin of a quiet river."[64] Their existence is clarified by a recognition of their shared membership in a larger biological community.

The narrator prefaces "The New Adam and Eve" with the declaration that "[w]e who are born into the world's artificial system can never adequately know how little in our present state and circumstances is natural, and how much is merely the interpolation of the perverted mind and heart of man."[65] What are humans naturally, when at their best and uninfluenced by human culture? This is the impossible question it addresses in "The New Adam and Eve." Such knowledge is made more difficult by our recognition that "Art has become a second and stronger nature; she is a stepmother, whose crafty tenderness has taught us to despise the bountiful and wholesome ministrations of our true parent."[66] "The New Adam and Eve" represents a thought experiment that tests Emerson's closing assertion in the first part of his essay *Nature*:

"Nature and art, all other men and my own body, must be ranked under this name, NATURE."[67] That is, humans are natural beings and so their creations are works of nature because they are the creations of natural beings, much as a beaver dam can be considered a work of nature.

Emerson proceeds to make a distinction that is helpful for understanding the narrative voice in Hawthorne's tale: "*Nature*, in the common sense, refers to essences unchanged by man; space, the air, the river, the leaf. *Art* is applied to the mixture of his will with the same things, as in a house, a canal, a picture."[68] Emerson's initial distinctions between nature and art break down, however, as he proceeds with his argument. "But [human] operations taken together are so insignificant, a little chipping, baking, patching, and washing, that in an impression so grand as that of the world on the human mind, they do not vary the result."[69] With this Hawthorne's narrator seems to agree, drawing his readers' attention to "marks of wear and tear, and unrenewed decay, which distinguish the works of man from the growth of nature!"[70] When the New Adam and Eve gaze upon the world for the first time, they are puzzled by the human "marks of wear and tear" they find in the city, and they embrace the natural elements they find inside and outside the city. Human operations puzzle them but do not detract them from their goal of returning to the natural world. Their brief foray into the human world suggests that nature (the grass, the flowers, the trees, the landscape) and art (sculptures, artistic clothing, architecture, books, mirrors, and cityscape) are not ultimately opposed but that human arts can become corrupted—as is most obvious in the gallows that are abhorred in both "The New Adam and Eve" and "Earth's Holocaust." For these two uncultured innocents, Nature remains remote from culture even while seeming to be somehow imbricated in the culture of a forgotten civilization. While this approaches ecological thinking, it functions finally as little more than a gesture in that direction. These two solitary humans in the world are able to sense their own connection with the natural world but without being able to imagine how human culture could operate out of such a connection.

The narrator's simplistic dualism between art and nature—the notion that nature is good and art is a cunning expression of deviant human intelligence—is ultimately undermined by the actions of the characters in Hawthorne's story. The new Adam and Eve's adulatory reactions to a marble statue of an "exquisitely idealized" child also undercut the narrator's assertions about the distinction between nature and art, and he hastens to explain that "[s]culpture, in its highest excellence, is more genuine than painting, and might seem to be evolved from a natural germ, by the same law as a leaf or flower."[71] Although the narrator excuses their interest in the statue by noting that it is a type of art most similar to nature, even the "pure" Adam and Eve show they are not immune to art's appeal. Eve questions whether the statue once breathed with life or if it is "only the shadow of something real, like [their] pictures in the mirror." Adam associates the statue with the "mysteries all around" them and declares his desire to catch hold of the idea communicated by it.[72] They cannot decide whether the sculpture was once a living being or not, and these responses to the statue serve as a critique of the narrator's earlier advocacy of simplistic natural "wisdom" that he asserts will "at once distinguish between art and nature."[73] While drawing upon the art versus nature dichotomy of conventional pastorals, this short story thus challenges too facile distinctions between art and nature. As the new Adam and Eve explore the abandoned city and its vicinity, the narrator's stated expectations are continuously stymied by the events of the story.

Ending in a graveyard beside the Bunker Hill Memorial, this story is, as Robert Levine notices, a cautionary tale about the extinction of human life. Whether through a catastrophe such as war or through old age, "death (extinction) will always remain the final stop in every individual's worldly journey."[74] When they see the image of a sleeping child engraved on a tombstone, Adam suggests that they join the child in its sleeping position and await the dawn of "another morn [that] will find us somewhere beneath the smile of God."[75] Eve's final comment is that regardless of where they wake, they will be happy just to continue being together. This story serves as a commentary on the tenure of human life on earth from the birth of humans into the world and the extinction of humans from that world. While recent environmental crises caused by human destruction of the environment and global warming makes it increasingly possible that life on earth may become altogether extinct, Hawthorne's story stands as a reminder of the extinction of each individual if not of the human species and the entire biological world as we know it. In either case, the specter of human extinction raises questions about the future that environmentalists are keen to address. The preexistence of the earth's processes and products calls into question any entirely anthropocentric rubric for understanding the ecosphere.

Hawthorne's celebration of nature's beauty and regenerative force does not undercut the dark strain of his writing, however, even in Concord where he is surrounded by his Transcendentalist friends and his new bride. In an 1837 entry in his notebooks, Hawthorne jotted a story idea that followed him to Concord: "A person to spend all his life and splendid talents in trying to achieve something naturally impossible,—as to make a conquest over Nature."[76] The characters who do not adequately respect the processes of nature pay the consequences either by misfortunes that occur or by becoming themselves unsympathetic characters, and this is perhaps nowhere more evident than in stories in which strong male figures undermine the sanctity and dignity of female characters.

Analyzing the deep satisfaction Hawthorne derived from gardening alongside his meditations of the interconnections between garden plants and fruit trees and humans, John Gatta observes, "More than most other male authors of the period, Hawthorne has frequently been associated with a culturally feminized sensibility."[77] If we take Hawthorne's gardening as a sign of such a "culturally feminized sensibility," it is little surprise that his greatest concerns about human interaction with nature during this period have to do with controlling male figures who poison gardens and women. Male figures who attempted to perfect or protect women by tampering with their natural bodies were special targets of his critique. The same impulse that drives less exemplary men in Hawthorne's stories to conquer nature also leads them to subjugate women.

Two of Hawthorne's stories that explore the common impulse of domineering male figures to control women and nature are "The Birthmark" and "Rappaccini's Daughter." These two stories represent an exploration of the concerns that motivate ecological feminism, which Karen J. Warren describes as "the connections between the domination of women (and other oppressed humans) and the domination of nature."[78] While Nina Baym and others have for several decades now debated Hawthorne's sympathy with feminism, his sympathy with ecofeminism bears closer scrutiny. Margaret Fuller, the Transcendentalist author most famous for her feminist essay-turned book titled *Woman in the Nineteenth Century*, mentions these two stories in her review of Hawthorne's collection of tales titled *Mosses from an Old Manse*; she characterizes them as a pair that both "embody truths of profound importance in shapes of aerial elegance."[79] These embodied truths have to do with his depiction of idealized love and what Fuller calls "feminine purity, (by which we mean no mere acts or absences, but perfect single truth felt and done in gentleness)."[80] The women of these tales are hard-pressed by men, and Georgiana in the earlier tale yields to her husband Aylmer either gracefully or (more likely) naively, while Beatrice directly rebukes her domineering patronizing father Rappaccini with a sternness that nonetheless exhibits a graciousness wholly lacking in her father. In both cases, the women are more self-aware of the actual condition of their bodies than the men, and Beatrice is also more aware that her personal identity and bodily well-being has been violated by the dominance of the male figure. As he exposes the hidden rhetorical purposes of Puritan John Endicott in his earlier tales, Hawthorne's fiction also exposes the underlying motivations of controlling men, particularly those who promote a vision of human perfection and execute a plan for achieving such perfection.

In "The Birthmark," Hawthorne pits the power of human love in the form of a marriage between Aylmer and Georgiana against the allure of scientific prowess. Aylmer, a late eighteenth-century scientist "proficient in every branch of natural philosophy," had recently gotten married, but in these exciting days the discovery of electricity and similar scientific findings had made it "not unusual for the love of science to rival the love of woman in its depth and absorbing energy."[81] The narrator is clearly skeptical of Aylmer but admits that it remains unknown whether Aylmer holds to the extreme scientific "faith in man's ultimate control over nature" that characterizes some of his contemporaries. The narrator warns at the outset of the tale that his love for his wife could only grow "by intertwining itself with his love of science."[82] When Aylmer wants to remove the birthmark in his bride's cheek, he notes that she "came so nearly perfect from the hand of Nature" and that the birthmark is the only blemish to her otherwise perfect beauty.

Georgiana has had lovers who found her birthmark quite attractive, and Aylmer's servant and lab assistant Aminadab later mutters, "If she were my wife, I'd never part with that birthmark."[83] Aminadab is compared to an animal since his responses to Aylmer's directions often consist of grunts rather than human speech, but his bodily attraction to Georgiana serves as a rebuke—however ineffective to Aylmer himself—of the high-minded idealism of a scientist such as Aylmer, who values scientific discovery above human love. Georgiana herself seems quite happy with the birthmark initially and is aghast at Aylmer's abhorrence of it, crying out, "You cannot love what shocks you!"[84] However, when he becomes moody and tormented by dreams, she eventually asks him to remove the birthmark at any cost. Aylmer exults prematurely in what he predicts "will be my triumph, when I shall have corrected what Nature left imperfect, in her fairest work!"[85] As Georgiana is dying shortly after Aylmer successfully removes the birthmark, she begs her husband not to regret his "high and pure a feeling" by which he "rejected the best the earth could offer."[86] And so Aylmer has converted his wife to his way of thinking and reduced her to the grave. He stands as an example of the kind of man determined to assert his sway of influence and ultimate power over women and nature alike.

While Georgiana is converted to her husband's way of thinking, Aylmer's assistant and the narrator of this story are not converted. The narrator's critique of Aylmer is most explicit in his closing observation that an all-engrossed scientist like Aylmer, seeking mastery over the natural world above all else, misses the happiness and beauty of the present world by trying to create a perfect future without recognizing either the unusual beauty of Georgiana's birthmark or the natural limits of bodily endurance. The narrator regrets what Aylmer fails to see, noting that "had Aylmer reached a profounder wisdom, he need not thus have flung away the happiness [of his marriage]."[87] It is clear to the narrator that Aylmer's shortsightedness has led to failure despite Aylmer's own self-satisfied sense of accomplishment: "He failed to look beyond the shadowy scope of time, and . . . to find the perfect future in the present."[88] Liz Rosenberg situates Hawthorne's tale as a critique of nineteenth-century mind/body theories and represents his commendation of "the imperfect and mortal quality of human nature."[89] This story represents a critique of Aylmer and any who would undermine the inviolable sanctity of human nature, however imperfect it might be. The sacred quality of nature that Hawthorne intimates in his earlier works extends to human nature as well.

Like Aylmer, Rappaccini in "Rappaccini's Daughter" is a scientist, but he is described as a scientific gardener in Renaissance Italy, and the garden he has created suggests his affinity to the natural world. But this affinity is motivated by an attempt to manipulate nature—taking a risk as Aylmer did—in order to obtain immortality for his daughter by making her untouchable by disease or human ill will. He does this by using herbs to make her poisonous. When Giovanni, the youth next door, realizes this, he tries to acquire Beatrice's ability to poison the world around him and successfully acquires the ability but also takes with him an antidote created by a family friend who distrusts Rappaccini. When Giovanni realizes that he too can breathe poison on the world around him, he brags to Beatrice that he now has her power and suggests that they use their power to vanquish the human world. He is mystified by her rejection of his plan and scorns her prayer to the "Holy Virgin," but Beatrice indicates that she thinks that her "accursed" status is the result of her father's machinations: she blames her father for making her "a monster" by using her as a tool for his scientific endeavors.[90] When Rappaccini shows up and calls Beatrice the "daughter of my pride and triumph," he urges her to join with Giovanni in a life untouchable, but she rebukes him with her question of why he "inflict[ed] this miserable doom" on her.[91] Rappaccini has made his own daughter Beatrice little more than a tool for his scientific experimentation, making her immune to poison while become dangerously poisonous herself.

Beatrice is no Georgiana, converted to the viewpoints of the men who want to "perfect" her. Instead, she values the beauties of the garden and her own body for their own sake and resists the sway of influence by her father Rappaccini and her would-be lover Giovanni who imagines that he may rescue her from human isolation despite the chemically poisoned composition of her body. The narrator calls her a "victim of man's ingenuity and of thwarted nature, and of the fatality that attends all such efforts of perverted wisdom" and reinforces her rebuke of both her father and Giovanni, with Baglioni yelling out his reproaches from a nearby window.[92] As Nina Baym has noted, Hawthorne's emphasis on Beatrice's victimization by her father as an instance of "thwarted nature" suggests Hawthorne's sympathy with Beatrice—a sympathy that is overlooked by critics who only focus on the conflicts between the men in the story. Hawthorne's tale is a qualified defense of Nature and womanhood against the subjugations of a testosterone-infused will to conquer. Both Georgiana and Beatrice suffer at the hands of scientific men who have adopted a mechanistic view of nature (including the nature of women in their lives) and are in the process of manipulating the natural mechanisms for their own benefit. In *The Death of Nature: Women, Ecology and the Scientific Revolution*, Carolyn Merchant issues a call to "reexamine the formation of a world view and a science that, by reconceptualizing reality as a machine rather than a living organism, sanctioned the domination of both nature and women."[93] Certainly, Hawthorne's scientist-husband (Aylmer) and scientist-father (Rappaccini) both adopt such an approach to the world, trying to fix the women in their lives by chemically altering them to turn the two women into "perfect" beings able to maneuver the world without fear of rivalry.

These stories lay the groundwork for Hawthorne's later book-length romances, preceding his lull in publication followed by another burst of productivity with the appearance of *The Scarlet Letter* (1850) and other book-length romances. Either way, describing the spectacle of nature provides at once a human connection to the processes of the physical environment and a more or less true representation of it. Power-seeking motivations tend toward less true representations since gaining power takes precedence over the accuracy of environmental renderings. Such an understanding of Hawthorne's earliest tales insists upon the reality of a natural world that cannot be ignored without consequence while recognizing that such a reality can be readily and maliciously manipulated by human language and action. Moving first from a conviction of the earth's processes as superior to human ingenuity, Hawthorne analyzes competing views of the natural world in US history. The historical and contemporary experiences of these early stories suggest that those who do not pay attention to nature and its processes bear the consequences. Those who do pay attention to nature and those who attempt to manipulate it for political or scientific advancement either fail in the attempt or succeed and become less than exemplary characters.

INTERPRETING NATURE FROM A 'POSITION BETWEEN'

In a brief preface to "Rappaccini's Daughter," Hawthorne directly addresses his relationship with the Transcendentalists, prefacing his story with a mock review of his own work, noting that the author "seems to occupy an unfortunate position between the Transcendentalists . . . and the great body of pen-and-ink men who address the intellect and sympathies of the multitude."[94]

Hawthorne's position is of course not unfortunate in its attraction of an extensive readership that draws one set of readers from those who admire the high-minded work of Transcendentalists such as Emerson and draws another set of readers who approach literature with a less theoretically minded approach. By positioning himself between these two classes, Hawthorne intimates his simultaneous interest in intellectual and popular culture. Even while adopting the Transcendentalist habit of philosophical inquiry into the natural world, Hawthorne joins other "pen-and-ink" writers who know how to capture the popular imagination of a broader swath of the American public. Perhaps this doubleness of purpose is one reason why Hawthorne's interest in the natural world has gone largely unremarked during the last few decades. Although he used fiction rather than nonfiction as a vehicle for his inquiry into nature, Hawthorne's writing does engage the intellectual concerns of the Transcendentalists who theorized the relation between humans and the environment. In Fuller's review of Hawthorne's *Mosses* for the *New-York Daily Tribune*, Hawthorne is praised for retaining "the same gentle and sincere companionship with nature" that characterizes his earlier work but also for making "his range of subjects is a little wider."[95] Hawthorne's relationship to Fuller, who frequently visited the Hawthornes and the Transcendentalists in Concord, no doubt influenced his interest in the subjects of nature and women alike—both of which eventually contribute to the thematic structure of his book-length romances. So while he has not often been regarded as a writer who cares about nature in recent years, his Transcendentalist contemporaries understood an attention to the natural world to be essential to his literary work.

In Hawthorne's short fiction, there emerges a persistent vision of the natural world as a source of ecological wisdom that posits humans as members of a larger sphere. Humans can learn from the natural processes of the environment, or they can ignore them at their own peril. Humans can manipulate nature without respecting inherent limitations of natural beings or processes, or they can learn to live in harmony with nature by treating the natural environment as an important part of the larger scope of reality rather than a threat to subdue or an object to subject to their every whim. Hawthorne's early writings explore the reality of nonhuman nature and the interpolations of "nature" and human nature. Nature and culture are intertwined in Hawthorne's stories such an extent that one cannot extricate one from the other without deforming it. As Georgiana's birthmark cannot be removed without doing violence to her, so culture cannot be extracted from nature without doing harm.

For Hawthorne, representing the natural world linguistically is a challenge best handled by acknowledging the limits of human language. Even near the beginning of his writing career, Hawthorne registered his awareness of the difficulty of any linguistic representation of reality in a letter to his fiancé, noting, "I have felt, a thousand times, that words may be a thick and darksome veil of mystery between the soul and the truth which it seeks. . . . Yet words are not without their use even for purposes of explanation,—but merely for explaining outward acts and all sorts of external things, leaving the soul's life and action to explain itself in its own way."[96] Notwithstanding the human refractions of linguistic communication, Hawthorne grants words the ability to bear witness to the external world of reality—the movements or scenery of nature and nature's creatures (including humans)—and to hint at the internal world of "the soul's life and action." Given this understanding of the necessary subjectivity of all human experience and understanding, the imagination is an essential component in the work of grasping the language that most adequately describes the natural world and communicates the responsibilities that arise from an adequate understanding of the relationship between humans and the environment. Since we necessarily represent the natural world through cultural forms by even attempting to describe it, we can only get part way there through visual and verbal representations, but this does not stop Hawthorne from attempting to engage the natural world in his fiction—a genre that openly acknowledges the human role in artistically shaping texts. Despite his frequent use of personification when representing the natural environment, Hawthorne's fiction gives a significant role to the natural environment not only as background but as a system of vital processes that involve humans.

Given Hawthorne's conviction of the need for artistic forms such as fiction to address the ever-looming gap between language and reality, it is no surprise that his representation of the natural world is less explicit and confident than that of his Transcendentalist contemporaries. In his later work, he is increasingly suspicious of the rhetoric of "Nature," particularly in *The Blithedale Romance* when the Transcendentalist dream of a utopian community close to nature becomes little more than what one character calls "the very emptiest mockery in our effort to establish the one true system."[97] In both his fiction and nonfiction, however, Hawthorne artistically intertwines human concerns and nonhuman nature to suggest a vision of the world that positions humans as members of a larger sphere. Hawthorne's descriptions of the attitudes of Puritans and non-Puritans give evidence of his growing awareness that culturally constructed understandings of the natural environment strongly influence how people perceive and interact with "Nature." Young Goodman Brown's experience and interpretation of the natural environment are clearly constrained by Puritan teachings of a sharp antagonism between humans and nature. For Hawthorne, the objectivity implied by a clear-cut distinction between nature and culture is impossible since our sight of anything, including the nonhuman reality of the natural environment, is always inflected through the subjectivity not only of our sight but also of the very words we use to represent what we see. While we may well misinterpret and misrepresent nature, we are left with the *idea* of nature and with it we must grapple as members of the natural environment in which we live and move and have our being. How humans can best acknowledge, understand, and interact with the rest of the natural world is a topic ripe for explaration, and Hawthorne explores a variety of responses to nature in the stories he writes.

NOTES

1. Hawthorne, *Complete Works*, vol. 2, 210.
2. Hawthorne, *Complete Works*, vol. 9, 301.
3. Thoreau, *Walden*, 88.
4. Emerson, *Nature and Selected Essays*, 35.
5. Hawthorne, *Centenary Edition of the Works of Nathaniel Hawthorne*, vol. 16, *The Letters, 1843-1853,* ed. William Charvat et al. (Columbus: Ohio State University Press, 1985), 22.
6. Hawthorne, *Complete Works,* vol. 2, 46.
7. Alfred Weber, Beth L. Lueck, and Dennis Berthold, *Hawthorne's American Travel Sketches* (Hanover: University Press of New England, 1989).
8. Hawthorne, *Complete Works*, vol. 2, 478.
9. Hawthorne, *Complete Works*, vol. 2, 476.
10. Hawthorne, *Complete Works*, vol. 1, 364.
11. Hawthorne, *Complete Works*, vol. 1, 364.
12. Hawthorne, *Complete Works*, vol. 1, 369.
13. Christopher Johnson, *This Grand and Magnificent Place: The Wilderness Heritage of the White Mountains* (Lebanon, NH: University of New Hampshire Press, 2006), 92–93.
14. Hawthorne, *Centenary Edition of the Works of Nathaniel Hawthorne*, vol. 15, *The Letters, 1813-1843,* ed. William Charvat et al. (Columbus: Ohio State University Press, 1984), 226–27.
15. John Sears, "Hawthorne's 'The Ambitious Guest' and the Significance of the Willey Disaster," *American Literature* 54, no. 3 (1982): 354, 356.
16. Ian Marshall, "Reading the Willey Disaster: An Evolutionary Approach to Environmental Aesthetics in Cole's *Notch of the White Mountains* and Hawthorne's 'The Ambitious Guest,'" *The Journal of Ecocriticism: A New Journal of Nature, Society and Literature* 3, no. 2 (2011): 7.
17. Hawthorne, *Complete Works,* vol. 1, 373.
18. Marshall, "Reading the Willey Disaster," 7.
19. Hawthorne, *Complete Works,* vol. 1, 173.
20. Hawthorne, *Complete Works,* vol. 1, 182.
21. Bowdoin College, *Laws of Bowdoin College*, 29.
22. John Locke, *An Essay Concerning Human Understanding*, ed. Roger Woolhouse (New York: Penguin, 1997), 560.
23. Johnson, *This Grand and Magnificent Place,* 93–94.

24. Hawthorne, *Complete Works,* vol. 1, 178.
25. Reginald Cook, "The Forest of Goodman Brown's Night: A Reading of Hawthorne's 'Young Goodman Brown,'" *The New England Quarterly* 43, no. 3 (September 1970), 473.
26. Max L. Autrey, "'My Kinsman Major Molineux': Hawthorne's Allegory of the Urban Movement," *College Literature* 12, no. 3 (Fall 1985): 221.
27. Hawthorne, *Complete Works,* vol. 3, 632.
28. Hawthorne, *Complete Works,* vol. 3, 631.
29. Hawthorne, *Complete Works,* vol. 2, 90, 104–105.
30. Paul Lindholdt, *Explorations in Ecocriticism: Advocacy, Bioregionalism, and Visual Design* (Lanham, MD: Lexington Books, 2015), 128.
31. Hawthorne, *Complete Works,* vol. 3, 631.
32. William Cronon, "The Trouble with Wilderness: or, Getting Back to the Wrong Nature," in *Uncommon Ground: Rethinking the Human Place in Nature* (New York: Norton, 1996), 80.
33. Hawthorne, *Complete Works,* vol. 3, 70.
34. Hawthorne, *Complete Works,* vol. 3, 79, 84.
35. Hawthorne, *Complete Works,* vol. 3, 72.
36. George Decker, *The American Historical Romance* (New York: Cambridge University Press, 1987), 156.
37. Decker, *The American Historical Romance,* 157.
38. Hawthorne, *Complete Works,* vol. 1, 491.
39. Hawthorne, *Complete Works,* vol. 1, 491.
40. Hawthorne, *Centenary Edition,* vol. 15, 113, 119, 138.
41. Hawthorne, *Centenary Edition,* vol. 15, 111.
42. Hawthorne, *Centenary Edition,* vol. 15, 141, 150.
43. James McIntosh, "Nature and Frontier in 'Roger Malvin's Burial,'" *American Literature* 60, no. 2 (1988), 191.
44. Hawthorne, *Complete Works,* vol. 2, 381.
45. Hawthorne, *Complete Works,* vol. 2, 389.
46. Hawthorne, *Complete Works,* vol. 2, 389.
47. Hawthorne, *Complete Works,* vol. 2, 398.
48. Hawthorne, *Complete Works,* vol. 2, 398.
49. Hawthorne, *Complete Works,* vol. 2, 390.
50. McIntosh, "Nature and Frontier," 199–200.
51. Hawthorne, *Complete Works,* vol. 3, 478.
52. Marx, *The Machine in the Garden,* 276–77.
53. Hawthorne, *Complete Works,* vol. 3, 498.
54. Hawthorne, *Complete Works,* vol. 2, 13.
55. Abel, *Moral Picturesque,* 10.
56. Hawthorne, *Complete Works*, vol. 2, 197.
57. Glotfelty, introduction to "Literary Studies in an Age of Environmental Crisis," xix.
58. Hawthorne, *Complete Works*, vol. 2, 209.
59. Hawthorne, *Complete Works*, vol. 2, 209.

60. Hawthorne, *Complete Works*, vol. 2, 210.
61. Hawthorne, *Complete Works*, vol. 2, 449.
62. Hawthorne, *Complete Works*, vol. 2, 455.
63. Hawthorne, *Complete Works*, vol. 2, 282.
64. Hawthorne, *Complete Works*, vol. 2, 298.
65. Hawthorne, *Complete Works*, vol. 2, 279.
66. Hawthorne, *Complete Works*, vol. 2, 279.
67. Emerson, *Nature and Selected Essays*, 36.
68. Emerson, *Nature and Selected Essays*, 36.
69. Emerson, *Nature and Selected Essays*, 37.
70. Hawthorne, *Complete Works*, vol. 2, 281–82.
71. Hawthorne, *Complete Works*, vol. 2, 290.
72. Hawthorne, *Complete Works*, vol. 2, 291.
73. Hawthorne, *Complete Works*, vol. 2, 280.
74. Robert Levine, "American Studies in an Age of Extinction," *States of Emergency: The Object of American Studies*, ed. Russ Castronovo and Susan Gillman (Chapel Hill: University of North Carolina Press, 2009), 176.
75. Hawthorne, *Complete Works*, vol. 2, 302.
76. Hawthorne, *Complete Works*, vol. 9, 106.
77. Gatta, *Making Nature Sacred: Literature, Religion, and Environment in America from the Puritans to the Present*, 106.
78. Karen J. Warren, "Ecological Feminist Philosophies: An Overview of the Issues," *Ecological Feminist Philosophies*, ed. Karen J. Warren (Bloomington: Indiana University Press, 1996), x.
79. Margaret Fuller, review of *Mosses from an Old Manse,* by Nathaniel Hawthorne, in *Nathaniel Hawthorne: The Contemporary Reviews*, 73.
80. Fuller, review of *Mosses*, 73.
81. Hawthorne, *Complete Works*, vol. 2, 47.
82. Hawthorne, *Complete Works*, vol. 2, 47.
83. Hawthorne, *Complete Works*, vol. 2, 55.
84. Hawthorne, *Complete Works*, vol. 2, 48.
85. Hawthorne, *Complete Works*, vol. 2, 53.
86. Hawthorne, *Complete Works*, vol. 2, 69.
87. Hawthorne, *Complete Works*, vol. 2, 69.
88. Hawthorne, *Complete Works*, vol. 2, 69.
89. Liz Rosenberg, "'The Best that Earth Could Offer': 'The Birthmark,' A Newly-Wed's Story," *Studies in Short Fiction* 30, no. 2 (1993): 145.
90. Hawthorne, *Complete Works*, vol. 2, 144.
91. Hawthorne, *Complete Works*, vol. 2, 144.
92. Hawthorne, *Complete Works*, vol. 2, 147.
93. Carolyn Merchant, *The Death of Nature: Women, Ecology and the Scientific Revolution* (New York: Harper Collins, 1980), xxi.
94. Hawthorne, *Complete Works*, vol. 2, 108.
95. Fuller, review of *Mosses*, 73.
96. Hawthorne, *Centenary Edition*, vol. 15, 462.
97. Hawthorne, *Complete Works*, vol. 5, 576.

Chapter 3

Reading Nature and the Human Body in *The Scarlet Letter*

> Nothing was more common, in those days, than to interpret all meteoric appearances, and other natural phenomena, that occurred with less regularity than the rise and set of sun and moon, as so many revelations from a supernatural source.
>
> —Nathaniel Hawthorne, *The Scarlet Letter*[1]

It is no great secret that Nathaniel Hawthorne frequently personifies nature and presents it allegorically. As a result, his comments about the natural world have frequently been discounted as little more than a romantic morass from which he fashions his fiction. Hawthorne writes about culture, not about nature—or so it is often thought. This assumption is perhaps nowhere more apparent than in the standard scholarly treatment of his title's significance to his story's meaning in *The Scarlet Letter*. The cultural signifiers embedded in the scarlet letter on Hester Prynne's breast are presumed to be the key for decoding the *real* meaning of the text. Cindy Weinstein, for example, observes, "The scarlet letter is one of those grand symbols in antebellum American literature that keeps company with a white whale, a pond, and leaves of grass. Unlike these others, however, which are simultaneously elements of the natural world and sites of cultural projection, the scarlet letter inhabits, unambiguously, the realm of culture."[2] Weinstein's comparison of Hawthorne's work with Herman Melville's *Moby-Dick*, Henry David Thoreau's *Walden*, and Walt Whitman's *Leaves of Grass* aptly brings together influential nineteenth-century texts that are taken to represent "Americanness," but her hasty dismissal of the scarlet letter semiology from the "elements of the natural world" is based on only one scarlet letter—the piece of enchanted needlework on Hester's breast. This is problematic because Hawthorne's text explicitly displays the scarlet letter in multiple instances as an element or object of the natural world, both in the natural environment of the Puritan village and in the corporeality of the human body. By viewing Hawthorne's direct references to nature as more than figurative language alone, we can gain a fresh perspective on the meaning of the scarlet letters that appear *in nature* in Hawthorne's text.

Two prominent instances of the scarlet letter in or as nature are located in the central chapter and in the penultimate chapter, in the two scenes where the major characters of his romance stand on the scaffold in the town center. In the first instance, Hester and Dimmesdale and Pearl are standing together on the scaffold as a meteor streaks through the night sky. The narrator scoffs at Dimmesdale's perception of the meteor as "an immense letter,—the letter A,—marked out in lines of dull red light."[3] Hester's red letter A, which she had embroidered and hung over her breast, stood for adultery; Dimmesdale supposes the red letter A in the sky is a sign that he—standing there on the scaffold with Hester—is being similarly judged as an adulterer by Providence. The nineteenth-century narrator breaks in with a condescending comment about the Puritan belief system: "Nothing was more common, in those days," he scoffs, "than to interpret all meteoric appearances, and other natural phenomena, that occurred with less regularity than the rise and set of sun and moon, as so many revelations from a supernatural source."[4] But he is quick to offer an alternate modern explanation, attributing the appearance of the letter to the colored perception of Dimmesdale's anxiety-ridden psychological state, saying, "it could only be the symptom of a highly disordered mental state, when a man, rendered morbidly self-contemplative . . . had extended his egotism over the whole vast expanse of nature, until the firmament itself should appear no more than a fitting page for his soul's history and fate."[5] Rather than dismissing the natural world, the narrator claims that his characters are misreading it.

The natural aspect of this scene was apparent to many of Hawthorne's early readers through the circulation of the painting by Tompkins Harrison Matteson, an artist who allegedly consulted Hawthorne for feedback on the painting, which has been aptly described as follows: "The painting includes Dimmesdale and Chillingworth as well as Hester and Pearl; it is in fact a representation of . . . 'The Minister's Vigil', when Hester, Pearl and Dimmesdale stand on the scaffold at night, as Chillingworth looks on, and the letter *A* appears in the sky."[6] (See figure 3.1.)

The next morning, however, when the sexton brings Dimmesdale's glove to him, the narrator is proven at least partially incorrect about his conclusions. For the sexton describes the same "great red letter in the sky,—the letter A." While they see the same shape, the sexton offers a different interpretation: it was a "portent . . . which we interpret to stand for Angel."[7] The aged, retired governor John Winthrop had died in the night. Despite declaring that the scarlet letter was not part of the natural world, Weinstein does notice the meteor's

Figure 3.1 The Scarlet Letter by Tompkins Harrison Matteson, 1860. *Source*: Wikimedia Commons. Public Domain.

appearance and wonders, "If other people have seen the letter, do they all suffer from Dimmesdale's 'disease'?"[8] Whether or not this is the purport of the narrator's commentary, the narrator's initial perceptions are also clearly suspect even though he is a more skeptical reader than the Puritans. Hawthorne's Puritans of all stripes assume that unusual occurrences or appearances in nature are nothing less than supernatural signs. If it looks like a letter A, it must mean something related to that letter since the supernatural that made the meteor into the shape of the letter is presumed to be "over" nature. The narrator remains noncommittal in the end, not trusting his own judgment yet not hiding this account of how the natural and the supernatural were thought to coincide.

The second scaffold scene that conspicuously displays a scarlet letter as a work of nature appears in the chapter Hawthorne titled "The Revelation of the Scarlet Letter." Here again Dimmesdale makes his way to the scaffold, but this time in the broad midday sun and in sight of all the people on the way from the church where he has just preached a moving Election-Day sermon. Drawing Pearl and Hester up beside him, Dimmesdale tells the crowd of curious and confused onlookers to look at Hester's scarlet letter, adding that "with all its mysterious horror, it is but the shadow of what he bears on his own breast."[9] When he tears away the front of his ministerial garb to reveal "his own red stigma," the narrator refuses to describe it, perhaps remembering he was wrong in his earlier dismissal of a scarlet letter shape that appeared in the sky. Of this letter on the minister's chest, the narrator claims, "But it were irreverent to describe that revelation."[10] Irreverent or not, the narrator does not hesitate to relate the onlookers' first-hand descriptions of what they see: "Most of the spectators testified to having seen, on the breast of the unhappy minister, a SCARLET LETTER—the very semblance of that worn by Hester Prynne—imprinted in the flesh."[11] The scarlet letter in this case amounts to something like a scar or branding of the human body, whether brought about by natural, supernatural, or unnatural forces. This physical stigma, like the declining health of Dimmesdale, marks his natural body as somehow failing.

In both of these prominent examples of the scarlet letter as something natural and possibly supernatural, the role of interpretation is emphasized. How do we read this letter? How do we read nature? Is it an allegory of human experience? Is it a communication from the great beyond, supernatural handwriting overlaid on the natural world for human interpretation? The narrator inserts nineteenth-century skepticism into the first instance by calling into question the shape of the meteor that Dimmesdale sees. When he is proven wrong, he ends the chapter abruptly with the minister's words, "I had not heard of it."[12] While the minister did not *hear* of the A-shaped meteor, he had indicated earlier that he had clearly *seen* it. The narrator gives no further commentary, however, moving immediately to the next chapter, "Another View of Hester," a deliberate change of scene.

When Dimmesdale's scarlet letter is revealed in the latter scene, the narrator is not so quick to give his interpretation of the letter. Instead, he simply repeats the various interpretations the Puritans give the scarlet letter burned into Dimmesdale's flesh, and then thrusts the work of interpretation upon the reader:

As regarded its origin, there were various explanations, all of which must necessarily have been conjectural. Some affirmed that the Reverend Mr. Dimmesdale, on the very day when Hester Prynne first wore her ignominious badge, had begun a course of penance . . . by inflicting a hideous torture on himself. Others contended that the stigma had not been produced until a long time subsequent, when old Roger Chillingworth, being a potent necromancer, had caused it to appear, through the agency of magic and poisonous drugs. Others, again,—and those best able to appreciate the minister's peculiar sensibility, and the wonderful operation of his spirit upon the body,— whispered their belief, that the awful symbol was the effect of the ever-active tooth of remorse, gnawing from the inmost heart outwardly, and at last manifesting Heaven's dreadful judgment by the visible presence of the letter.[13]

So here, the letter—according to those with the most knowledge of the situation—becomes an act of nature, an act of God, an example of the way the spirit works on the body, or the effect of some combination of these causes. The narrator's response is subdued, and he refuses even to say which theory of the letter's origin he favors, although this time even he considers it a "portent" of some sort: "The reader may choose among these theories. We have thrown all the light we could acquire upon the portent."[14] And so the role of the reader in the work of interpreting the natural world is foregrounded. How should we read nature? Unlike the skeptical nineteenth-century narrator, the seventeenth-century Puritans do not pause to question whether the spiritual world and the material world are coexistent realities. They simply assume that it is. Yet the narrator's apparent errors call into question his own nineteenth-century interpretive strategies just as strongly as he questions the interpretations of the deeply religious Puritans.

To address such perplexing questions, Hawthorne brings natural theology alongside the science of human development, juxtaposing older Puritan understandings of the natural world alongside nineteenth-century biological modes of naturalistic inquiry. Problems of perception and representation destabilize the inquiries of Puritans and skeptics alike, and the narrator leaves us with a jumble of clues to interpret. Like Hester, we are left to wander, almost "without rule or guidance, in a moral wilderness; as vast, as intricate and shadowy, as the untamed forest."[15] What the narrator does give us, however, are the perceptions and interpretations of various characters in the forests and villages of seventeenth-century New England in order that readers may make up their own minds how to interpret with the help of the clues he has scattered before us.

PURITAN ALLEGORY—PARADISE OR WILDERNESS

Hawthorne's Puritans read the natural world as a kind of allegory of the spiritual world. Whether responding with joy or recoiling in fear, the

Puritans routinely approached nature as an allegorical message shaped by God to show them how to live. Even though the narrator generally takes a condescending tone toward the seventeenth-century Puritans he describes, he nonetheless adopts some of their interpretive strategies for understanding nature. Puritan allegory offers a clear method for reading nature: it is treated as the handwriting of God in the earth and sky. In this romance, Hawthorne employs elements of Puritan allegory to focus pastoral by examining human and nonhuman nature for any evidence of a divine imprint. While the divine is typically at least in the background of Renaissance pastoral, Hawthorne's use of Puritan allegory draws it more conspicuously to the foreground. Hawthorne questions Puritans' tendency toward formulaic interpretations of allegory, however, offering alternative ways to read nature. Such multiplicity of meaning suggests that while allegorical readings may rightly implicate the divine within Nature, such implication does not necessarily lead to the kind of clear-cut interpretation of Nature that both Puritans and Transcendentalists hoped for.

As the Puritans saw it, nature was a site of divine mediation with nature as the signifier, the divine message as the signified, and humans as the receivers and interpreters. Such common interpretive assumptions do not always result in identical conclusions, however. For Hawthorne's Puritans, nature can be alternately good or evil, but it is invariably a site on which the handwriting of God can be found. Whether appearing as "awful hieroglyphics, on the cope of heaven" or conceived of as a space in some other way portentous of an individual's or a nation's destiny, nature is something to be read.[16] Hawthorne's Puritans consider nature an allegory for a religious life, but they disagree on what the allegory of Nature suggests or teaches. Some Puritans view the new world as a new Garden of Eden and the forest as a place of beauty and harmony between humans, Nature, and God. Others consider the forest a place of evil, where witches and devils mix with Native Americans and wild animals to produce threats to Puritan civilization. In *The Scarlet Letter*, Hawthorne rewrites the nineteenth century's understanding of the Puritan history of seventeenth-century America—a history in which the allegory of wilderness largely displaces the allegory of paradise.

Drawing on elements of Puritan allegory as he does, Hawthorne shapes *The Scarlet Letter* as an investigation of theological claims of a divine imprint in or influence on nature. This same sense of "the Laws of Nature and Nature's God" was written into the Declaration of Independence. American history—official and unofficial, political and literary—undergoes the scrutiny of Hawthorne's pastoral and allegorical scope. An already old genre when John Bunyan used it in *Pilgrim's Progress* for a seventeenth-century English readership that included many Puritans, allegory has sometimes been considered an inferior literary form. However, allegory (*allos* [other] + *agoria* [speaking, in the open square]) can signify any number of ways of speaking about something by referring to something other than itself and does not necessarily fall into the mode of didactic parallels. Hawthorne continued to find allegory useful for his composing processes even as many other nineteenth-century writers were abandoning it. Samuel Taylor Coleridge, for example, considered allegory inferior to symbolism, and Edgar Allan Poe considered it too mechanical to be true art.[17]

The allegorical method of typology, a method of interpretation that purported to find Christ in the Old Testament scriptures and to find truth within the human or natural world, was sprinkled liberally throughout Puritan sermons. Typology was a kind of allegory whose meaning was already known. All that remained was to determine *how* a text was a type, or shadow, of the larger truth. Typological representations of this sort generally comprised a very strict form of allegory. All that had to be done is to match the type to the original, and the message would be known. Hawthorne's allegorical method of composition is not so strictly parallel. In fact, it is one of the loosest forms of allegory. As David Berkeley points out, allegory or quasi-allegory can be categorized in at least three different ways: it may lead to "one of many possible interpretations" (e.g., Melville's *Moby-Dick*), it may be "nuanced, some shades of meaning being discerned by readers rather than being obtruded on their sensibilities" (e.g., Spenser's *Faerie Queene*, Book II), or it may represent a "one-for-one allegory whose force perhaps gains from lack of such a polysemous texture" (e.g., Bunyan's *Pilgrim's Progress*).[18]

Hawthorne shares the Puritan approach of investigating possible analogies between nature and humans or nature and the divine, but he does not share their confidence that what he discovers will be a straightforward analogy. In *The Scarlet Letter*, Hawthorne presents the reader with clear interpretive choices rather than insisting on a single possibility. Representative of Hawthorne's approach is the narrator's final statement of his introductory exposition in which the narrator focuses on the rosebush against the backdrop of the prison, the "black flower of civilization": "[The rose-bush] may serve, let us hope, to symbolize some sweet moral blossom, that may be found along the track, or relieve the darkening close of a tale of human frailty and sorrow."[19] Nature, beauty, and a sense of morality are intrinsically linked in this image, suggesting that Puritans who eschew beauty and nature cannot expect to be truly moral either. The story of *The Scarlet Letter* is in some sense the story of characters attempting to realize the possible meanings of the rosebush in their own lives. As readers travel with the narrator along the track of this romance and the characters of the romance travel along the track of their lives, the beauty of art and nature brightens the darkness of a tale otherwise brimming with gloom and doom. Morality without beauty and passion is both unnatural and farcical.

In early American Puritan depictions of nature with which Hawthorne was acquainted, two themes are apparent. Samuel Danforth called the American landscape a "waste and howling Wilderness."[20] John Winthrop, on the other hand, presented America as a "good Lande" and a potential "soule's paradise."[21] Despite their disparate viewpoints, Danforth and Winthrop both situate nature primarily as a place in which humans live out their relation to the divine—whether in grateful or oppositional terms with nature. Some Puritans read divine love and some read divine wrath; some view nature antagonistically and some read it sympathetically. Hawthorne's writing privileges a middle position between these polarities, neither trusting wholly in nature's sympathies nor consigning it entirely to witches and devils. Indeed, the American situation represents a new attempt to ask the questions that humans in Western civilization had repeatedly asked about our relationship with nature and the divine. The open-endedness of Hawthorne's allegorical method emphasizes the problems inherent in formulating an accurate understanding of our interrelations.

It is significant that Hawthorne's interest in American history gestures toward the fading optimism of John Winthrop, the dying governor who is repeatedly mentioned but who never actually appears in *The Scarlet Letter*. For Puritans who followed the example of Winthrop, a religious strain of the pastoral myth offered the promise of a new life in an idealized landscape away from the corruptions of English and European decadence. This idealized new world is immediately revealed in Hawthorne's retelling as yet another postlapsarian setting in which the drama of humanity is played out: "The founders of a new colony, whatever Utopia of human virtue and happiness they might originally project," the narrator states in the opening scene of *The Scarlet Letter*, "have invariably recognized it among their earliest practical necessities to allot a portion of the virgin soil as a cemetery, and another portion as the site of a prison."[22] This new world is not, however, *just* another such setting for Hawthorne: it is a real place in which the relations between humans and nature can be examined anew, a place where city-building is ostensibly less threatened by the corruptions of European civilization.

As Winthrop first envisioned America, its "new world" setting invited a revitalization of the myths and hopes of harmonious relations between humans and their natural environment. The rhetoric of the new world as a land of opportunity whose borders had not yet been established, a promised land that provided the space for religious and political freedom from the constraints of European (and especially British) control, a place where humans could live in harmony with the natural world made way for the rebirth of the pastoral. Puritans, however, had a thorny relation with the new world. For while many of them viewed it at first as a pristine place to build the kingdom of God away from a corrupt Europe, the standard Puritan rhetoric soon became one of surviving in the wilderness where they found themselves and their neighbors in tempted by the devil. Hawthorne's awareness of the undercurrents of his own Puritan lineage gave him a unique creative sensibility, leading him to examine early American conceptions of nature even before writing about his association with the Transcendentalists. Hawthorne's much-taught "Young Goodman Brown," for example, highlights the Puritans' association of the forest with devil worshippers, witches, and Native Americans. In other historical accounts of Puritans and Indians, such as "The May-pole of Merry Mount," Hawthorne also depicts stern leaders who associate the unredeemed forest with the unredeemed pagan Native Americans.

In Hawthorne's literature, the harshest Puritan views toward human and nonhuman nature come not from original leaders like Winthrop but from his more intransigent successors in the leadership of Boston. Hawthorne's treatment of Winthrop as a man of charity echoes the tone of Caleb Snow's *History of Boston*.[23] Emphasizing Winthrop's contribution to the trajectory of Boston history, Snow recounts the leniency of Winthrop and his deathbed regret for even his own harsher actions, concluding, "We consider the death of Gov. Winthrop to have completed an epoch in the history of Boston."[24] In the games of the Puritan children, Hawthorne shows the growing Puritan hostility toward the natural world and those in it who were not just like them. Hester watched these little Puritans "disporting themselves in such grim fashion as the Puritanic nurture would permit; playing at going to church, perchance; or at scourging Quakers; or taking scalps in a sham-fight with the Indians; or scaring one another with freaks of imitative witchcraft."[25] These little Puritans' games would be their adult activities all too soon.

Many Election-Day sermons in Puritan New England thrust aside Winthrop's Edenic vision of America and replaced it with an allegory of surviving in the wilderness of the world as a test of faith. One of the most significant sermons in this vein is Samuel Danforth's "Errand into the Wilderness," a sermon made famous by Perry Miller's use of the title for a book on the Puritans. In this sermon, Danforth suggests that the Puritans may well have "in a great measure forgotten our Errand into the Wilderness."[26] He uses this suggestion as his basis for warning the Puritans:

> You have solemnly professed before God, Angels and Men, that the cause of your leaving your Country, Kindred and Fathers Houses, and transporting your selves with your Wives, Little Ones and Substance, over the vast Ocean into this waste and howling Wilderness was *your Liberty to walk in the Faith of the Gospel with all good Conscience according to the Order of the Gospel, and your enjoyment of the pure Worship of God according to His Institution, without Humane mixtures and Impositions.*[27]

Danforth frames the new world as a howling wilderness and emphasizes the fact that the Puritan colonists have exposed their children to the wilds of America, adopting the biblical trope of a prophet's voice crying in the wilderness and urging them to keep the faith even in this testing ground of the so-called howling wilderness. Danforth's sermon was collected with similar ones in a volume of historical Puritan Election-Day sermons that Hawthorne began perusing over two decades before writing *The Scarlet Letter*. Hawthorne's familiarity with this theme likely also grew through his reading of Felt's *Annals of Salem* and numerous books of early New England sermons that he checked out of the Salem Athenaeum.[28] In the *Annals*, Felt mentions that Francis Higginson, a clergyman who arrived in Boston before Winthrop's group, greeted the newcomers arriving with Winthrop by treating them to a wilderness sermon.[29] The wilderness motif of such sermons—a theme Dimmesdale adopts in *The Scarlet Letter*—challenged visions of a new Eden and advocated in its place a vision of pious struggle.

No doubt Winthrop's own wilderness sermon would have caught Hawthorne's attention as he read through Winthrop's journals, especially since it seems to cave to the growing Puritan consensus that the new world is a wilderness rather than a paradise. Winthrop's reluctance to take up this trope is apparent in this sermon, which focuses not so much on wilderness language as on Winthrop's fear that self-interest and material prosperity are about to replace the commitment to charity he had earlier envisioned as an integral part of experiencing the new world as a paradise. As settlers began to move away from the community to better their economic prospects, Winthrop addressed them in the form of a sermon. Though he uses the wilderness motif, Winthrop frames the appearance of wilderness as the result of abandoning faithful religious principles in favor of selfish economic ones: "Ask thy conscience, if thou wouldst have plucked up thy stakes, and brought thy family 3000 miles, if thou hadst expected that all, or most, would have forsaken thee here. Ask again, what liberty thou hast toward others, which thou likest not to allow others toward thyself; for if one may go, another may, and so the greater part, and so the church and commonwealth may be left destitute in a wilderness, exposed to misery and reproach, and all for thy ease and pleasure."[30]

These words signal Winthrop's regretful awareness of the Puritan community's apparent rejection of his model of Christian charity, an overwhelming of the new world paradise that he had envisioned. He adopts the language of wilderness with the lingering hope that a new world paradise might not be wholly beyond their grasp, which he indicates by repeating the word "may"—one person "may" leave, another person "may" follow, the community "may be left destitute in a wilderness." Winthrop's tone provides a decided contrast from the more typical Puritan use of the wilderness sermon as an authoritarian jeremiad, which Sacvan Bercovitch describes as an endeavor "to sustain process by imposing control, and to justify control by presenting a certain form of process as the only road to the future kingdom."[31] Kristin Boudreau characterizes Winthrop's "wilderness speech" as a regretful statement that "[c]harity might have held the community together, but selfishness and love of liberty threatened the ruin of the colony.... [Winthrop] could take little joy in overall prosperity when it was merely the sum total of private gains." Boudreau also notes that Hawthorne represents Winthrop more favorably than most historical Puritans, noting that upon Winthrop's death in *The Scarlet Letter*, "charity seems to have evaporated among the political and religious leaders of New England; consequently, so have the real bonds of community."[32]

In *The Scarlet Letter*, Dimmesdale's Election-Day sermon draws upon the wilderness motif of Puritan sermons but without quite the sense of impending doom that marked so many of these other sermons Hawthorne had read. In this sermon is the suggestion that the Puritans could yet experience ideal relations with each other and with the natural world, in the manner advocated by Winthrop's sermon. Though the narrator declines to give the actual words of the sermon, he provides a description of the sermon as one that conflated the earlier categories between land as paradise and land as wilderness to issue perhaps the most conflicted jeremiad of them all:

> His subject, it appeared, had been the relation between the Deity and the communities of mankind, with a special reference to the New England which they were here planting in the wilderness. And, as he drew toward the close, a spirit of prophecy had come upon him, constraining him to its purpose as mightily as the old prophets of Israel were constrained; only with this difference, that, whereas the Jewish seers had denounced judgments and ruin on their country, it was his mission to foretell a high and glorious destiny for the newly gathered people of the Lord. But, throughout it all, and through the whole discourse, there had been a certain deep, sad undertone of pathos, which could not be interpreted otherwise than as the natural regret of one soon to pass away.[33]

Gone are the questionings, the strivings to change their ways; here is sheer prophecy of goodness to come, paradise soon to be regained! But his prophecy must later appear as madness, for Winthrop's dream—parallel in many ways to what Dimmesdale here predicts—disintegrates, and both men pass away, their visions passing with them.

NATURAL THEOLOGY FROM THE BOOK OF NATURE

Hawthorne would have been familiar with Puritan rhetoric about nature through his reading of Cotton Mather, the most prolific and perhaps the most controversial writer of Puritan history. Mather provides an important alternative to the "wilderness versus paradise" paradigm of the Puritans. In his responses to Mather and his view of the natural world, Hawthorne practices a mixture of censure and respect. Although Mather advocates the necessity of controlling the more natural world of Native Americans, Mather also presents nature as a Book of God that can be read. Mather's method of studying nature as one of the two books of a divine creator comes from an older religious and intellectual tradition: "*Chrysostom,* I remember, mentions a *Twofold Book* of GOD; the Book of the *Creatures,* and the Book of the *Scriptures,* GOD having taught first of all us διαπραγματων, by his *Works,* did it afterwards γραμματων, by his *Words.* We will now for a while read the *Former* of these *Books,* 'twill help us in reading the *Latter:* They will admirably assist one another."³⁴

Mather, like other Puritans, searched the Book of Nature for signs of the divine. Mather records the wilderness trope of some of his predecessors with only limited agreement, advocating a more receptive attitude toward the natural world that is not exactly the paradise of Winthrop but is expectant rather than hostile. And Mather is not without precedent, as his citation indicates. He might have cited John Calvin on the same issue. Or he might have pointed to a prominent example of a Puritan view of nature as a work of God and a delightful place in Anne Bradstreet's *Contemplations* (1678):

> Under the cooling shadow of a stately Elm
> Close sate I by a goodly Rivers side,
> Where gliding streams the Rocks did overwhelm;
> A lonely place, with pleasures dignifi'd.
> I once that lov'd the shady woods so well,
> Now thought the rivers did the trees excel,
> And if the sun would ever shine, there would I dwell.³⁵

Trees and the stream feature prominently in her poem, as they do in the forest scenes of *The Scarlet Letter.* Bradstreet finds solace, delight, even joy in the natural world, much in the way that Hawthorne's main characters do. Puritan poets like Bradstreet offered Hawthorne actual examples of Puritan views of nature that are more admirable than that of Endicott and perhaps more realistic than that of Winthrop.

Even within a Puritan context and allegorical framework, Hawthorne's text opens up questions about how to read nature. As Nina Baym notes, the harshest Puritan significations concerning nature and civilization do not hold in *The Scarlet Letter*: "Wildness and evil are not necessarily identical; the forest, where Indians and the Devil dwell, is also the abode of nature, which the community must destroy in order to erect its civilization. Is nature evil, or only untamed? Is everything that is untamed evil? Why does every heart have secrets, and if every heart does, might not the forest, where they can be shown, be more the abode of honesty than the town, where law and order require inhibition, suppression, and concealment?"[36] For Hawthorne and some of his characters, the natural world and human society are not at odds with each other, but are twin realities.

The simultaneous fallenness and goodness of the natural world is brought to the fore when the earth is considered in the contrasts between forest and civilization. In *American Adam*, R.W.B. Lewis depicts the contrast between nature and civilization in *The Scarlet Letter* as "a decision about ethical reality" that "most of Hawthorne's heroes and heroines eventually have to confront":

> That is why we have the frantic shuttling, in novel after novel, between the village and the forest, the city and the country; for these are the symbols between which the choice must be made and the means by which moral inference is converted into dramatic action. . . . And while [Hawthorne] was responsive to the attractions of the open air and to the appeal of the forest, he also understood the grounds for the Puritan distrust of the forest. He retained that distrust as a part of the symbol. In the forest, possibility was unbounded; but just because of that, evil inclination was unchecked, and witches could flourish there. For Hawthorne, the forest was neither the proper home of the admirable Adam, as with [James Fenimore] Cooper, nor was it the hideout of the malevolent adversary, as with [Robert Montgomery] Bird. It was the ambiguous setting of moral choice, the scene of reversal and discovery in his characteristic tragic drama. The forest was the pivot of Hawthorne's grand recurring pattern of escape and return.[37]

As Lewis intimates, Hawthorne's reaction to Puritan ideas about nature reveals not a dichotomy of opposing relations as in country versus city, nature versus civilization. Instead, Hawthorne displays in the natural world both "dark nature" and harmonious nature.

In a thorough going study of the "historical romance of New England," Michael Davitt Bell traces nineteenth-century conceptions of the divergences between *wild* nature and *tame* nature. As Bell claims, however, Hawthorne fits all of nature under one heading: "Nature with a capital N. Nature as meaning both universal human nature and natural landscape."[38] Pearl's "wild" character, like Hester's "voluptuous" nature, and Dimmesdale's "animal nature" find relief from Puritan grimness in the sanctity of "wild" nature. Bell studies the characteristics of the "Indian stories" of Hawthorne's period and finds that "[a] special figure again and again emphasized in these noble savages is their 'natural' piety—a quality particularly well suited to expose by contrast the cruelty of the professedly 'Christian' Puritans."[39] Hawthorne, Bell suggests, is working against typical romances of his time that depict a strong contrast between the "natural" religion of the Native Americans and the "unnatural" religion of the Puritans. Further, Bell claims that Hawthorne is indeed employing the standard motifs of Native American romances of his time by presenting Hester as a "natural heroine"; however, by showing her flaws as well as her heroism, Hawthorne undermines "the cult of nature through the figure usually used to support it."[40] For Hawthorne, nature is not wholly pure, as many nineteenth-century writers of Native American tales implied, but neither is it wholly impure as seventeenth-century Puritans increasingly assumed.

Unlike most of Hawthorne's Puritan characters, Hester and Dimmesdale exhibit uncertainty about how to read the Book of Nature. This uncertainty results in their dilemma about whether to flee into the heart of the forest or to escape to Europe: "Whither leads yonder forest-track? Backward to the settlement, thou sayest! Yes; but onward, too! Deeper it goes, and deeper, into the wilderness, less plainly to be seen at every step, until, some few miles hence, the yellow leaves will show no vestige of the white man's tread. There thou art free!"[41] They decide instead to go together to Europe where Dimmesdale can continue to develop his studious nature, but Dimmesdale's death precludes any such move by them together. When Hester does go to Europe, it is with her daughter Pearl, but Hester returns in the end to take up residence once again between the forest and the Puritan community in her cottage located "[o]n the outskirts of the town, within the verge of the peninsula, but not in close vicinity to any other habitation . . . on the shore, looking across a basin of the sea at the forest-covered hills, toward the west."[42] Hester is at home it seems both nowhere and everywhere. The forest, the seashore, and the Puritan community—this new world Book of Nature—has become her home.

Hawthorne's characterizations of Hester and Pearl especially offer congenial readings of Nature. In one scene where Pearl is skipping through the forest as Hester and Dimmesdale sit in a secluded nook, Hawthorne describes the natural world as a dynamic place:

> The great black forest—stern as it showed itself to those who brought the guilt and troubles of the world into its bosom—became the playmate of the lonely infant. . . . It offered her the partridge-berries, the growth of the preceding autumn. . . . A pigeon, alone on a low branch, allowed Pearl to come beneath, and uttered a sound as much of greeting as alarm. A squirrel, from the lofty depths of his domestic tree, chattered either in anger or merriment. . . . A fox, startled from his sleep by her light footsteps, looked inquisitively at Pearl. . . . A wolf, it is said,—but here the tale has surely lapsed into the improbable,—came up and smelt of Pearl's robe, and offered his savage head to be patted by her hand. The truth seems to be, however, that the mother-forest, and these wild things which it nourished, all recognized a kindred wildness in the human child.[43]

This description directly challenges darker Puritan views of nature as a threat to humans by showcasing the safety and beauty enjoyed by a *natural* child like Pearl. By transforming the "great black forest" into a "mother-forest," Hawthorne turns the wild forest into a place of beauty and invigorating vitality and suggests that some of the first Puritans in America may have done the same.[44] Hawthorne's description of nature in this passage transfigures Puritan suspicions of the evil of the natural world into more romantic Puritan views of nature as a place of goodness and beauty.

Pearl stands in stark contrast to her peers, the second-generation Puritans whom Hawthorne designates as "being of the most intolerant brood that ever lived."[45] The first-generation of Puritans are depicted as being only in "the first stages of joyless deportment, and the offspring of sires who had known how to be merry, in their day," while the second-generation Puritans are associated with "the blackest shade of Puritanism." It is they who earn Hawthorne's censure of this second generation as "the blackest shade of Puritanism."[46] When Hester and Pearl are walking through the woods, Pearl asks Hester to tell her a story about the devil, who "haunts this forest" and "offers his book and an iron pen to everybody that meets him here among these trees."[47] Hester asks her where she heard this story, which she recognizes as "a common superstition of the period," and Pearl tells her she heard it from an "old dame in the chimney-corner" who thought Pearl was asleep at a sick house Hester was visiting in Boston.[48] This superstition may be common at this time, but it has not yet resulted in the witch-hunting frenzy that will occur not long after the close of the events of Hawthorne's romance.

In the Puritan village too, Pearl reads nature as a happy text. This is shown in her response to the wild men of the forest and the sea. Their nature finds a counterpart in Pearl's passionate affinity with nature. All those who see Pearl as they are milling about Boston on Election Day are entranced by her bird-like vivacity, but she has an especially significant effect on the mariners and Native Americans:

> She ran and looked the wild Indian in the face; and he grew conscious of a nature wilder than his own. Thence, with native audacity, but still with a reserve as characteristic, she flew into the midst of a group of mariners, the swarthy-cheeked wild men of the ocean, as the Indians were of the land; and they gazed wonderingly and admiringly at Pearl, as if a flake of the sea-foam had taken the shape of a little maid, and were gifted with a soul of the sea-fire, that flashes beneath the prow in the night-time.[49]

Pearl is a natural person whose likeness to the wild men of the earth and the wild men of the ocean emphasizes her affinity to nature. But the Native Americans are not the wildest folks described gathering in the marketplace.

That designation belongs to the Spanish mariners: "They were rough-looking desperadoes, with sun-blackened faces, and an immensity of beard; their wide, short trousers were confined about the waist by belts, often clasped with a rough plate of gold, and sustaining always a long knife, and, in some instances, a sword. From beneath their broad-brimmed hats of palm-leaf, gleamed eyes which, even in good-nature and merriment, had a kind of animal ferocity."[50] More like pirates than simple sailors, these mariners exemplify the natural "animal ferocity" of man at his worst, when greed and murder are let loose at will. Hawthorne may have been drawing on family stories of his own seafaring ancestors for his description of the mariners.[51]

Through her visits to the forest, Hester like her daughter ignores Puritan suspicions of nature as the domain of witches and devils and finds the wilderness amenable to her occasional need for space outside of the Puritan community. At the very beginning, however, Hester cannot catch the sunshine dancing in the forest as her daughter does. Pearl skips along the forest trail, and, "as Hester smiled to perceive, did actually catch the sunshine, and stood laughing in the midst of it, all brightened by its splendor, and scintillating with the vivacity excited by rapid motion."[52] When Hester approaches, the light moves away, but it returns when she finds Dimmesdale: "All at once, as with a sudden smile of heaven, forth burst the sunshine, pouring a very flood into the obscure forest, gladdening each green leaf, transmuting the yellow fallen ones to gold. . . . The course of the little brook might be traced by its merry gleam afar into the wood's heart of mystery, which had become a mystery of joy."[53] Passages like these show Hawthorne's treatment of select individuals in and about the Puritan community who do not find nature a hostile territory.

For some of Hawthorne's Puritans, unrestrained passion and witchcraft are closely linked, and the forest is read as a site of such illicit activity. Many of his Puritan characters consider the forest as the place the devil "haunts" while plotting "the ruin of [the human] soul."[54] Mistress Hibbins names the forest as the physical location where she consorts with "fiends and night-hags." Despite the dubious nature of her wild assertions, Mistress Hibbins has actually been to the forest in more than dreams or fantasies for she is described with "twigs of the forest clinging to her skirts."[55] The forest, however, is the place frequented most by Hester and the other major characters in those moments when they deliberately contemplate their place within the natural order.

Although Hester considers leaving human civilization behind, she ultimately remains in the Puritan community. Even after spending a number of years back in the old world with her daughter Pearl, she return to New England after Pearl is grown and stays there for the rest of her life. Hester's relation to society and to the natural world remains undetermined until the end, and it is only through her charitable actions in society and her intimacy with the natural world that she achieves a sense of equilibrium. Despite what some critics claim about Hester as a static character, a definite change in her character can be observed between the time she takes her first tremulous steps out of the prison house to the time she serves as a counselor for young women who seek her out as a wiser, older person who has overcome her detractors through her charitable work for the Puritan community.

Hester's less suspicious reading of the natural world and social world avoids the cynical turn of the eponymous Young Goodman Brown in the earlier Hawthorne tale after his dreamlike witch-meeting in the forest—"[a] stern, a sad, a darkly meditative, a distrustful, if not a desperate man did he become . . . [H]is dying hour was gloom."[56] Like Young Goodman Brown, Hester is threatened with disillusionment in the face of her suspicions that the apparent purity of the Puritan community may be a cover for licentious behavior. Mistress Hibbins, a suspected witch whom the narrator tells us will later be hanged, tells Hester that she has seen Dimmesdale "take an airing in the forest" where she claims she has often danced "when Somebody was fiddler, and, it might be, an Indian powwow or a Lapland wizard changing hands with us! That is but a trifle," she adds, "when a woman knows the world."[57] Hester suspects Mistress Hibbins not of witchcraft but of having an "infirm mind."[58] Earlier, when she sees Dimmesdale returning from the forest, Mistress Hibbins teasingly asks him if he has been meeting with the devil there and promises him that they will have "other talk" when they meet "[a]t midnight, and in the forest," thereby hinting of unsanctioned passion as well as devil worship.[59] Indeed, Dimmesdale knows from experience that he may lose control of his passions in the forest away from the strictures of Puritan society.

Other Puritan parishioners take a very different view of Dimmesdale's forays into nature, viewing it as a place of divine sanctity. When Dimmesdale is described "coming forth [from the forest], when occasion was, with a freshness, and fragrance, and dewy purity of thought, which, as many people said, affected them like the speech of an angel."[60] Thus, Dimmesdale and a number of other Puritans do not take the view espoused by Mistress Hibbins and the old dame from whom Pearl picks up on the local superstitions. Instead, they view the natural world as a delightful place in a manner reminiscent of Anne Bradstreet.

Dimmesdale's forest rambles sometimes lead him to secret meetings with Hester but more often down the path to the "Apostle Eliot." John Eliot, a missionary to the Native Americans, is the one white man whom Hawthorne suggests tried to bridge the gap between the whites and Native Americans. In *Grandfather's Chair*, a book of historical American tales for children which Hawthorne gives in the voice of "Grandfather," Eliot's attitude toward the Native Americans is portrayed as unusual but exemplary: "I have sometimes doubted whether there was more than a single man among our forefathers, who realized that an Indian possesses a mind, and a heart, and an immortal soul. That single man was John Eliot. All the rest of the early settlers seemed to think that the Indians were an inferior race of beings, whom the Creator had merely allowed to keep possession of this beautiful country, till the white men should be in want of it."[61] By associating Dimmesdale with Eliot, Hawthorne projects at least one Puritan character who sees the people of the wilderness as fully human. Upon Dimmesdale's return from the forest after one of his visits to Eliot, Chillingworth exclaims, "Methinks, dear Sir, that you look pale; as if the travel through the wilderness had been too sore for you."[62] Dimmesdale brushes him off, saying that the "free air" has been good for him in his frail state of health. And he proceeds to write the best sermon he has ever delivered, fresh from the woods where the beauty and passion he found in Hester, Pearl, and even Eliot have again given him the impetus to bring life to his own art—the art of eloquent rhetoric.

Yet despite her enjoyment of the forest, Hester wonders whether the apparent chaos of the forest "imaged not amiss the moral wilderness in which she had so long been wandering."[63] And she is strangely unsettled by the chattering brook that "still kept telling its unintelligible secret of some very mournful mystery that had happened—or making a prophetic lamentation about something that was yet to happen—within the verge of the dismal forest."[64] Although the natural environment takes part in the mysterious prophecies seemingly uttered here, the mystery of the setting seems as important as the darkness of the setting. This parallel between inner and outer world is again delineated in the narrator's reflections on Hester's situation: "Her intellect and heart had their home, as it were, in desert places, where she roamed as freely as the wild Indian in his woods. . . . Shame, Despair, Solitude! These had been her teachers,—stern and wild ones,—and they had made her strong, but taught her much amiss."[65] So the inner conflicts and the outer world of nature coincide in a stroke of artistic license that seems to bend the outer to the inner. And the outer world of nature so personified, so allegorized, is pronounced insufficient as a model for or reflection of the inner life of humans.

Reading nature is no easy task for Hawthorne's Puritans or his nineteenth-century narrator. When nature is written upon—whether in the sky or the human body—reading nature becomes even trickier. Meteors and comets received much public attention during Hawthorne's lifetime, most significantly with the loudly hailed discovery of a new comet—alternately called Miss Mitchell's Comet, Comet Mitchell, or Maria's Comet—on October 1, 1847, a few years before *The Scarlet Letter* was published. Discovered by an American woman, Maria Mitchell, the comet was said to portend great things for women.[66] Perhaps this is one reason Hawthorne pairs such celestial imagery with Hester's "recognition" in the last chapter of *The Scarlet Letter* that "[t]he angel and apostle of the coming revelation must be a woman indeed, but lofty, pure, and beautiful; and wise, moreover, not through dusky grief, but the ethereal medium of joy; and showing how sacred love should make us happy, by the truest test of a life successful to such an end!"[67] This statement suggests some degree of sympathy in the women's movement in the nineteenth century as well as wishing for a renewed spiritual vision and communion with nature.

A notice of the appearance of a meteor later in 1847 was printed in the November 6 edition of the *Salem Tri-Weekly Gazette*. In this brief announcement, the meteor is described in terms of light, much as the meteor in *The Scarlet Letter* is: "A very brilliant Meteor was seen last evening just before ten. Its course was from South to North, and passed very near the Pleiades. The light was so bright for the moment, as to light up the street. It left a bright train behind it."[68] Richard Kopley points out that Hawthorne's attention would have been drawn to this article because of its appearance alongside "Intelligence Office," the title of one of his own sketches, in a newspaper he likely read.[69] Astronomy and cosmology were together subsumed under the Puritans' theocentric rubric, and theories of the universe were theories of the relation between the earth, the physical heavens, and the supernatural—theories that place humans within a kind of terrestrial and celestial divine cosmology. Hiroko Washizu notes the early American Puritans' interest in astronomy as attested to by Samuel Danforth's *An Astronomical Description of the Late Comet*. Washizu traces additional examples of Hawthorne's attention to meteors, concluding that Hawthorne's "elaborate narrative strategy" in discussing the A-shaped meteor in *The Scarlet Letter* "shows that Hawthorne was well-aware of the transformations in the view of comets/meteors between the ages of 1650 and 1850: he could just as easily be both sympathetic and critical of decoding the celestial hieroglyphics."[70]

The meteor that turns the midnight into an uncanny midday also fits the providential structure Kopley identifies in *The Scarlet Letter*: "a symmetrically framed Sun of Righteousness, Christ come in judgment, and a chiastic expression of that judgment."[71] Kopley is drawing here on a formal tradition with pagan and Christian roots that he traces from medieval sources to John Donne and John Milton in England and on to Defoe's *Robinson Crusoe*, a favorite childhood book of Hawthorne's. Kopley concludes his analysis with this summation: "Though very different in myriad ways, the novels *Robinson Crusoe* and *The Scarlet Letter*—both of which do, in fact, concern Original Sin, Divine Providence, and spiritual redemption—may be considered as homologous texts, distinct instances of providential form."[72] Kopley's observations about the formal resonances of Hawthorne's work with regard to the seeming inscrutability of an ultimately righteous Providence finds its parallel in the seeming inscrutability of the hieroglyphic portents of that Providence upon the natural world—in this instance, upon the sky. Certainly, the Puritans are looking there for signs of the divine to give form to the world they see.

Reading the human body as part of Nature is also a fearful thing for most of the Puritans. Hester covers her body in drab gray much of the time but literally lets down her hair while in the forest with Dimmesdale. After casting off her stigma, as the narrator calls the scarlet letter, Hester frees some of the constraints on her body:

> By another impulse, she took off the formal cap that confined her hair; and down it fell upon her shoulders, dark and rich, with at once a shadow and a light in its abundance, and imparting the charm of softness to her features. There played around her mouth, and beamed out of her eyes, a radiant and tender smile, that seemed gushing from the very heart of womanhood. A crimson flush was glowing on her cheek, that had been long so pale. Her sex, her youth, and the whole richness of her beauty, came back from what men call the irrevocable past.[73]

For Hawthorne, writing his own revisionary history of the Puritans, the past may not be quite revocable, but it certainly can be examined in a new light. Like Hester, Hawthorne is able to go back to what was before, to remember and to seek out the beauty and charm of a past that has been forgotten or misrepresented. And in that remembering, a closeness to nature may be found that is overlooked by those who remember only the howling wilderness proclaimed by Puritan clergymen. Hester loves nature, and nature seems to love her back even when she hides her sin of adultery there. Her adultery is enough to make the narrator at least tentatively side with those Puritans who feared that the sympathy of "that wild, heathen Nature of the forest, never subjugated by human law, nor illumined by higher truth."[74] In this case, the narrator responds to nature in sympathy with adultery as something even less desirable than the austere Puritan laws whose claims to higher truth strictly forbade adultery.[75] Nature may be both a redeemer and a temptress.

Another difficulty in reading the human body has to do with the scarlet letter on Dimmesdale's chest. Is there an actual stigma, imposed on his physical body by natural or supernatural means? His natural body represents a site of divine inscriptions, but his natural body is also the site of his adultery. Nature becomes less clearly a message of God for the Puritans when the human body becomes the subject of consideration. While the Puritan onlookers uniformly report witnessing the glowing A on Dimmesdale's chest as he is dying, a variety of differing meanings are attached to that stigma and manner of death. Despite their varying interpretations, the Puritans uniformly attempt to find some explanation other than the possibility that the stigma was a punishment placed upon Dimmesdale by God, as Dimmesdale claimed. Some of the onlookers say that it is the result of self-inflicted tortures Dimmesdale undertook in penance, while others suggest that Chillingworth is a magician as well as a physician and that he made it appear. Still others consider it the bodily effects of Dimmesdale's godly remorse for sin. While there are a few who say—presumably like many of Hawthorne's nineteenth-century readers—that there probably never was an actual stigma in his physical body and that Dimmesdale chose his manner of death to be a parable, the narrator asserts: "The reader may choose among these theories. We have thrown all the light we could acquire upon the portent."[76] Here, the narrator gives over the task of interpretation to the reader, but in so doing he signifies that his earlier confident statements may not be trustworthy—they have, after all, been undermined repeatedly. With such a move, Hawthorne cautions readers against being too ready to adopt the perspective of the narrator instead of becoming careful interpreters themselves.

It is worth noting that Dimmesdale's failing health makes his body "inadequate to sustain the hardships of a forest life" in a literal sense quite as much as in a metaphoric sense.[77] On the morning of his Election-Day sermon, the village square is filled with people who know physical reality intimately, for it is "thronged with craftsmen and . . . rough figures, whose attire of deerskins marked them as belonging to some of the forest settlements."[78] The natural world has clearly influenced the apparel of the people who lived there, deerskins indicating their connection to the natural world through the literal food chain rather than just through metaphorical patterns. To disregard the literal, or physical, implications because of the obvious metaphoric ones is to miss Hawthorne's interest in the human body as well as the human soul.

THE NATURE AND CONSTITUTION OF HUMAN BODIES

The Scarlet Letter contains multiple hints that the nature of the body can be understood in terms of nineteenth-century scientific theories about human development. Reflecting on the situation to which he finds himself reduced by his job indoors at the Salem Custom House, Hawthorne writes in his preface: "Nature,—except it were human nature,—the nature that is developed in earth and sky, was, in one sense, hidden from me; and all the imaginative delight, wherewith it had been spiritualized, passed away out of my mind."[79] And he does make a study of human nature by observing his fellow workers even though he wishes again for "that invigorating charm of Nature, which used to give me such freshness and activity of thought, the moment that I crossed the threshold of the Old Manse."[80] The study of human nature as part of nature is in fact an increasingly important component of Hawthorne's consideration of life. By focusing on the human body itself—its constitution and its responses to stimuli in its environment—Hawthorne's questions about nature turn to the realm of natural philosophy, the mother of science. What are we by nature? How does understanding our nature help us to understand the significance of human life? Hawthorne addresses such questions by imaginatively investigating the nature of a developing child and the nature of a woman. Both the child Pearl and the woman Hester as described by Hawthorne demonstrate a nature in tune with the rest of the natural world more than the men around them do—even if those men seem to be in control. Despite the antagonism of the people around them, there is also something in the nature of Pearl and Hester that enables them to experience a surprising level of agency, given the constraints of their social environment.

Through Hester, the narrator closely observes Pearl for clues of her nature. "Day after day, she looked fearfully into the child's expanding nature; ever dreading to detect some dark and wild peculiarity, that should correspond with the guiltiness to which she owed her being."[81] Clearly, Hester expects a direct correlation between the moral world and the natural world. In Pearl's body, however, she can see "no physical defect." Instead, she sees the opposite: "By its perfect shape, its vigor, and its natural dexterity in the use of all its untried limbs, the infant was worthy to have been brought forth in Eden; worthy to have been left there, to be the plaything of the angels, after the world's first parents were driven out."[82] Given her strong belief in moral and natural correspondence, Hester sometimes doubts that her adultery was really a sin, telling Dimmesdale on one occasion, "What we did had a consecration of its own. We felt it so!"[83] The narrator, on the other hand, sometimes casts doubt on Hester's belief in the exact correspondence of the moral and natural worlds. Spiritual meaning may not always flow from a directly allegorical interpretation of the natural world after all.

This ambivalence is particulary pronounced in Pearl's physical form, which is described repeatedly as a thing of nature. In Pearl, we see "the full scope between the wild-flower prettiness of a peasant-baby, and the pomp, in little, of an infant princess. Throughout all, however, there was a trait of passion, a certain depth of hue, which she never lost. . . . This outward mutability indicated, and did not more than fairly express, the various properties of her inner life. Her nature appeared to possess depth, too, as well as variety."[84] A child of nature, then, rather than of the Puritan community, Pearl offers an opportunity to see how a little child might develop naturally in this time and place. When Hester calls upon Dimmesdale to weigh in on the question of whether the Puritan officials would take Pearl away from her, Dimmesdale defends Hester by linking God to a mother's "instinctive knowledge of [her child's] nature and requirements."[85] Even the Puritans give in to arguments about a mother's natural instincts.

Little Pearl's gorgeous red outfit with gold embroidery covers her warm little body, much as the scarlet letter on Hester's breast covers a substance that creates a burning sensation. She seems to be another natural scarlet letter, or, in the narrator's words, "the scarlet letter in another form; the scarlet letter endowed with life!"[86] The unkind little Puritans call Pearl "the likeness of the scarlet letter."[87] When begging the Puritan magistrates not to take her child from her, Hester declares, "See ye not, she is the scarlet letter."[88] Out in the forest, Pearl creates her own letter A, but it is a green letter A made of "eel-grass" as Pearl tries to make herself appear to be a mermaid. Hester tries to laugh it off, but when Pearl asks what Hester's scarlet letter means, Hester refuses to answer.[89] In another incident, Pearl says old Mistress Hibbins had informed her that the letter was the devil's mark on her mother. Through it, certainly, Hester found a "passport into regions where other women dared not tread" and enjoyed the wild forest "where she roamed as freely as the wild Indian in his woods."[90]

Hawthorne's characterization of Pearl as a living letter for her mother to read follows many of the naturalist theories of Robert Mudie in his *Popular Guide to the Observation of Nature*, a book Hawthorne borrowed from the Salem Athenaeum more than once. In this book, Hawthorne would have read Mudie's insistence that our empirical senses serve as "the organs of observation," which "will not cease from making their revelations to us, if the circumstances under which we are placed will at all admit of their acting."[91] The act of observation, Mudie claims, "is, indeed, in the very constitution of our nature; and though our own memories do not reach back to that period and those who are very near it cannot inform us, yet we have every reason to believe that life and observation begin at the same instant, and hold on their course, and close together."[92] If it is in our nature to be observers, we may find our observations acutely informed by those who have not yet been trained to observe in a way that is contrary to nature. Unlike the rest of the little Puritans in *The Scarlet Letter*, Pearl observes the patterns of nature without interference. She represents Mudie's romantic "little child on the meadow" who serves as one of "our schoolmasters in the study of nature."[93] Yet even if she is not herself frightened of her nature or of the natural world around her, she is always shadowed by Puritan fears of the natural. Darrel Abel's characterization of Pearl as both a "romantic child of nature" and a "Puritan child of nature" describes the complexity of Pearl's significance to the text.[94] But the romantic child of nature is clearly favored by Hawthorne, for the Puritans would have learned much from schoolmaster Pearl if they had only observed her as Hester did.

Young Pearl, so different from the Puritan community in most ways, was well acquainted with the Puritan conception of original sin and the story of the Garden of Eden. "In Adam's fall, we sinn'd all," declared the *New-England Primer* that routinely instructed young New Englanders into the nineteenth century. Hawthorne refers to this text while assuring the reader that, though the three-year-old Pearl refused to answer the clergyman's question about who made her, she had been instructed by her mother: "Pearl knew well enough who made her . . . [S]o large were the attainments of her three years' lifetime, [she] could have borne a fair examination in the New England Primer, or the first column of the Westminster Catechisms, though unacquainted with the outward form of either of those celebrated works."[95] Later when they are at the seashore, Pearl replies to Hester's question about whether she knows what the A stands for: "Yes, mother . . . It is the great letter A. Thou hast taught it me in the horn-book."[96] In these cases, Hawthorne emphasizes that the "A" of *The Scarlet Letter* represents original sin (associated with Adam), even though the "A" literally stands for adultery in this story of America. In this Puritan conception of original sin, Nature—whether human or nonhuman nature—is in need of redemption.

But Pearl seems a possible exception to all this fallenness. She has "a native grace" about her and appears to be "the plaything of the angels" in the Garden of Eden "after the world's first parents were driven out."[97] She does not fit snugly into a Puritan theological framework. And if Pearl is the child of Adam and Eve and Hester is Eve, who then is Adam—the one whose fall the New England Primer would claim had started it all? Indeed, that is the question the Puritan leaders so insistently ask, first in the words of Dimmesdale himself (at the urging of those around him), then in the entreaties of the older Reverend Wilson, both men charging her on the public scaffold to "speak out the name."[98] While no such mystery of identity surrounds the characters of *Paradise Lost*, the dilemma of what to do after the entry of original sin is a central concern of both texts, and a change in the characters' relations to their society and to the natural world seems the obvious result. While Milton's epic is a dramatic expansion upon the Genesis account of Eden with parallels to the political situation in England after the Restoration, Hawthorne's version of the fall exposes the vulnerability of Puritan New England as a reenactment of the fall in stark contrast to the "city on a hill" envisioned by the first Puritans. The fall of Dimmesdale and Hester is not itself the central focus: that crucial event has already transpired before the beginning of the story. Instead, the characters' reactions to their fallen condition gain the narrator's greatest attention.

In his descriptions of Pearl's nature, Hawthorne's choice of language also shows an emerging interest in biological development, more particularly in what is known today as embryogenesis and genetics. In connection with human nature, Hawthorne frequently uses terms such as "embryo" and "germ" and "transmute" and "transform." When Pearl is first born, the narrator draws attention to the "faint, embryo smile of the little mouth" when she first gazed upon the scarlet letter at Hester's breast.[99] Responding to the enmity of the little Puritans who jeered at her, Pearl reflects characteristics "inherited" from her mother: "in the nature of the child," remarks the narrator, "seemed to be perpetuated those unquiet elements that had distracted Hester Prynne before Pearl's birth."[100] Such thinly veiled references to Jean Baptiste de Lamarck's theory of acquired characteristics that are formed during embryonic development represent Hawthorne's oblique method of engaging scientific observations as ongoing discussions rather than conclusions about the natural world. The germ theory of embryonic development is encoded by the narrator's comment that "Providence, in the person of this little girl, had assigned to Hester's charge the germ and blossom of womanhood, to be cherished and developed amid a host of difficulties," followed by Hester's suspicion that "[t]he child's own nature had something wrong in it, which continually betokened that she had been born amiss,—the effluence of her mother's lawless passion."[101]

According to Ron Amundson's study of the history of embryonic theory, "Prior to Linnaeus and his botanical colleagues, beliefs in transmutation and spontaneous generation were extremely widespread."[102] Besides reading Linnaeus and Lyell and Cuvier, Hawthorne heard scientists and other speakers at the Lyceums in Massachusetts, particularly at the Salem Lyceum, where he served as an officer for a term. The frequent scientific lecturer Louis Agassiz, for example, popularized Linnaeus's more traditional ideas and rejected theories of transmutation. Thomas Pennant, whose *British Zoology* Hawthorne checked out of the Salem Athenaeum, also praises "the admirable Linnaeus . . . that great naturalist . . . [who urged] his countrymen to the study of nature."[103] Hawthorne's interest in inherited characteristics is not quite in line with the principle of genetic fixity advocated by zoologists such as Pennant and Linnaeus, suggesting that he had access to these vying nineteenth-century theories of biological development.

Besides being the husband Hester has cuckolded, Chillingworth is a physician well-versed in European knowledge and speculations about the human body. And while living with Native Americans, he learns the remedies of the so-called new world as well. "the healing talents and herbal medicinal knowledge . . . [of] his Indian captors."[104] This gives Chillingworth both the motivation and tools to attempt to learn the identity of Pearl's father. A practitioner of medical science and a student of natural philosophy, Chillingworth is a scientist of sorts in seventeenth-century New England. Like the floral and weed imagery associated earlier with Pearl, the herbal imagery associated with Chillingworth suggests that natural growths hold secrets just waiting to be discovered. Like Pearl, Chillingworth has a secret identity and a stronger affinity for the natural world than the other Puritans do. His knowledge of Native American herbal secrets of the new world combined with the learning of old world scientists make Chillingworth almost a miracle to the Puritan community: "He was heard to speak of Sir Kenelm Digby, and other famous men,—whose scientific attainments were esteemed hardly less than supernatural,—as having been his correspondents or associates" (121).

Chillingsworth's association with Kenelm Digby aligns him with a more materialist philosophy than the Puritans would have accepted. According to Dugald Stewart's *Philosophical Essays*, which Hawthorne borrowed from the Salem Athenaeum on more than one occasion, Digby was an early believer in "the doctrine of the *materiality of our ideas*."[105] Such a materialist might seem out of place in the world of the seventeenth-century Puritans, but Chillingworth clearly represents an interest in the interworkings of the material and the spiritual. Chillingsworth's reliance on Digby's materialist philosophy is further apparent when he suggests, "It is easy to see the mother's part in her. Would it be beyond a philosopher's research, think ye, gentlemen, to analyze that child's nature, and, from its make and mould, to give a shrewd guess at the father?"[106] The elderly clergyman Reverend Wilson rebukes Chillingworth for what he deems a highly inappropriate suggestion about how to address a religious issue: "It would be sinful, in such a question, to follow the clew of profane philosophy."[107] Mr. Wilson leaves it to Providence rather than turning to the theories of natural philosophy. Chillingworth, however, apparently subscribes to the then-prescient but now-outdated blended inheritance theory of heredity prevalent before Charles Darwin's postulation of natural selection. According to the blended inheritance theory, the phenotypes (physical traits) of a developing baby take form as the fusion of the two parents' physical traits. By subtracting the known "mother's part," Chillingworth hoped to identify the shape of the unknown father.

Old science, whether seen as medical progress or alchemy, as magic or poison, is sometimes treated seriously and sometimes treated as pseudoscience in *The Scarlet Letter*. By representing old science as a set of unproven realities better left alone, Hawthorne adopts Mary Shelley's tactic of depicting old science as a hazardous venture into the secrets of nature. But rather than offering a caution against playing God, as Shelley's *Frankenstein* does, Hawthorne's story cautions against playing the part of the devil, as Chillingworth does. *The Scarlet Letter* asserts the narrator's belief that the Puritans were wrong to depict the natural world as the abode of the devil, but the narrator does begin to wonder if his dismissal of a connection between the natural and the supernatural has been premature. And he also moves much closer to the obsessively allegorical Puritans' grim conviction of the devilish potential of human nature left to its own devices. By giving us an ambiguous narrator who changes his tune as events unfold contrary to his expectations, Hawthorne invites readers to think through issues of the connection between nature and spirit for themselves. In the end, the narrator hopes for an ultimate resolution in the afterlife—a resolution where an "earthly stock of hatred and antipathy" may be "transmuted into golden love."[108] Again using the language of alchemy and natural philosophy, Hawthorne uses natural processes as metaphors for internal human processes of transformation. As creatures of nature, humans can find mirrored in the natural order principles for their own health and flourishing. If we learn how to read and interpret nature, Hawthorne seems to be suggesting, we can expect to enjoy a more harmonious world.

Hawthorne's use of the term "transmutation" has typically been addressed as a reference to the discredited old science of alchemy. Given Chillingworth's study of alchemists, such a reference makes sense. In nineteenth-century America, however, "transmutation" most often referred to theories of the "transmutation of species," a term for evolution before Darwin popularized the current terminology. Hawthorne's use of the term "transmutation" is often figurative but also works as a literal change resulting from the effects of the environment on the body. The effects are usually short term, but sometimes have long-term implications as well. In one instance when Hester is alone in the forest with Pearl and Dimmesdale, for example, she finally feels the rhythms of nature relieving her from the rhythms of the Puritan community. The sun "pour[ed] a very flood into the obscure forest, gladdening each green leaf, transmuting the yellow fallen ones to gold, and gleaming adown the gray trunks of the solemn trees."[109] This transmutation that is happening in the natural world mirrors the transmutation that happened in their adulterous act and the conception of Pearl almost a decade earlier.

In seventeenth-century Puritan America, Hester is pushed to the margins of civilization. But she has learned to blend nature and culture, transmuting them into a place where she can exist. She ends her life at her cottage, situated at the border between the forest, the sea, and the village. Here she lived with Pearl: "On the outskirts of the town, within the verge of the peninsula, but not in close vicinity to any other habitation, there was a small thatched cottage. . . . It stood on the shore, looking across a basin of the sea at the forest-covered hills, towards the west. A clump of scrubby trees, such as alone grew on the peninsula, did not . . . much conceal the cottage from view. . . . A mystic shadow of suspicion immediately attached itself to the spot."[110] Hester is pushed to the margins of the Puritan community, comfortable on both sides of the border between nature and civilization where she lives in her cottage by the seashore—in a location that allows her to experience equilibrim with nature and culture. Her transmutation has been accompanied by painful changes, but she shows a high degree of adaptability. She survives and thrives, passing on something of herself to her European granddaughter, for whom she knits little dresses, and to the women she counsels when they fall into disfavor with the Puritan leaders.

Unlike Hester, Dimmesdale and Chillingworth remain shrouded in their individual failures to reveal the truth about their intimate connections to Pearl and her mother. When Dimmesdale wonders if some men are silent "by the very constitution of their nature," Chillingworth waxes philosophical on the self-deception of such people.[111] When Dimmesdale tells people from the pulpit that he is a vile sinner, they suppose he is speaking in general terms of the sinfulness of all people. And he is only considered more saintly for this admission of guilt, which means, the narrator tells us, that he "had only gained one other sin . . . without the momentary relief of being self-deceived. He had spoken the very truth, and transformed it into the veriest falsehood. And yet, by the constitution of his nature, he loved the truth, and loathed the lie, as few men ever did. Therefore, above all things else, he loathed his miserable self!"[112] So while the true natures of the handsome Dimmesdale and the hump-backed Chillingworth remain unknown, the Puritans—and we along with them—are given occasion to examine Hester's nature very carefully. The voyeuristic male gaze is enabled by the Puritan legal system, and the harsh treatment a woman in Hester Prynne's situation can receive may have contributed to the narrator's statement that "[t]he angel and apostle of the coming revelation must be a woman."[113] In any case, the men renege on their responsibilities, wanting only absolution for their sins or vengeance on those who have done them wrong.

Breaking down the gender roles that play such a prominent role in seventeenth-century Puritan culture, the narrator notes that the "long hereditary habit" that is sometimes taken to be the "nature" of women needed to be "essentially modified" in order for women to exert their influences in reforming the public sphere.[114] Hester may be moving in the right direction for this to happen since her habits do not conform to the norm for Puritan women. Even in the very first scene, when she appears in the prison doorway with her baby in her arms, the narrator remarks on her "natural dignity and force of character" in refusing the arm of the beadle on the path from the prison to the scaffold where she was to be shamed.[115] While she stands on the scaffold, steeling her "impulsive and passionate nature" against the fierce stares of the onlookers, her "preternaturally active" mind recalls scenes of public amusements from her childhood in England.[116] As this scene plays out, the narrator describes her physical demeanor as enabled by an active mind—forceful and dignified, spontaneous and passionate. An active mind and an active body are linked. When the clergymen and governor emerge to join the crowd, the elder clergyman remarks that Dimmesdale knows Hester's "natural temper" and has already argued that it would be "wronging the very nature of woman" to compel an open confession. Dimmesdale does not have the strength of mind that Hester does, quickly acceding to the demands of others who inisist that he question Hester anyway.[117] Hester steadfastly refuses to yield to their questioning and by the time they are finished, the narrator admires her for enduring "all that nature could endure; and as her temperament was not of the order that escapes from too intense suffering by a swoon, her spirit could only shelter itself beneath a stony crust of insensibility, while the faculties of animal life remained entire."[118] In tune with her biological existence as a young woman and bearing up under the demands placed upon her body by the

Puritan community, Hester shows her nature. She is both spirit and animal, her temperament and faculties alike taking part in her essential nature.

Hawthorne does make it clear that Hester's womanly passions as shaped by nature rather than by the Puritan community constitute her character. But Hester does not always act in accordance with her nature. She does not, for example, disappear into "the passes of the dark, inscrutable forest open to her, where the wildness of her nature might assimilate itself with a people whose customs and life were alien from the law that had condemned her."[119] Her wild nature, the narrator suggests here, makes her more like the *wild* Indians than the *civilized* Puritans. Similarly, when speaking of the forest where Hester and Dimmesdale consummated their act of adultery, the narrator suggests that "the sympathy of Nature—that wild, heathen Nature of the forest, never subjugated by human law, nor illumined by higher truth" is well aligned "with the bliss of these two spirits!"[120] Nature gives its blessing to the couple, but it is a "heathen" Nature. The narrator hesitates to approve this sympathy since it is not elevated by ultimate truths. His constant ridicule of the ruling Puritans throughout *The Scarlet Letter* suggests that he is less concerned that the act of adultery shows disregard for human law than that it may demonstrate disregard for higher truth. In light of his own method of seeking to understand humans as part of nature and part of something else and his emphasis on "heathen" nature, the narrator implies here the need for a rational spirituality to interpret nonhuman nature.

In the events that preceded the book's opening chapter, Hester seemed to be acting in accordance with her nature by falling for a young man close to her in age and physical location. Dimmesdale was a young man, and she was a young woman. And they were together at the edges of the American forests far away from the more elderly man she had married who had stayed behind in Europe bent over his books. Even when the man she married joins them in America, he too suggests that Hester's adultery with Dimmesdale was not entirely unnatural. Chillingworth even suggests that Hester's marriage to himself—an elderly man bent over his studies—was less natural than the act of adultery that joined two young bodies in the bloom of life as Dimmesdale and Hester had both been when Pearl was conceived. "Mine was the first wrong," Chillingworth tells her, "when I betrayed thy budding youth into a false and unnatural relation with my decay."[121] To one of Chillingworth's ilk, natural philosophy—like "heathen Nature"—seems to dictate the natural mating of two young bodies rather than an old body with a young one. It is Chaucer's old story of January and May in "The Merchant's Tale," the old man cuckolded by a young wife who finds a young lover who is more in tune with her.

Hester's nature involves a "taste for the gorgeously beautiful," and "a rich, voluptuous, Oriental characteristic."[122] Chillingworth speaks of her nature in materialist terms, telling Hester, "Thou hadst great elements . . . I pity thee, for the good that has been wasted in thy nature."[123] But Hester's actions prove that her nature is not wasted. The narrator notices this, pointing out that she uses her body to serve others:

> Hester's nature showed itself warm and rich; a well-spring of human tenderness . . . Her breast, with its badge of shame, was but the softer pillow for the head that needed one. She was self-ordained a Sister of Mercy; or, we may rather say, the world's heavy hand had so ordained her. . . . The letter was the symbol of her calling. Such helpfulness was found in her,—so much power to do, and power to sympathize,—that many people refused to interpret the scarlet A by its original signification. They said it meant Able; so strong was Hester Prynne, with a woman's strength.[124]

She uses her natural and passionate love of beauty to serve other human beings, others with a common human nature. The narrator changes his first description of her as a "self-ordained . . . Sister of Mercy" to suggest instead that "the world's heavy hand had so ordained her."[125] In this case, circumstances have conspired to allow her true nature as a passionate woman to move her to the aid of other humans. Whether nature or culture is the world being referred to is irrelevant in this case because the cultural can be seen as an outworking of the natural.

Despite the way Hester redeems herself in the eyes of at least some of the Puritan community, the narrator does not approach the natural world as an unmediated purveyor of truth. Instead, nature itself bears the same marks of fallenness that mark the human condition. Human nature bears an organic resemblance to Mother Nature and losing that resemblance disfigures humans. Thus, Hawthorne's romantic view of nature always retains a shred of Puritan suspicion of the natural world. Nature is not proven to be the equivalent of good or evil in *The Scarlet Letter*: instead, it is a dynamic and actual place in which humans can better recognize their own condition as creatures of a world they share with others.

HARMONY WITH NATURE IN PURITAN AMERICA

In *The Scarlet Letter*, nature and beauty are brought together in the major characters, who adapt to the natural world in various fairly explicit ways. The characters in this romance are evaluated, sometimes directly and sometimes indirectly, according to their relation to nature and society, and their status as Puritans bears directly on this scrutiny. In each case, the artist figures are praised or damned by the text in accord to the quality of their interactions with the world around them. Hyatt Waggoner claims that "[a]s Chillingworth is associated with weeds, Pearl with flowers, and Dimmesdale with no natural growing thing at all, so Hester walks her ambiguous way between burdock and rose, neither of which is alone sufficient to define her nature and her position."[126] Waggoner correctly connects these characters to nature in that Chillingworth gathers herbs and such suspicious looking plants as "the deadly night-shade" for his medical remedies, Pearl gathers flowers as her attire, and Hester draws on the sympathy of the rosebush. However, Hester does not incline toward the burdocks, and both she and Dimmesdale find the natural world a refreshing place that embraces them even when the Puritan community would not.

Although Hawthorne's personifications of nature typically serve to nurture a romantic impulse toward the natural world, his treatment of nature is neither merely reactive to the Puritan sensibility nor wholly romantic in the Transcendentalist sense. The narrator's voice alternately applauds, questions, and rejects the characters' attitudes but generally intimates that healthy relations with the natural world are an important signifier of a character's wholeness as a person. Hawthorne's text is a reminder that humans are interlinked with nature and the divine in ways worth searching out. Where that search ends is not entirely clear. However, Hawthorne's *Scarlet Letter*, with its interpolation of allegorical and pastoral motifs, turns to nature as a way of reaching for an understanding of nonhuman reality as a part of the human condition.

For both pessimistic and optimistic Puritans, nature serves as a place of supernatural possibility. The narrator's personifications of nature—whether the sunshine dancing through the trees, the trees gently groaning, the brook murmuring its secrets, the heart of nature offering its sympathy to the humans in its bosom—are often offered through the eyes of Hester or as the narrator. While I do not agree with Janice Daniel that nature itself is the narrator of *The Scarlet Letter,* Daniel does effectively show that Hawthorne distances himself from the voice of his nineteenth-century narrator—in this work as well as in his other romances. My reading closely aligns with Daniel's overall contention that the narrator's personifications of nature indicate more sympathy with nature than is allowed by the abrasive attitudes espoused by harsher Puritans of Hawthorne's text.[127] Hawthorne's main characters, regardless of their status in society, adopt less hostile views toward the natural world than do most of their austere counterparts. The nature of earth, human nature, and human charity all spring from a divine source—this much conviction Hawthorne shares with his Puritans. And with them he also shares a sense that the goodness of these three things are threatened by a fallenness that inheres in the natural condition. But Hawthorne's insistence on the good potential of nature, nonetheless, sets him apart from the harsher Puritan views even as his conviction of fallenness sets him apart from his Transcendentalist contemporaries.

Hawthorne's personification and allegorization of nature do not foreclose his ability to attend to the natural world as a reality of its own—a reality that precedes and outlives any representation of it. Like religious conceptions of nature, ascendant scientific theories also influence Hawthorne's portrayal of the natural world in *The Scarlet Letter*. For in this book are clear signs of Hawthorne's interest in the natural development of humans, transmuting from embryos into babies and growing from babies into adulthood and old age. Drawing together the questions of natural philosophy and theology, physical health, and human biology, Hawthorne approaches the workings of the natural world as clues to help the human subject discern the ultimate meaning of human existence and our best possibly harmony with the nonhuman world.

Thus, nature is not mere metaphor in *The Scarlet Letter*. When Hester suggests that Dimmesdale leave the Puritan community, she first expresses her wish to pass deep into the forest beyond even the "vestige of the white man's tread" and asks, "Is there not shade enough in all this boundless forest to hide thy heart from the gaze of Roger Chillingworth?"[128] Certainly this literal benefit of the forest breaks it out of a strictly allegorical form even if Hester seems to have forgotten that Chillingworth knows more about the forest than they do. For Chillingworth, the forest serves as the source of "medicinal herbs and roots" that he learns from "the savage people" who live there.[129] Puritans like Hester Prynne and Arthur Dimmesdale and even the cuckolded villain Roger Chillingworth find in nature a panacea of restorative power—whether through medical or spiritual or familial connections to the earth.

Through her recognition of nature and human society as complementary rather than opposing forces, Hester offers an affirmative model for humanity in the world of *The Scarlet Letter*. Her change from dualistic thinking to an understanding of nature and society as reciprocal and necessary parts of human life is typically demonstrated by her actions rather than reflected by her thought. As readers, we are given many of her confused thoughts at the beginning but fewer thoughts and more actions as time progresses. The only major exception at the end occurs as she thinks about the future and her role in it. In the woods with Dimmesdale, Hester mentions "yonder town, which only a little time ago was but a leaf-strewn desert, as lonely as this around us."[130] And she finds herself comfortable at the edge of society and in the woods. Although her return to Europe is a blank within the text, we are told the details of her reentry into Boston life when she returns to America again to take up her residence in the cottage on the seashore. Once again—and permanently this time—she establishes her home at the margin between the wilderness and the Puritan community and transforms it into a refuge for women alienated in various ways from the Puritan community.

Yet "Nature" remains a much contested term in *The Scarlet Letter*. Puritan suspicions of the natural world as the devil's territory are offset by the paradisiacal experiences of those who find the natural world restorative. Nature is neither fully transcendent nor merely immanent in Hawthorne's telling. Pastoral romance and Puritan allegory combine splashes of sunlight and water, the nature of sky and earth, the body and soul of humans to hypothesize an interconnectivity between humans and the natural world that remains open to the divine without imposing strict Puritan conceptions of God upon the reader.

The spectral and corporeal webs that connect the human, the natural, and the divine in *The Scarlet Letter* open the human subject to prospects both biological and spiritual. And while the Puritans are perhaps too quick to relegate the natural to the supernatural, most of them do not reduce Nature to a reality that is simply a reflection of human desires. The variant views of the natural world held by Hawthorne's characters demonstrate that religiously infused ways of thinking about the natural world do not always yield identical attitudes toward the natural world. It does become apparent, however, that one's sympathies with or antagonisms against the natural world influence one's capacity to read the world in good faith.

As other nineteenth-century American epics do, *The Scarlet Letter* challenges artificial divisions in our knowledge of the world while attempting to tell the story of what it means to be an American. In Hawthorne's study of human nature, the supposed division between *nature* and *culture* quickly breaks down. While this text raises more questions than it answers about the natural world and our relationship to it, some tentative conclusions are allowed to stand. First of all, human and nonhuman nature are not ultimately divided but come from the same source. Or, to use current terminology, the division between nature and culture is an artificial one since the humans creating culture are part of nature. Accordingly, some correspondences between human and nonhuman nature exist. Furthermore, some connections between spirit and nature exist but the complicated work of understanding that relationship is an ongoing project since all descriptions of the natural world are interpretations and representations rather than the thing itself. By drawing attention to the need for interpretation and refusing to give an authoritative interpretation for his readers, Hawthorne gives us an unreliable narrator who leaves us searching for the best way of approaching nature, reason, and the imagination in our thinking about the natural world in which we find themselves.

NOTES

1. Hawthorne, *Complete Works,* vol. 5, 188.
2. Cindy Weinstein, introduction to *The Scarlet Letter,* by Nathaniel Hawthorne, ed. Brian Harding (New York: Oxford University Press, 2007), ix.

3. Hawthorne, *Complete Works,* vol. 5, 189.

4. Hawthorne, *Complete Works,* vol. 5, 188.

5. Hawthorne, *Complete Works,* vol. 5, 188.

6. Stephen Matterson, *Melville: Fashioning in Modernity* (New York: Bloomsbury Publishing, 2014), 28. Matterson is one of many to allude to this common account of Hawthorne being consulted about this painting. Matterson also notes that this painting was on display at the National Academy of Design in 1860, which would have further increased its influence on Hawthorne's readers during the last half of the nineteenth century.

7. Hawthorne, *Complete Works,* vol. 5, 192.

8. Weinstein, introduction, xxix.

9. Hawthorne, *Complete Works,* vol. 5, 302.

10. Hawthorne, *Complete Works,* vol. 5, 302.

11. Hawthorne, *Complete Works,* vol. 5, 305.

12. Hawthorne, *Complete Works,* vol. 5, 192.

13. Hawthorne, *Complete Works,* vol. 5, 305.

14. Hawthorne, *Complete Works,* vol. 5, 305–6.

15. Hawthorne, *Complete Works,* vol. 5, 239.

16. Hawthorne, *Complete Works,* vol. 5, 188.

17. Poe particularly lambasts Hawthorne's use of allegory, a departure from his earlier praise of Hawthorne's originality, criticizing "the strain of allegory which completely overwhelms the greater number of his subjects, and which in some measure interferes with the direct conduct of absolutely all." See his Review of *Twice-Told Tales* and *Mosses from an Old Manse* (1847), in *Poe: Essays and Reviews,* ed. Gary Richard Thompson (New York: The Library of America, 1984), 582.

18. David Berkeley, "Allegory," in *A Dictionary of Biblical Tradition in English Literature,* ed. David L. Jeffrey (Grand Rapids: William B. Eerdman's Publishing, 1992), 29–31.

19. Hawthorne, *Complete Works,* vol. 5, 68.

20. Samuel Danforth, "A Brief Recognition of New-England's Errand into the Wilderness: An Online Electronic Text Edition," 1670, ed. Paul Royster (Digital Commons, University of Nebraska-Lincoln, UNL Libraries, 2006), 11.

21. John Winthrop, "A Modell of Christian Charity," in *Collections of the Massachusetts Historical Society,* vol. 7 (Boston: Little and Brown, 1838), 44.

22. Hawthorne, *Complete Works,* vol. 5, 67.

23. See also Charles Ryskamp, "The New England Sources of *The Scarlet Letter,*" *American Literature* 31, no. 3 (1959): 257–58. Ryskamp notes that Hawthorne used Snow's *History* "for authentication of the setting of *The Scarlet Letter.*"

24. Caleb Hopkins Snow, *A History of Boston, the Metropolis of Massachusetts, from Its Origin to the Present, with Some Account of the Environs* (Boston: A. Bowen, 1825), 104.

25. Hawthorne, *Complete Works,* vol. 5, 118–19.

26. Danforth, "A Brief Recognition," 10.

27. Danforth, "A Brief Recognition," 10–11.

28. See Marion Louise Kesselring, *Hawthorne's Reading, 1828-1850: A Transcription and Identification of Titles Recorded in the Charge-books of the Salem*

Athenaeum (New York: Haskell House, 1975), 50, 60–61. Hawthorne checked out Boston Lecture sermons, Fast sermons, Funeral sermons, occasional sermons, and other sermons between the years of 1828 and 1830. He checked out Felt's *Annals* repeatedly, in 1833, 1834, and again in 1849 just prior to writing *The Scarlet Letter*.

29. Joseph Barlow Felt, *The Annals of Salem: From Its First Settlement* (Salem, MA: Ives, 1827), 46.

30. John Winthrop, *The Journal of John Winthrop, 1630–1649*, ed. Richard S. Dunn, James Savage, and Laetitia Yeandle (Cambridge: Harvard University Press, 1996), 416.

31. Sacvan Bercovitch, *The American Jeremiad* (Madison: University of Wisconsin Press, 1978), 24.

32. Kristin Boudreau, *Sympathy in American Literature: American Sentiments from Jefferson to the Jameses* (Gainesville: University Press of Florida, 2002), 69–71.

33. Hawthorne, *Complete Works,* vol. 5, 295.

34. Cotton Mather, *The Christian Philosopher*, ed. Winton U. Solberg (Urbana: University of Illinois Press, 1994), 17–18.

35. Anne Bradstreet, "Contemplations," in *The Works of Anne Bradstreet in Prose and Verse,* ed. John Harvard Ellis (Charlestown: Cutter, 1867), 377.

36. Baym, *The Scarlet Letter: A Reading,* 44.

37. R.W.B. Lewis, *The American Adam: Innocence, Tragedy and Tradition in the Nineteenth Century* (Chicago: University of Chicago Press, 1971), 113–14.

38. Michael Davitt Bell, *Hawthorne and the Historical Romance of New England* (Princeton: Princeton University Press, 1971), 166.

39. Bell, *Hawthorne and the Historical Romance,* 94.

40. Bell, *Hawthorne and the Historical Romance,* 184.

41. Hawthorne, *Complete Works,* vol. 5, 295.

42. Hawthorne, *Complete Works,* vol. 5, 104.

43. Hawthorne, *Complete Works,* vol. 5, 244–45.

44. Hawthorne, *Complete Works,* vol. 5, 245.

45. Hawthorne, *Complete Works,* vol. 5, 119.

46. Hawthorne, *Complete Works,* vol. 5, 276–77.

47. Hawthorne, *Complete Works,* vol. 5, 222.

48. Hawthorne, *Complete Works,* vol. 5, 222.

49. Hawthorne, *Complete Works,* vol. 5, 291.

50. Hawthorne, *Complete Works,* vol. 5, 277.

51. The elder Nathaniel Hathorne, a sea captain who traveled to far-off ports including Calcutta and the South Atlantic island of St. Helena, died of yellow fever in Suriname when Hawthorne was four years old. Captain Hathorne's logbooks, which track his sea voyages, are housed in the Phillips Library in Salem, Massachusetts. My thanks to the librarians there who facilitated my visit in 2011.

52. Hawthorne, *Complete Works,* vol. 5, 221.

53. Hawthorne, *Complete Works,* vol. 5, 248.

54. Hawthorne, *Complete Works,* vol. 5, 100.

55. Hawthorne, *Complete Works,* vol. 5, 181, 184.

56. Hawthorne, *Complete Works,* vol. 2, 106.

57. Hawthorne, *Complete Works,* vol. 5, 287.

58. Hawthorne, *Complete Works,* vol. 5, 287.
59. Hawthorne, *Complete Works,* vol. 5, 265.
60. Hawthorne, *Complete Works,* vol. 5, 88.
61. Hawthorne, *The Complete Works of Nathaniel Hawthorne,* vol. 4, *A Wonder-Book, Tanglewood Tales, and Grandfather's Chair,* with Introductory Notes by George Parsons Lathrop. Riverside Edition (Boston: Houghton Mifflin, 1883), 468–69.
62. Hawthorne, *Complete Works,* vol. 5, 266–67.
63. Hawthorne, *Complete Works,* vol. 5, 220.
64. Hawthorne, *Complete Works,* vol. 5, 225.
65. Hawthorne, *Complete Works,* vol. 5, 239–40.
66. Renée L. Bergland, *Maria Mitchell and the Sexing of Science: An Astronomer among the American Romantics* (Boston: Beacon Press, 2008), 53–58.
67. Hawthorne, *Complete Works,* vol. 5, 311.
68. In Richard Kopley, *The Threads of The Scarlet Letter: A Study of Hawthorne's Transformative Art* (Newark: University of Delaware Press, 2003), 98.
69. Kopley, *The Threads of the Scarlet Letter,* 98.
70. Hiroko Washizu, "Celestial Hieroglyphics," *Hawthorne in Salem,* Web. 31 July 2011.
71. Kopley, *Threads of the Scarlet Letter,* 97.
72. Kopley, *Threads of the Scarlet Letter,* 101–3.
73. Hawthorne, *Complete Works,* vol. 5, 243.
74. Hawthorne, *Complete Works,* vol. 5, 243.
75. Hawthorne, *Complete Works,* vol. 5, 243.
76. Hawthorne, *Complete Works,* vol. 5, 305–6.
77. Hawthorne, *Complete Works,* vol. 5, 257.
78. Hawthorne, *Complete Works,* vol. 5, 270.
79. Hawthorne, *Complete Works,* vol. 5, 43.
80. Hawthorne, *Complete Works,* vol. 5, 54.
81. Hawthorne, *Complete Works,* vol. 5, 114.
82. Hawthorne, *Complete Works,* vol. 5, 114.
83. Hawthorne, *Complete Works,* vol. 5, 234.
84. Hawthorne, *Complete Works,* vol. 5, 114–15.
85. Hawthorne, *Complete Works,* vol. 5, 140–41.
86. Hawthorne, *Complete Works,* vol. 5, 127.
87. Hawthorne, *Complete Works,* vol. 5, 128.
88. Hawthorne, *Complete Works,* vol. 5, 139.
89. Hawthorne, *Complete Works,* vol. 5, 214.
90. Hawthorne, *Complete Works,* vol. 5, 239.
91. Robert Mudie, *Popular Guide to the Observation of Nature, Or, Hints of Inducement to the Study of Natural Productions and Appearances, in Their Connexions and Relations* (New York: Harper, 1833), 34, *Google Books.*
92. Mudie, *Popular Guide to the Observation of Nature,* 34.
93. Mudie, *Popular Guide to the Observation of Nature,* 54.
94. Abel, *The Moral Picturesque: Studies in Hawthorne's Fiction,* 190, 193.

95. Hawthorne, *Complete Works,* vol. 5, 138.
96. Hawthorne, *Complete Works,* vol. 5, 215.
97. Hawthorne, *Complete Works,* vol. 5, 114.
98. Hawthorne, *Complete Works,* vol. 5, 89–90.
99. Hawthorne, *Complete Works,* vol. 5, 121.
100. Hawthorne, *Complete Works,* vol. 5, 119.
101. Hawthorne, *Complete Works,* vol. 5, 200.
102. Ron Amundson, *The Changing Role of the Embryo in Evolutionary Thought* (New York: Cambridge University Press, 2005), 35.
103. Thomas Pennant, *British Zoology 1* (Warrington: Benjamin White, 1776), iv, *Google Books.*
104. See the chapter 4 section of "Literature Related to Native Americans and the Scarlet Letter," http://www.hawthorneinsalem.org/page/11445/.
105. Dugald Stewart, *Philosophical Essays,* 2nd edn (Edinburgh: George Ramsay and Company, 1816), 195, *Google Books.*
106. Hawthorne, *Complete Works,* vol. 5, 143.
107. Hawthorne, *Complete Works,* vol. 5, 143.
108. Hawthorne, *Complete Works,* vol. 5, 308.
109. Hawthorne, *Complete Works,* vol. 5, 243.
110. Hawthorne, *Complete Works,* vol. 5, 104.
111. Hawthorne, *Complete Works,* vol. 5, 162.
112. Hawthorne, *Complete Works,* vol. 5, 176.
113. Hawthorne, *Complete Works,* vol. 5, 311.
114. Hawthorne, *Complete Works,* vol. 5, 200.
115. Hawthorne, *Complete Works,* vol. 5, 73.
116. Hawthorne, *Complete Works,* vol. 5, 78.
117. Hawthorne, *Complete Works,* vol. 5, 87.
118. Hawthorne, *Complete Works,* vol. 5, 91.
119. Hawthorne, *Complete Works,* vol. 5, 102.
120. Hawthorne, *Complete Works,* vol. 5, 243.
121. Hawthorne, *Complete Works*, vol. 5, 97.
122. Hawthorne, *Complete Works,* vol. 5, 107.
123. Hawthorne, *Complete Works,* vol. 5, 209.
124. Hawthorne, *Complete Works,* vol. 5, 195–96.
125. Hawthorne, *Complete Works,* vol. 5, 196.
126. Hyatt Howe Waggoner, *Hawthorne: A Critical Study* (Cambridge: Harvard University Press, 1963), 141.
127. Janice B. Daniel, "'Apples of the Thoughts and Fancies': Nature as Narrator in *The Scarlet Letter,*" *American Transcendental Quarterly* 7, no. 4 (1993): 307.
128. Hawthorne, *Complete Works,* vol. 5, 236.
129. Hawthorne, *Complete Works,* vol. 5, 92.
130. Hawthorne, *Complete Works,* vol. 5, 236.

Chapter 4

Mapping Blood and Biology in *The House of the Seven Gables*

> The Author . . . would feel it a singular gratification, if this romance might effectually convince mankind—or, indeed, any one man—of the folly of tumbling down an avalanche of ill-gotten gold, or real estate, on the heads of an unfortunate posterity, thereby to maim and crush them until the accumulated mass shall be scattered abroad in its original atoms.
>
> —Hawthorne, Preface of *The House of the Seven Gables*[1]

Nathaniel Hawthorne's second major romance strongly suggests his rising skepticism of nineteenth-century rhetorics of race and legal rights of ownership even while continuing the focus on nature of his earlier work. Like many other American publications in the early 1850s—most notably Harriet Beecher Stowe's *Uncle Tom's Cabin*—Hawthorne's *House of the Seven Gables* represents a response to the Fugitive Slave Law that was included in the Compromise of 1850. Requiring Northerners to cooperate with Southern slaveholders retrieving their "property" of runaway slaves, this bill was highly controversial as soon as it was signed into law. Hawthorne found it easier, or maybe safer, given the political climate, to address a corollary of slavery rather than directly taking on the issue of slavery itself. While this evasion is disappointing, Hawthorne's *House* nonetheless registers a political critique of national policies by engaging national property disputes that focus on competing claims of land ownership during the Puritans' colonization of seventeenth-century America. This choice of historical matter also allows Hawthorne to wrestle with his own personal Puritan ancestry and the wrongdoing that extended even further back in the nation's history as national borders and Native Americans have continually been pushed westward.

Some readers have considered *Seven Gables* an affirmation of the superiority of the Anglo-Saxon race and middle-class values. Shawn Michelle Smith, for example, draws attention to Hawthorne's use of terminology that would be used later in the nineteenth century to argue for white supremacy. Hawthorne's text, according to Smith, "prefigures" biological racism and "the eugenicist conceits that were to dominate the middle-class discourses of identity and cultural privilege in the late nineteenth century."[2] While it is clear that Hawthorne focuses on the situations of white Americans of European descent, *Seven Gables* repeatedly refers to the "blood" of different "races" and "breeds." And the voices in this text are all too explicitly prescribed by their limited experiences to be considered authoritative. Hepzibah and Clifford have been removed from human interaction for so long that they have a hard time translating their thoughts into words. Holgrave changes radically during the course of the text, but we are given little information about why he changes or which of his understandings of the world is more trustworthy. Judge Pyncheon is a clearly devious villain not to be trusted, and Phoebe—angelic though she may be—has no great depth of understanding about the undercurrents of what is happening around her.

As in Hawthorne's other romances, the narrator of *Seven Gables* has limited information and a limited perspective that makes him somewhat unreliable. For instance, he reports various sources throughout the course of his narrative but declines to verify or deny the accuracy of these sources. In the space of two paragraphs near the end, for example, he keeps hemming and hawing about the veracity of his story until we have little idea which version of events to consider most likely: "Whencesoever originating, there now rose a theory. . . . Many persons affirmed. . . . According to this version of the story . . . Now it is averred,—but whether on authority available in a court of justice, we do not pretend to have investigated."[3] And yet his famous mockery of the dead judge makes him less than a disinterested outsider telling a tale about this place, even raising the possibility that he is a hidden character whose identity remains unrevealed in the story. The narrator has secrets to hide as well as secrets to uncover; thus, we cannot be sure that his voice is more trustworthy than that of another character in *Seven Gables*.

Like Robert Levine, I remain unconvinced that *Seven Gables* serves as an "upbeat celebration of the nation's middle-class values."[4] I find much more persuasive Levine's argument that the text suggests deep misgivings about "blood-based Anglo-Saxonist nationalism and expansionism," that it ultimately "challenges belief in the superiority of Anglo-Saxon 'blood' and remains highly unclear, even suspicious, about whether race even exists as a workable category of human identity and difference."[5] Certainly in *Seven Gables*, Hawthorne uses the term "race" in various ways and with various emphases, fraught with scientific and sociopolitical implications for the nation and typically weighted with Hawthorne's signature ambiguity. In the preface, we are told that the author "would feel it a singular gratification if this romance might effectually convince mankind—or, indeed, any one man—of the folly of tumbling down an avalanche of ill-gotten gold, or real estate, on the heads of an unfortunate posterity, thereby to maim and crush them, until the accumulated mass shall be scattered abroad in its original atoms."[6] Grasping for real estate, like grasping for gold, creates illegitimate wealth and establishes an atomistic prototype of wrongdoing as one generation inherits the property that is "tumbled down" upon them by their predecessors. Thus, the sins of the fathers visit the children in the form of disputable property claims. More than a decade before writing his major romances, Hawthorne jotted down a story idea about human nature that informs *The House of the Seven Gables* as well as many of his other stories: "A story to show how we are all wronged and wrongers, and avenge one another."[7] It is about wrongs committed within the fabric of American nationhood rather than about the celebration of unabashed American nationalism.

To investigate the environmental implications of *The House of Seven Gables*, it is essential to recognize the regional as well as the national anxieties embedded in this text and to account for the way race works as a scientific designation in Hawthorne's nineteenth-century world. Both of these considerations feed into issues that have surrounded American land claims since before the founding of the United States. What becomes clear after this analysis of Hawthorne's romance is that the sunny resolution prognosticated at the end of *Seven Gables* is fragile—nearly as fragile as the sense of uneasiness created by the narrator's uncanny exposition in the first chapter. For under the conventional closure of a comedy ending with a marriage between warring families of New England's founders, many readers sense a dissatisfaction with the ending. Notions of landownership in America have been proven faulty despite what may have been settled in a court of American law. The narrator leaves us with many unanswered questions about the future of the nation, of the region, and of the races and families whose histories are being traced in Hawthorne's narrative.

Embedded in the second paragraph of Hawthorne's romance, we find what the narrator calls "the little-regarded truth, that the act of the passing generation is the germ which may and must produce good or evil fruit in a far-distant time; that, together with the seed of the merely temporary crop, which mortals term expediency, they inevitably sow the acorns of a more enduring growth, which may darkly overshadow their posterity."[8] What kind of offspring, or "fruit" is produced by this germ, which is more than the immediate seed? The emphasis in *House* is that "more enduring growth" will eventually eclipse "the merely temporary crop" planted by American forebears. The organic emphasis of this text, though "little-regarded" by scholars since Hawthorne's publication, suggests that Hawthorne's second major romance comprises a more naturalist narrative than is often recognized.

Hawthorne's use of organic language here is no accident. Humans can take the patterns of the botanical world as patterns for their own regeneration. Each biological generation activates "the germ," drops "the seed," and plants "the acorns" that come to life in subsequent generations. Such implantation is not only metaphoric but is also what we do with the land and with our bodies. The breeds of plants, the breeds of animals, and the breeds of people are continuously engaged in the work of generation, degeneration, and regeneration. If reproduction is to be more than cyclical degeneration that stultifies the life it creates, if a "House" is to thrive in America, it must generate new blood. Otherwise, what follows will indeed overshadow subsequent generations. Blood and biology are more important to the establishment and maintenance of a "house" than the American Dream suggests, and the undercurrent of violence that accompanies this dream haunts this most Gothic of Hawthorne's romances.

GENERATING RACE IN HAWTHORNE'S *HOUSE*

Published exactly a year before *Uncle Tom's Cabin*, Hawthorne's *House of the Seven Gables* was published during an outpouring of antislavery literature sparked by the Fugitive Slave Law of 1850. Readers of Hawthorne have not generally connected his book to this deluge of antislavery literature. We need to reassess, however, the assumption that Hawthorne was removed from the problems of race embedded within American history since before the founding of the United States and increasingly dominating national conversations. In *House*, Hawthorne does address issues of race—albeit much less directly than abolitionist writers like Harriet Beecher Stowe. The word "race" appears two dozen times in *The House of the Seven Gables*, sometimes in reference to the main human or animal families in the text, sometimes referring to ethnicities, and sometimes referring to "the human race." For in the years prior to the mid-nineteenth century, race was not treated as a fixed category and did not always have to do with skin color. The *Oxford English Dictionary* identifies one of the earliest usages of the term race as designating "a group of people belonging to the same family and descended from a common ancestor; a house, family, kindred."[9] This is the usage we see in the opening chapter as the lines are drawn between the aristocratic Pyncheons and the plebian Maules—two "houses" separated by religious belief, social class, and political standing.

The actual reason for the competing claims of Matthew Maule and Colonel Pyncheon is made obvious in the narrator's observation that "after some thirty or forty years, the site covered by this rude hovel had become exceedingly desirable in the eyes of a prominent and powerful personage, who asserted plausible claims to the proprietorship of this, and a large adjacent tract of land, on the strength of a grant from the legislature."[10] But the narrator intimates that these "plausible claims" are not wholly convincing after a distance of two centuries, especially given the dubious manner of Maule's death:

> [I]t appears to have been at least a matter of doubt, whether Colonel Pyncheon's claim were not unduly stretched, in order to make it cover the small metes and bounds of Matthew Maule. What greatly strengthens such a suspicion is the fact, that this controversy between two ill-matched antagonists—at a period, moreover, laud it as we may, when personal influence had far more weight than now—remained for years undecided, and came to a close only with the death of the party occupying the disputed soil. The mode of his death, too, affects the mind differently, in our day, from what it did a century and a half ago. It was a death that blasted with strange horror the humble name of the dweller in the cottage, and made it seem almost a religious act to drive the plough over the little area of his habitation, and obliterate his place and memory form among men. Old Matthew Maule, in a word, was executed for the crime of witchcraft.[11]

Colonel Pyncheon's personal animosity in Matthew Maule's case was noted by observers even during "the frenzy of that hideous epoch," and they afterward also "remembered how loudly Colonel Pyncheon had joined in the general cry, to purge the land from witchcraft."[12] When Maule was executed, "his humble homestead had fallen an easy spoil into Colonel Pyncheon's grasp."[13] Thus, the Maules were wronged by the Pyncheons, and the place of a "humble homestead" began being treated as a possession or battle trophy to be used and abused at will. The difference between land as homestead and land as possession indicate radically different conceptions of the land and humans' place on it. While the Colonel considers the land as a commodity to add to his wealth, Matthew Maule considers it his home.

As in many Gothic works, ancestral houses and landownership and violent crimes create issues for the characters. Jack G. Voller aptly characterizes Hawthorne's American Gothic as less eerily supernatural than its British predecessors but more heavily steeped in disturbing topography.[14] Vermin inhabit the dark shadows of the House, the well dries up, the chickens refuse to lay many eggs, and the earth grudgingly produces fruit and flowers. The land itself seems to reject the wrongs being done there. Even the aggressive Pyncheons' inherited cause of death seems both natural (the result of apoplexy) and supernatural (caused by a gurgling of "miraculous blood" in their throats). The squatting rights of the Maules are unjustly overturned by the legal rights (or manipulations) of the Pyncheons. But the old Indian deed that

Judge Pyncheon is seeking also reminds readers that the land was first taken from the Native Americans. The idea that human relations to the land can lead to injustice not only to other people but also to the land provides Hawthorne with the material of a Gothic romance that highlights the workings of nature as well as supernatural and human contrivances.

In the Pyncheon family, there is a "hereditary liability" to the medical disorder of apoplexy.[15] Hawthorne's reading of *Medical Jurisprudence* would have acquainted him with accounts of apoplexy present in the seventeenth-century world of his text. In the case of the death of Joseph Lane, a British man whose suspicious death was investigated to determine whether he died of poisoning or apoplexy, the court decided he was poisoned but the case is built on circumstantial evidence. During the questioning, Mr. John Hunter, an anatomist who dissects bodies, is asked for his opinion, and he allows that poison and apoplexy can produce the same symptoms within a body that seemed in sound health only a moment earlier.[16] When asked if apoplexy is constitutional, Hunter replies that some people have "a hereditary disposition" for apoplexy, but that "most diseases are constitutional" and apoplexy appears to be "as much constitutional as any disease whatever." The transcript of the case ends with Hunter's words, "I can give nothing decisive."[17] Earlier in his testimony, he mentions that animals have been killed by alcohol that gets into the lungs while they are working their throats to reject it, then states, "I wish, in this case, the head had been opened to remove all dates," explaining that "an apoplexy arises from an extravasation in the brain."[18] Earlier in the case, it was established that there were almost two pints of "extravasated blood in the thorax" and that cats who are forced to take some brandy can die of alcohol poisoning if they "get some of the liquor in their lungs."[19] On the fateful day when the judge visits the House of the Seven Gables for the last time, he has many activities on his schedule, including a doctor's visit to check out some symptoms: "dimness of sight and dizziness of brain . . . a disagreeable choking, or stifling, or gurgling, or bubbling, in the region of the thorax, as the anatomists say."[20] Certainly, all the conditions for an attack of apoplexy are present when the judge meets his death.

Holgrave, the secret descendant of the Maules, tells Phoebe a story that shows he knows the hereditary disposition toward apoplexy that runs in the Pyncheon family. His story also reveals that Holgrave knows more about the antagonism between the Maules and the Pyncheons than he has revealed. The Colonel's grandson Gervayse Pyncheon, the father of the beautiful Alice Pyncheon, had exhibited the symptoms of apoplexy during an outburst of rage at the grandson of Matthew Maule, who has placed his daughter into a hypnotic trance. The symptoms had followed soon after the younger Maule urged him to drink some sherry, which Alice's father found "too potent a wine for me; it has affected my brain already."[21] And when Alice's now-anxious and angry father cannot break her from her trance, the younger Maule refuses to reveal the secret Alice's father has wanted. The result is that Mr. Pyncheon "with fear and passion—could make only a gurgling murmur in his throat," leading to the younger Maule's taunt: "So, you have old Maule's blood to drink!"[22] Gervayse Pyncheon does not die at that moment, however, and "when his choked utterance could make way," he calls Maule a devil and Maule releases Alice from her trance.[23] The Pyncheons do not get what they want—the lost deed to Pyncheon land claims. But it seems from Holgrave's story that the Maules have some awareness of how to trigger an apoplectic attack in the "race" of their enemies.

The Maules' secretive descendant Holgrave, who relates the story to Phoebe, explicitly suggests that his wrongfully executed ancestor may have known of "this physical predisposition in the Pyncheon race."[24] Whether he or the narrator who taunts the dead judge somehow vexed the judge into a tantrum that brought on the apoplexy as he sat waiting for Hepzibah to bring Clifford back is anyone's guess. Certainly, Holgrave has demonstrated his abilities in the nineteenth-century trance-setting "science" of Mesmerism by putting a rooster to sleep and by seemingly casting a spell on Phoebe while he tells the story of Alice.[25] But he does not take advantage of her, as Alice's antagonist had done earlier, exhibiting instead "the rare and high quality of reverence for another's individuality" that differentiates him from his more vengeful ancestor.[26]

Colonel Pyncheon promoted the view of his family as a special race, considering "the race of his fallen antagonist" Matthew Maule distinct from his own.[27] Even though the Maule descendants are not accused of witchcraft, as Matthew Maule had been, they have been thought to have magical powers, at least "[s]o long as any of the race were to be found."[28] Before revealing that Holgrave is descended from the Maules, the narrator pretends they have disappeared: "At last, after creeping, as it were, for such a length of time, along the utmost verge of the opaque puddle of obscurity, they had taken that downright plunge, which, sooner or later, is the destiny of all families, whether princely or plebeian."[29] The narrator's remark that all families, regardless of class, regardless of race, are destined for extinction serves as a reminder of our common humanity and our common limits—a reminder that is further illustrated by Clifford Pyncheon later in the text.

The Puritan clergyman who gives the sermon at Colonel Pyncheon's funeral says that the Colonel's "race and future generations" are well provisioned, and the narrator adds that even "the poorest member of the race" of Pyncheons felt himself superior, supposing that he "might yet come into the possession of princely wealth."[30] But here the narrator steps in to say that "the better specimens of the breed" were characterized by "an ideal grace over the hard material of human life."[31] Phoebe, one those "better specimens," cannot help but shudder when she reflects on "the progenitor of the whole race of New England Pyncheons, the founder of the House of the Seven Gables."[32] The Pyncheon family are a breed, a race. And they are haunted by the Matthew Maule's curse that God will give him (and his race after him) "blood to drink!"[33]

Like the Pyncheons, the Maules are represented as a race, albeit a typically "quiet, honest, well-meaning race of people, cherishing no malice against individuals or the public, for the wrong which had been done them."[34] By presenting two European families as separate races, Hawthorne appears initially to be suggesting that white European races need to interbreed—that the best intermixture might in fact bring about the best white race. Indeed, Shawn Michelle Smith assumes this to be the case when she notes that despite the "striking" appearance of "Holgrave's celebration of blood mixing," this celebration is strictly limited to "mixing across class lines" and "is literally supported by white supremacist alliances."[35] Smith emphasizes the "segregation" of blacks in Hawthorne's text by delineating a "cameo role" for Scipio, the African American servant of the Pyncheons, and describing little Ned's gobbling of the Jim Crow gingerbread cookies in Hepzibah's shop.[36] As she points out, the use of such racial categories is soon to invigorate the eugenics movement of the later nineteenth and early twentieth centuries.[37] Hawthorne's handling of racial issues is not quite this simplistic, however. Scipio considers himself enough on the level of the Maules, for example, to chastise one of them for presuming to think he can openly admire Alice's beauty.

But it is even more significant that Hawthorne encodes black and Native American racial categories into a text that is—as Smith indicates—at least ostensibly focused on the situation of white races. Levine also discusses the black racial terms that are used in descriptors associated with and against the judge and other characters. Levine aptly notes, for example, that Matthew Maule is described in terminology often reserved for black people while Scipio is associated (even by his name) with black minstrelsy and *performs* race rather than claiming it as a natural trait.[38]

The Maule race is associated not only with African Americans but also with Native Americans. The Maules occupy a position that parallels Native American tribes which have increasingly been pushed out of New England by the forced removals of the nineteenth century. The narrator's language about the Maules encodes racial terminology often used to describe the "vanishing Indian":

> As for Matthew Maule's posterity, it was supposed now to be extinct. For a very long period after the witchcraft delusion, however, the Maules had continued to inhabit the town, where their progenitor had suffered so unjust a death. . . .

> For thirty years past, neither town-record, nor gravestone, nor the directory, nor the knowledge or memory of man, bore any trace of Matthew Maule's descendants.[39]

This description of the Maule race employs nineteenth-century rhetoric about the Native American tribes of New England.[40] Like the "vanishing Indian," the Maules are said to vanish or at least they are "supposed now to be extinct," although the narrator also supposes that their "blood might possibly exist elsewhere; here, where its lowly current could be traced so far back, it had ceased to keep an onward course."[41] The same could be said for many of the tribes that had once populated the Salem area—most nearby surviving Native Americans who hadn't moved west had moved to southern Massachusetts to the reservations in and around Martha's Vineyard or had mixed into the white population.[42] So even though they were said to be extinct, a number of their offspring did actually exist. The falsity of the myth of American Indian extinction is more evident today than in Hawthorne's time, now that some tribal rights have again been recognized at least in some areas by the US government.

Racial terminology also raises the specter of scientific differentiation in *Seven Gables*. At a time when species of animals were also sometimes called races, the fowl of the Pyncheon place are rumored to be "pure specimens of a breed" once superior in size and taste, but by the time we are introduced to them, the narrator tells us, "It was evident that the race had degenerated, like many a noble race besides, in consequence of too strict a watchfulness to keep it pure."[43] Maintaining pure bloodlines has been the cause of disease and devastation rather than preservation. Hawthorne's views have likely been influenced by his reading of George Combe's *The Constitution of Man Considered in Relation to External Objects*. This book engaged the public in scientific controversy even before Darwin's *Origin of Species*, effectively laying the groundwork for the changed way of thinking required to accept Darwin's conclusions. In 1858, the *Illustrated London News* would claim, "No book published within the memory of man, in the English or any other language, has effected so great a revolution in the previously received opinions of society. . . . The influence of that unpretending treatise has extended to hundreds of thousands of minds which know not whence they derived the new light that has broken in upon them, and percolated into thousands of circles that are scarcely conscious of knowing more about Mr. Combe than his name, and the fact that he was a phrenologist."[44] Combe posits an "organic law of the animal kingdom [that] deserves attention; viz, that by which marriages betwixt blood relations tend decidedly to the deterioration of the physical and mental qualities of the offspring."[45] Disregarding Combe's advice that people of high standing should be "united with strangers in blood of *equal vigor and cerebral development*," however, Hawthorne allows Phoebe and Holgrave—characters of differing mental capacities—to get married.[46] Combe's words provide a clear example of racially coded language, given nineteenth-century assumptions of inferior brains in black people, but Hawthorne clearly does not follow Combe's advice, suggesting that he is at least less committed to racial purity than Combe was.

The Pyncheon chickens are also a race: designated first as an "antiquated race," the Pyncheon chickens are also called an "illustrious race," and an "ancient feathered race."[47] Hawthorne does not regard their antiquity as guarantee of their continued existence: "These feathered people had too long existed in their distinct variety."[48] The narrator pauses at the sight of the idea that these chickens apparently "communicating their sage opinions" to each other, suspecting that they are "not merely . . . the descendants of a time-honored race, but that they had existed, in their individual capacity, ever since the House of the Seven Gables was founded, and were somehow mixed up with its destiny. They were a species of tutelary sprite, or Banshee; although winged and feathered differently from most other guardian angels."[49] That the Pyncheons would have their own Banshee suggests—in the words of Sir Walter Scott—that they are descended of an old "original" family, "an undisturbed and native race," one of a number of "certain families of ancient descent and distinguished rank."[50] The Banshee was a spirit of the land and the water, a spirit that gave warning of the impending death of a family member. After we see and hear the voices of the banshee chickens, Judge Pyncheon accordingly dies in the parlor of the House of the Seven Gables.

But the spirits of the land seem to be awakened in another more literal way. The term "feathered people" was more typically associated with the Native American tribes than with chickens. And certainly Native Americans are constantly hovering in the background of Hawthorne's text. Although no living Native Americans actually appear in this text, their very absence is made glaringly apparent by repeated references to the elusive Indian deed being sought by the Pyncheons. The memory of Native Americans is also preserved in the illustrations of Native Americans on the map of the supposed Pyncheon "Eastern Lands" hanging alongside the portrait of Colonel Pyncheon:

> One was a map of the Pyncheon territory at the eastward, not engraved, but the handiwork of some skilful old draughtsman, and grotesquely illuminated with pictures of Indians and wild beasts, among which was seen a lion; the natural history of the region being as little known as its geography, which was put down most fantastically awry. The other adornment was the portrait of old Colonel Pyncheon, at two thirds length, representing the stern features of a Puritanic-looking personage, in a skull-cap, with a laced band and a grizzly beard; holding a Bible with one hand, and in the other uplifting an iron sword-hilt.[51]

"Indians and wild beasts" are mentioned in one breath as are "a Bible" and "an iron sword-hilt" in another. To Colonel Pyncheon, Native Americans seem little more than wild animals—barely human inhabitants. A figure of religious intolerance, the Puritan Colonel's warlike attitude toward those who opposed his ownership of the land is symbolically rendered by the pairing of this picture with the etchings on the map next to it. The narrator's disapproving tone reflects Hawthorne's own earlier castigation of the famous Puritan divine Cotton Mather in his 1836 retelling of Hannah Duston's massacre of her Indian captors and their children. While Mather justifies Hannah, a white captive, Hawthorne finds Mather's justification the result of bigotry rather than respect: "Mather, like an old hard-hearted, pedantic bigot, as he was, seems trebly to exult in the destruction of these poor wretches, on account of their Popish superstitions."[52] Hawthorne's political aversion to violence of any kind, on the other hand, no doubt contributes to his conviction of national guilt for the wrongs committed against the Native Americans. In *Devils and Rebels: The Making of Hawthorne's Damned Politics* (2008), Larry Reynolds offers a probing and persuasive reassessment of Hawthorne's political positions, situating Hawthorne as a man whose political persuasions made him deeply uneasy about nationalist rhetoric. Reynolds outlines Hawthorne's version of Christian pacifism, which he characterizes as a profound suspicion of "the notion of righteous violence." This, as Reynolds notes, put Hawthorne vastly at odds with nationalist rhetoric of a nation headed toward civil war.[53]

One important source that links the Maules and the Native Americans is the historical Thomas Maule, a Quaker accused of witchcraft who successfully defended himself against the Salem witch judges even while condemning them.[54] In two pamphlets—*Truth Held Forth and Maintained* (1695), followed by *New-England Pesecutors [sic] Mauled with Their Own Weapons* (1697)—Thomas Maule takes the Puritans to task for their dealings with others. Maule especially castigates them for "how they have turned the Native Indians . . . in to the Grave, where there is no Repentance" and adds that such actions by the Puritans, "a People that pretended so much to Gods Truth" against "the poor Natives" is both hypocritical and inexcusable. And he goes further, suggesting that the Native Americans' attacks on Puritan settlements are God's judgment against the Puritans for "their unrighteous dealings towards the Native Indians, whom now the Lord hath suffered to reward the Inhabitants with a double measure of Blood, by Fire and Sword."[55] Hawthorne likely encountered the historical Thomas Maule in Cotton Mather's *Magnalia Christi Americana*, where Mather discusses Maule as the writer of "a volume of *nonsensical* blasphemies and heresies, wherein he sets himself to defend the Indians in their bloody villanies, and revile the country for defending itself against them." Mather warns them not to "own this *bloody stuff*," and suggests making as a proverb to scorn Maule, the saying "He is as verily a liar as Tom Maule."[56] Hawthorne registers his criticism of Mather by adopting the Maule name for the man being wronged by the worst Puritan in *The House of the Seven Gables*.

As in the Hannah Duston story related earlier, Hawthorne's disagreements with Mather likely stem at least in part from his pacifist leanings. Certainly, if he read Thomas Maule's original pamphlet, he would have realized that the Quaker Maule's castigation of the Puritan's treatment of Native Americans is part of a broader polemic against war itself. And even if he hadn't read it, the pacifism of Quakers was no secret. Hawthorne makes the same connections as Maule (against Mather) in *The Scarlet Letter* when the narrator remarks that in the very earliest days of the Puritan colony, the crowd gathered in front of the prison door might have assembled to witness "an Antinomian, a Quaker, or other heterodox religionist, was to be scourged out of the town, or an idle and vagrant Indian, whom the white man's fire-water had made riotous about the streets, was to be driven with stripes into the shadow of the forest."[57] Like Thomas Maule, Hawthorne closely associates those peoples whom the Puritans have wronged through their harsh judgments and violent actions.

Thomas Maule was one of the few—perhaps the only, and certainly the most well-known and published—to criticize the Salem judges for their handling of the witchcraft trials while the trials were happening and live to tell about it. That he would come back to haunt New England through Hawthorne's story is a stroke of literary genius that calls into question the integrity of the founders of New England rather than supporting their dynasty through pernicious doctrines like manifest destiny. Hawthorne uses the name Maule for the condemned and executed Maule from whom Colonel Pyncheon filches the land at the beginning, but Matthew's son Thomas is the carpenter employed to build the house of the seven gables. And it is Thomas who outwits the stern Puritan Colonel by hiding the Indian deed in the house he is building. As Holgrave reveals at the end: "The son of the executed Matthew Maule, while building this house, took the opportunity to . . . hide away the Indian deed, on which depended the immense land-claim of the Pyncheons. Thus, they bartered their eastern-territory for Maule's garden-ground."[58]

Despite recent reconsiderations of Hawthorne's treatment of Native Americans, their importance in Hawthorne's *Seven Gables* has gone largely unnoticed. Anna Brickhouse rightly detects a prominent note of regret in Hawthorne's facetious statement, "I do abhor an Indian story," but she only mentions *Seven Gables* in passing: "The ancestral secrets of identity in *The House of the Seven Gables* include, ultimately, a long-hidden but useless deed to Indian lands."[59] Hawthorne's proclaimed abhorrence for an "Indian story," as Brickhouse and others point out, does not square with his own writing, and his proclamation functions more as an invective against the ease of national acclaim offered by writing these kinds of "Indian stories," and not by any means as a justification for displacing Native Americans from their lands. But of course, Hawthorne does write some "Indian stories" of a sort—perhaps most strikingly in the "Main Street" story being told by a traveling showman whose mechanical diorama is churning out a story of American history. Here the Native Americans are curious about the arrival of the Europeans on their shores, and "the white man's . . . deep track" and "heavy tread" soon sound ominously through the story, culminating in the showman's whitewashed statement: "The pavements of the Main Street must be laid over the red man's grave."[60] Michael Colacurcio suggests that this story represents Hawthorne's attempt to take into consideration a pressing national issue without disturbing his focus on the Puritans and the Revolution: "The effect is not to tip the balance of his cultural criticism away from the matter of the Puritans or of the Revolution but, in partially redressing a crucial omission, to remind his audience that certain issues may matter out of all proportion to the power of fiction satisfactorily to represent them. Art has indeed its limits."[61] Contemporaries and predecessors of Hawthorne, such as James Fenimore Cooper, Catharine Maria Sedgwick, and Lydia Maria Child, eagerly wrote "Indian stories" for the public. While he clearly noticed other authors engaging more directly with "the Indian question," Hawthorne resisted writing this kind of story, preferring to treat such issues from a kind of artistic distance.[62]

More recently, Yael Ben-Zvi has argued that "native-born settlers" in Hawthorne's texts are represented as rightful owners of the land whose claims are superior to those of people who were not born in the land they have come to inhabit. While Ben-Zvi uncovers an important difference between those who know the land on which they live and those who merely own the land, he rather too quickly concludes that this differentiation serves as a justification for "Hawthorne's antebellum cultural milieu, [in which] the native status of white citizens was perceived as a cultural birthright, which marginalized presumably disappearing Native Americans while naturalizing native-born settlers."[63] What Ben-Zvi does not sufficiently account for is the manner in which Hawthorne's writing registers his skepticism of the Puritans' land-grabbing rhetoric. Hawthorne, however, shows more concern for the wrongs being perpetrated than for the rights of anyone to own the land. Thus, Hawthorne participates at least obliquely in the national myth of the "vanishing Indian," not by taking sides for or against Native Americans but by troubling assumptions about white settlers' claims to land ownership.

One influence that may have contributed to any uneasiness Hawthorne was feeling with regard to Native American removals is a book titled *Indian Biography* that he checked out of the Salem Athenaeum in 1837. The author of this book, Samuel Gardner Drake, seems disinclined to simply accept as regrettable but inevitable the disappearance of Native Americans from their eastern lands. Beginning with a brief "advertisement," he states that this book is not a book of apologies but a book that represents "the first general attempt to embody Indian history in the only proper manner."[64] Hawthorne's focus on national wrongdoing is a parallel sentiment to the snippet of a poem by Charles Sprague, which serves as an opening epigraph for this book:

> We call them Savage—O be just!
> Their outraged feelings scan!
> A voice comes forth, 'tis from the dust—
> The savage was a man!
> *   *   *   *   *   *
> I venerate the Pilgrim's cause,
> Yet for the red man dare to plead;
> We bow to Heaven's recorded laws,
> He turned to nature for a creed![65]

Despite the seemingly noble and religious goals of the firstcomers, then, this book suggests that at least part of their success came at the expense of Native American peoples. Hawthorne's text touches upon two concerns Drake gives in Sprague's poem: (1) "the doomed Indian leaves behind no trace," and (2) "His heraldry is but a broken bow, His history but a tale of wrong and wo."[66] Here we see Hawthorne paying attention to laments of the ways whites mistreated Native Americans. One likely reason for Hawthorne's attention to the concomitant issues of Native Americans and landownership in the nineteenth century was the Indian Removal Act two decades earlier in 1830, which codified the US governmental policies toward Native Americans. This act led to voluntary and forced removals for many tribes east of the Mississippi.

When we turn to individual characters within the races represented in *Seven Gables*, we find variances within the family "races." These variances are almost always environmentally shaped. When Phoebe arrives on the doorstep of the old house, the narrator notes that she is "one little offshoot of the Pyncheon race . . . a native of a rural part of New England, where . . . it was regarded by no means improper for kinsfolk to visit one another without invitation, or preliminary and ceremonious warning."[67] In the rural parts of New England, the Pyncheon race has been changed by its environment. Clifford Pyncheon also shows the effects of his environment when he returns home after a long imprisonment and is about to leap from the balcony, "a wild, haggard figure . . . a lonely being, estranged from his race, but now feeling himself man again, by virtue of the irrepressible instinct that possessed him."[68] Clifford's imprisonment and newfound freedom have affected his personality and psychological makeup, yet what remains is his instinct for connection to the human race rather than to the Pyncheon race. Later when Clifford has fled the house with Hepzibah, he philosophizes on the human race:

[A]ll human progress is in a circle; or, to use a more accurate and beautiful figure, in an ascending spiral curve. . . . In the early epochs of our race, men dwelt in temporary huts, of bowers of branches, as easily constructed as a bird's nest . . . which Nature, we will say, assisted them to rear. . . . Transition [now] being so facile, what can be any man's inducement to tarry in one spot? Why, therefore, should he build a more cumbrous habitation than can readily be carried off with him? Why should he make himself a prisoner for life in brick, and stone, and old worm-eaten timber, when he may just as easily dwell, in one sense, nowhere,—in a better sense, wherever the fit and beautiful shall offer him a home?[69]

Why not, in other words, live like nomadic Bedouin tribes, like the birds of the air, or perhaps like migratory American Indian tribes who move from camp to camp rather than laying claim to one piece of land? From this perspective, wrongdoing represents not a necessity of life but a failure to respect the rhythms of nature and stems from a dreadful willingness to use violence to achieve our ends.

REGIONAL ANXIETIES, NATIONAL ANXIETIES

While questions of biological racism and genetic predisposition are clearly referenced by *The House of the Seven Gables*, another question related to race is also raised. What is the relationship of humans to the land on which they build their habitations? This question is foregrounded as an issue of race because of the constant search for the lost deed of Pyncheon land in Maine and the map of that territory, embellished with Indians and wild animals—some of them (like the presence of a lion) quite inaccurate portrayals of the American landscape, as the narrator points out. Hawthorne's excoriation of his Puritan ancestors for their intransigence against Indians and Quakers and other dissidents hints of the ways race and religion will become touchstones of American culture building. In her classic essay on regionalism, Mary Hunter Austin identifies two characteristics of regionalism that are pertinent to ecocriticism and to Hawthorne's text. The first is that "the region must enter constructively into the story, as another character, as the instigator of plot" rather than being "used merely as a back drop." Secondly, regionalist fiction "must not only be about the country, but of the country, flower and stalk of its root . . . taking its movement and rhythm, its structure and its tension, or lack of it, from the scene."[70] Austin identifies *Seven Gables* as a clear example of the regionalist fiction of New England. Not only is it of New England. It is of Salem, one of the founding Puritan settlements in colonial America. Walter Michaels explores the connection between the Salem witch trials and landownership extensively, drawing numerous obvious parallels that situate the Colonel's actions against Matthew Maule as an issue of property rights rather than a genuine attempt at godliness. "Hawthorne," Michaels notes, "revives the connection between witchcraft and quarrels over property by beginning his narrative with a title dispute."[71]

At the end of Hawthorne's preface, he belabors his attempt to distance his work from regionalist literature, managing only to establish it as a work of Gothic romance rather than to extricate it from its region. This romance, he avers, is composed "of materials long in use for constructing castles in the air," and the tale ought to be read as if it had "a great deal more to do with the clouds overhead, than with any portion of the actual soil of the County of Essex."[72] His allusion to "castles in the air" invokes the Gothic by its focus on the physical structure and imaginative framework that serves as the site of many Gothic romances in the British literature Hawthorne read. With regard to the Gothic texture of this story, what Hawthorne's prefatory statement does is twofold: it invokes the architectural framework of the Gothic, with its mention of castles, hinting at the same time of an ethereal atmosphere by having it be a "castle of the air." Hawthorne picked up this metaphoric phrase, of course, from his wide range of readings. Although this phrase was widely used to mean "visionary project or scheme, day-dream, idle fancy" since the seventeenth century, the phrase's appearance in Lewis's Gothic novel *The Monk* may have added a specially Gothic twist to it for Hawthorne, giving him the impetus to project "castles" into his vision of America.[73] Which parts of his book constitute a "visionary project" and which parts are "idle fancy" could be debated, but there is too much of a project being obviously shaped before the reader's eyes for *Seven Gables* to be wholly "idle fancy."

At first glance, however, Hawthorne's creaky Gothic tale may seem no more than a dreamy romance with little connection to real life. Hawthorne does himself much to create this sense with the anticipatory protest that "[t]he Reader" will probably be tempted to fixate on the locale of the event, but that "the Author" is trying to avoid any such fixation and prefers that this story "be read strictly as a Romance."[74] Mentioning the "soil of the County of Essex" actually serves to draw readers' attention to the physical location, the home of the infamous Salem witch trials. The implication is not that Salem or the soil of Essex County is immaterial to Hawthorne's tale—far from it, as the events come to show—but that it serves as a synecdoche not only for New England but for the young nation of America. *The House of the Seven Gables*, like the House of America, stands as a framework whose interiors may be inspected for crumbling supports. And, in America, one such crumbling support is the governmentally sanctioned mistreatment of Native Americans hinted at continuously in Hawthorne's text. Writing in the genre of romance allows Hawthorne to stretch his readers' imaginative capacity to find connections between the House and the Nation, and his description of romance in the preface of *Seven Gables* indicates that he is approaching this work in terms of Gothic romance. In this description, Hawthorne emphasizes the role of the imagination in considering a wide range of possibilities in a way that realist novels would be hard-pressed to achieve.

Hawthorne gives many indications that the house participates in a real history, but this text is clearly taking into consideration more than just one house and one greedy land baron. Instead, Hawthorne's text and the house in that text both function as synecdoche. The individual Pyncheon history is analogous to the history of the nation. The house is not merely a random haunted house but the dwelling place of a family much as the House of America is the dwelling place of a people. Both Stuart Borrows and Robert K. Martin recognize Hawthorne's use of synecdoche in *Seven Gables*, with Borrows pointing out that the text of *Seven Gables* is a synecdoche for the Pyncheon history associated with the house from which Hawthorne's romance obtains its name.[75] In addition, it is fairly obvious that the house of Pyncheon serves as a synecdoche for the House of America. The wrongs committed on a small scale in removing the Maules from the land the Pyncheons wanted, a removal enabled by accusing Matthew Maule of witchcraft and executing him henceforth, are recapitulated on a national scale by the removal of Native Americans from the lands the Anglo-Americans wanted. Robert K. Martin similarly argues that the text represents more than "a grotesque landscape of the imagination. Among the secrets [the house] conceals is a racial history of slavery which at least in part shifts the novel's theme away from family guilt to national guilt or uses the family as a synecdoche of the nation."[76] While there is a rough equivalence between the national wrong of slavery and the Pyncheon wrong of ill-gotten property (not to mention the presence of a slave named Scipio in the House's history), the more direct connection given in Hawthorne's text is between the wrongs of the land-grabbing Pyncheons and land-grabbing opportunists who disinherited Native Americans from the lands they had inhabited.

By viewing the House as a synecdoche not only of Salem but of America—and particularly of New England—we can productively assess the national guilt that Hawthorne is displaying in his text. Three primary historical wrongs have been committed—all having to do with land claims and individual views of human relations to the land. The first view is that of Colonel Pyncheon, who asserts his control over everything around him and desires to own as much "real estate" as possible. He wrongs whoever he must in order to get that land. The second view is that of squatters like Matthew Maule who come to know the land through their personal relations with it, and the final view is that of the Native Americans who have been displaced by the squabbling white Europeans. The first and most glaring wrong—one might say the *original sin*—is the forced displacement of Native Americans.

Hawthorne indicates his concern about landownership as it pertains to European colonizers, demarcating his own project of romance in the preface of *Seven Gables* as a way of avoiding the kind of imposition practiced by writers of novels. Novels, he claims, are even more susceptible than the romance "to an inflexible and exceedingly dangerous species of criticism, by bringing [their] fancy-pictures into positive contact with the realities of the moment," typically through unsuccessful attempts "to describe local manners" and "to meddle with the characteristics of a community."[77] Such statements seem to indicate at first that Hawthorne is simply demarcating an apolitical space in order to write an inoffensive text, but such an assumption belies the actual content of the tale itself—a tale which castigates the Salem witch trial judges of centuries past as well as the actions of Judge Jaffrey Pyncheon in the present. Like the Colonel before him, Judge Pyncheon, "with all the show of liberal expenditure, was said to be as close-fisted as if his gripe were of iron" but effectively fooled "most people" of the town into thinking he had "the genuine warmth of nature."[78] Such statements indicate a desire not merely to write something inoffensive but to write something that may in fact make readers rethink too hasty assumptions about the social and political issues of the day—particularly when such issues could be corrupted by the desire for wealth or political gain.

Comparing Shirley Jackson's *The Haunting of Hill House* with earlier haunted house narratives, Christine Wilson takes Jackson's novel as the first of many haunted house narratives that "express explicitly spatial anxieties."[79] Briefly noting the connection between environmental criticism and haunted house narratives in which the house itself is presented as a wilderness of sorts, Wilson clarifies, "Haunted house narratives typically do not propose that the house is a literal wilderness, but they most certainly imagine them as spaces of animation, unruliness, and often desolation. In fact, one of the reasons that Hill House and its descendants are so frightening is because they are unnaturally natural. They defy the boundaries between domestic and natural space, the wild and the domesticated, subject and object, the animate and inanimate."[80] Despite Wilson's claim that such narratives begin with Jackson's Hill House, this description applies just as well to Hawthorne's *House*. For in the first chapter, the narrator of *Seven Gables* introduces us to the haunted house of the Pyncheons in just such terms. It is a place with an "aspect" that, the narrator tells us, "has always affected me like a human countenance." It is a place whose "oozy" interior "was itself like a human heart, with a life of its own, and full of rich and sombre reminiscences."[81] But the narrator hastens to inform us that this imposing house, "antique as it now looks, was not the first habitation erected by civilized man, on precisely the same spot of ground."[82] By thinking about the "first habitation," we are drawn backward to earlier inhabitants but stopped at the point of the first "civilized man" who lived here. That is, until we notice the multitude of references to the Native Americans whose presence on the continent predates that of the European settlers or their African slaves.

Hawthorne's attention to Native Americans in this text is apparent not only in his mentions of the map and lost deed, however untrustworthy they are in the end. In the situation of the wrongs endured by the Maules who settled on the very site of the Pyncheon house before being displaced, Hawthorne also draws attention to Native Americans by creating a situation somewhat analogous to that of the Native Americans, goading his readers to see the wrongs they are participating in, most likely without even being aware of it. For while a squatter may not be a Native American, the squatter's relation to the land is more congenial than that of a legal thief like Colonel Pyncheon. Even the land responds to the difference in ownership. The nineteenth-century narrator reveals that the street known to him as Pyncheon Street had once been called "Maule's Lane" and consisted of little more than "a cow-path" that ran along the front of Maule's cottage. Matthew Maule, whom the narrator calls "the original occupant of the soil," had been attracted to this spot because of the presence of a "natural spring of soft and pleasant water—a rare treasure on the sea-girt peninsula."[83]

Like Matthew Maule himself, the land seems to curse the Pyncheons, who have taken it unjustly to satisfy their own greed. The land-grabbing Colonel "dug his cellar, and laid the deep foundations of his mansion, on the square of earth" where Matthew Maule's hut had stood for several decades.[84] The Colonel's house is made to impress, and the whole town is invited for an open house celebration of the Colonel's new residence. The narrator emphasizes the way the House is cut into the landscape and juts up against the sky:

> All, as they approached, looked upward at the imposing edifice, which was henceforth to assume its rank among the habitations of mankind. There it rose, a little withdrawn from the line of the street, but in pride, not modesty. Its whole visible exterior was ornamented with quaint figures, conceived in the grotesqueness of a Gothic fancy, and drawn or stamped in the glittering plaster, composed of lime, pebbles, and bits of glass, with which the woodwork of the walls was overspread. On every side the seven gables pointed sharply towards the sky, and presented the aspect of a whole sisterhood of edifices, breathing through the spiracles of one great chimney. . . . All around were scattered shavings, chips, shingles, and broken halves of bricks; these, together with the lately turned earth, on which the grass had not begun to grow, contributed to the impression of strangeness and novelty, proper to a house that had yet its place to make among men's daily interests.[85]

The imposing edifice which scars the face of the earth presents a visual contrast to Maule's hut which required little more than the sweeping of leaves from the forest floor. The house does not look natural in its position against the earth, for the grass has not yet grown over it. In precisely this state of things, Colonel Pyncheon dies his purportedly apoplectic death.

Land inheritance in this place is not as straightforward as it seems. The narrator remarks that property inheritance is a "custom, so immemorial, that it looks like nature. In all the Pyncheons, this feeling had the energy of disease."[86] But because of Clifford's long unjust imprisonment, he seems less concerned about this than the typical Pyncheon. When expostulating about human edifices during his trip on the train, for example, Clifford exclaims:

> In the early epochs of our race, men dwelt in temporary huts, or bowers of branches, as easily constructed as a bird's nest, and which they built—if it should be called building, when such sweet homes of a summer-solstice rather grew than were made with hands—which Nature, we will say, assisted them to rear where fruit abounded, where fish and game were plentiful, or, most especially, where the sense of beauty was to be gratified by a lovelier shade than elsewhere, and a more exquisite arrangement of lake, wood, and hill. This life possessed a charm, which, ever since man quitted it, has vanished from existence.[87]

This mention of "vanishing," in such close conjunction to an "early epoch" with simple dwellings, resounds with the myth of the vanishing Indian. As Holgrave comes to realize and Phoebe exemplifies, it takes a mutually sustaining relationship between the land and its inhabitants to restore the relations between humans and the nonhuman world. The House, the garden, the fountain, the chickens are all participants in nature, for nature has taken hold of them all in ways as varied as the moss and posies growing on the house or the ancient chickens pecking through the land for sustenance.

Under the Gothic stroke of Hawthorne's pen, the house becomes so intimately linked with the land that it seems itself a part of nature. Nature itself is wronged by those who, like Colonel Pyncheon, attempt to own the land without developing any intimate knowledge of the land. And nature participates plays a role in right at last some of the wrongs that occur at the House. For almost immediately after the Pyncheons seize the land and dig up the soil to build Pyncheon mansion, the spring water inexplicably becomes "hard and brackish."[88] Jane Lundblad takes note of Colonel Pyncheon's acquisition of Maule's soil as part of the "mysterious crime" that contributes to the Gothic texture of *The House of the Seven Gables*. She also alludes to the "lost Indian contract" that was said to prove that Colonel Pyncheon had "acquired a large and fertile piece of land from an Indian tribe," but she does not recognize them as crimes against nature.[89] The crimes in this story are specific to America: abuse of the land and its inhabitants in the hope of economic self-improvement has perpetuated great wrongs, whether through slavery, Native American removals, or simply the destruction of the natural world through careless industrialization or greedy use of the land.

Thus, Hawthorne's *The House of the Seven Gables* invites an exploration of the question of rightful habitation of the land and the question of who the "real" owners of the land are. However, who the owners are is, in the end, less significant to Hawthorne than the kind of ownership being practiced. The land reacts against greedy, violent owners but responds graciously to those who cultivate and nourish it. More importantly, this house becomes linked with the land so much that it seems itself a part of nature. Likewise, the backstory being related exposes the greed of some of the land speculators who roamed the territories in colonial America. For in *Seven Gables*, the Pyncheon land claims are built on dubious deals with Native Americans or simply stolen from others by bearing false witness against them for self-serving purposes—all wrapped within a perfectly hypocritical guise of godliness. The narrator's disapproval is barely hidden all throughout the text.

THE WORK OF RECONSTITUTING LAND CLAIMS

Landownership was a fraught issue in the British colonies from their beginnings, but most of the public discussion on these issues in the 1850s did not focus so much on the rights of landownership as on the kind of land being annexed—slave state or free state, slave territory or free territory. In 1850, just as he was finishing *The Scarlet Letter* and about to turn to *The House of the Seven Gables*, Hawthorne published one of his short stories in an abolitionist newspaper, *National Era*. In this issue, Hawthorne's contribution is one of several to mention Native Americans. Hawthorne's texts consistently suggest that even prior to the pressing issue of slave ownership in America was the haunting issue of landownership. While Native Americans are the most obvious group of non-Puritans in *Seven Gables,* other races also have an uneasy existence in the text (as in the nation). African Americans were often brought to America as slaves under the pretext that they were not civilized, which was often taken as proof that they were less than human.

Native Americans did not own the land in the same way that European Americans did, laying claim individually to specific plots of land. Ownership of the land—the very thing that seems to mark "civilized man" for the narrator in chapter one—is also the very thing criticized in the preface as the source of fraud, of "wrong-doing."[90] Hawthorne shapes the story of the conflict between the Pyncheons and the Maules so as to emphasize that land claims in early America were sometimes spurious. The judicial system did not always provide justice when property issues were at play. Even in discussions of natural rights, European Americans were clearly favored by a system that was set up with their laws and customs.

The fact that Native Americas are mentioned as frequently as they are in Hawthorne's text, and so often in connection with a land deed held by an unscrupulous land-grabber like Colonel Pyncheon, suggests that they are more than mere background for Hawthorne's stage work. Several scholars have noted at least in passing the significance of landownership in *The House of the Seven Gables*. As Robert K. Martin observes, "Hawthorne's text was written in the midst of a national—even international—debate over the right to property, the right to hold and sell slaves, and the connections between the enslavement of women and that of black Americans."[91] Like others before him, Martin accuses Hawthorne of "evad[ing] the issue of the Indian lands by staging a conflict between two white families in the absence of the dispersed and now dispossessed Indians."[92] Walter Benn Michaels simply claims that *Seven Gables* is like other "haunted house stories" and thus "involve[s] some form of anxiety about ownership."[93] While Michaels uncovers evidence that Hawthorne was well attuned to laws concerning property rights, he pays little heed to Native American claims to the land as perhaps a chief reason for Hawthorne's interest in issues of landownership. Like many other critics, however, he does aptly connect issues of landownership with the legal or effectual ownership of women and slaves in the nineteenth century.

Hawthorne's treatment of landownership in *Seven Gables* correlates to Emerson's comments on the natural landscape in his essay *Nature*: "Miller owns this field, Locke that, and Manning the woodland beyond. But none of them owns the landscape." Emerson characterizes this landscape variously as a "charming landscape" and a "tranquil landscape" in which "man beholds somewhat as beautiful as his own soul." Although Emerson further notes that the "rich landscape" has a "minuteness of details," these details are ultimately less important to him than achieving an overriding "tranquil sense of unity."[94] Emerson vaguely troubles the notion of human ownership of the land only to assert the ultimate tranquility of landscape that cannot be owned. Hawthorne, on the other hand, highlights the violence that landownership can entail and the effect that such violence continues to have upon future generations who live on that land. Hawthorne further suggests that the landscape itself will be affected by what individual landowners do with their land. When mutually nurturing relations are not developed, nature becomes grotesque and horrifying rather than beautiful or sublime. Viewed in this light, *The House of the Seven Gables* becomes a commentary on the difficulties attendant upon the realization of a "tranquil landscape." While Emerson simply argues that though one man may own a plot of land yet nobody can own the landscape,

Hawthorne goes a step further by suggesting not only that the titles are of dubious authority but that the very idea of owning land is suspect because claims of ownership are too often based on wrongs rather than rights.

Attempting to lay hold of Nature, Hawthorne implies, may have brought down upon the heads of Americans the guilt of "ill-gotten . . . real estate," and the righting of such a wrong is not easily achieved. In the nineteenth-century, competing views of landownership also contributed to the now-infamous Indian removals. The legality of landownership was often settled by the arbitration of the courts without careful consideration of Native American rights, and Hawthorne's attention to the role of the courts can be seen in his comment that Colonel Pyncheon's land claims had been "confirmed by a subsequent grant of the General Court."[95] At a time when slavery was emerging in the national consciousness as the most obvious national wrong, Hawthorne promotes another vision of the original sin of America—that of Anglo-Americans' treatment of the land and its inhabitants upon their arrival. Written the year after the Fugitive Slave Act that was part of the Compromise of 1850, *The House of the Seven Gables* suggests that even before slavery was brought to British America, wrongdoing had been part of the story of America and that until "the accumulated mass" had been finally been once more "scattered abroad in its original atoms," that wrongdoing would never be made wholly right.[96] Since landownership by the Puritans often came through displacement of the Native Americans, Hawthorne's link between historical issues of landownership and Native Americans is fitting, yet troubling.

Although Native Americans are not visibly lurking in the corners of *The House of the Seven Gables* as they are in the streets of colonial Boston in *The Scarlet Letter*, their very absence is made glaringly apparent by repeated references to land deeds gotten through Native American sagamores and their similarities with the wrongfully disinherited Maules. The ghostly narrator's repeated references to an elusive Indian deed being sought by the greedy Pyncheons sounds a note of obvious absence. The memory of the Native American presence is preserved alongside Colonel Pyncheon's portrait by the sketches of Native Americans and animals on the map of the supposed Pyncheon territories of Eastern Lands that hung beside the Colonel's portrait. The Native Americans seem little more than wild animals to Colonel Pyncheon—barely human inhabitants. As he attempted to establish legal claims to Maule's land, so his ancestor had laid legal claim to Native American lands in Maine but most likely against their will. The Puritan portrait is a figure of religious intolerance, his warlike attitude toward those who opposed his ownership of the land made apparent in the pairing of this picture with the etchings on the map next to it. The sword is next to the map of the territories coveted by Pyncheons from the colonial Colonel to the nineteenth-century judge. The etchings on the map, however, perhaps unwittingly show the Native Americans' relation to the land, in stark contrast to the Puritan Colonel's. The map itself—with its demarcations of Pyncheon property—indicates the possessive characteristics of the Pyncheon's coveted ownership, indicating not a mutuality between land and inhabitant but an imposing and destructive master/slave kind of relationship between landowner and land.

As Hawthorne's text intimates, Colonel Pyncheon and Native Americans often have radically opposed notions of humans' relation to the land. In addition to his "rich estate" in Salem, the Colonel wanted to extend his holdings elsewhere in New England; the narrator draws attention to the Colonel's attempt to establish "a claim, through an Indian deed" to a large territory in Maine:

> [T]here was a claim . . . to a vast, and as yet unexplored and unmeasured tract of Eastern lands. These possessions—for as such they might almost certainly be reckoned—comprised the greater part of what is now known as Waldo County, in the State of Maine, and were more extensive than many a dukedom, or even a reigning prince's territory, on European soil. When the pathless forest that still covered this wild principality should give place—as it inevitably must, though perhaps not till ages hence—to the golden fertility of human culture, it would be the source of incalculable wealth to the Pyncheon blood.[97]

Here Hawthorne notes the movement from Native American territory to Pyncheon possession, hinting of the doctrine of Manifest Destiny to which Colonel Pyncheon obviously ascribes. The word "inevitably" in this context is a marker of the doctrine of Manifest Destiny, and it is significant that Hawthorne ascribes this attitude to the villain Colonel Pyncheon. The description of the grant brings Native Americans firmly into focus. The Colonel's claim is found at last in the "sheet of parchment" found in the recess in the wall of the House behind the portrait. Inside lies "an ancient deed, signed with the hieroglyphics of several Indian sagamores, and conveying to Colonel Pyncheon and his heirs, forever, a vast extent of territory at the Eastward."[98] The "several Indian sagamores" are reminiscent of the few who were often consulted by white treaty-makers. Rather than working within Native American frameworks of treaty-making and relational practices toward the land, white courts operated as if one person in a tribe had the power to make treaties and other agreements.

The Maules too were wrongfully disinherited by corrupt legal proceedings. Many years after the Pyncheons had displaced the previous inhabitants of the land, a Pyncheon heir who was an antiquarian became convinced that the Maules had been unjustly deprived of their living quarters. The narrator's comments here come close to the expression of the book as a whole: "To a man living so much in the past, and so little in the present, as the secluded and antiquarian old bachelor, a century and a half seemed not so vast a period as to obviate the propriety of substituting right for wrong."[99] In like manner, *The House of the Seven Gables* is a reminder that no amount of time of lost opportunity is too "vast a period" for a romancer like Hawthorne to participate in righting the wrongs of his nation against the "original inhabitants" of the land. But Hawthorne does not broach such a politically charged topic directly—only at a slant. *The House of the Seven Gables* serves as a national caution: land gotten by unjust and greedy means is sure to bring a curse rather than a blessing upon the heads of those who have participated directly or indirectly in the original wrongdoing, and lack of care for that land only compounds the problem. The Pyncheons attempt to *own* the land while the Maules, like the Native Americans, attempt to *know* the land.

Landownership did not mean the same thing to Native Americans as to most whites, as Hawthorne's reading would have told him. When the Indian sagamores signed the deed for Colonel Pyncheon, what did they think they were signing? Native Americans viewed the land not as a commodity and not only as a home but as a gift to be enjoyed and treated with respect. Instead, the most terrible secrets are dark ones that hide behind pious or nationalistic pretenses that mask the exploitation and greed of the land-grabbers of America from its earliest European settlers in the seventeenth century to its position as a young republic in the early nineteenth century. The Colonel is an advocate of progress primarily as it benefits him materially with lands and wealth.

By focusing on the eastern lands of Maine rather than the western territories into which American expansionist policies were extending the borders of the nation, Hawthorne draws attention to the wrongs already committed centuries earlier by the original settlers who took over Native American lands. Thus, rather than commenting directly on the current situation, Hawthorne suggests that past wrongs have already contributed inextricably to the current situation with regard to landownership in the America east. Hawthorne's language suggests his displeasure with the land-grabbing self-justification of Pyncheon-like settlers: the General Court has "confirmed" the Indian deed, which ironically suggests that "Indian deeds" were not always authentic or valid documents. Some may have been forged, and others may have been gotten by tricking the Native Americans who typically could not read the documents for themselves. Further troubling the validity of this particular deed, the narrator notes the powerful influence of the Colonel in making people see things as he wanted to see them, and his influence may well have extended to the General Court that had "confirmed" the validity of the deed: "Had the Colonel survived only a few weeks longer, it is probable that his great political influence, at home and abroad, would have consummated all that was necessary to render the claim available."[100] But the narrator's skeptical attitude toward Colonel Pyncheon comes most clearly into his focus in his comparison of the Colonel's force of persuasion with that of his surviving son: "His son lacked not merely his father's eminent position, but the talent and force of character to achieve it: he could, therefore, effect nothing by dint of political interest; and the bare justice or legality of the claim was not so apparent, after the Colonel's decease, as it had been pronounced in his lifetime."[101]

In *Seven Gables*, then, Hawthorne indicates that he is not satisfied with trying to settle the question of whose claims to the land are the most valid in a court of law even though the courts have commonly been used for such settlement ever since disputes first broke out between Native Americans and white settlers. That question, he suggests, is itself the cause of much wrongdoing and legal manipulation that treats the land merely as an object to be owned and used. The kind of relationship established between land and tenant and the means of living on the land are more meaningful than the legal documents that establish land claims. Since the claims of nature are stronger than the claims of the law, a relationship with nature is essential. Knowledge of the land, intimacy with the land, and participation with the land are crucial parts of "natural" relations to the land. Native Americans may have had such a relationship, but their removal—unjust though it was—suggests that their way of life may be gone forever in the eastern lands of nineteenth-century New England. Squatters like old Matthew Maule may have had a somewhat "natural" relationship with the land as well, but land-grabbers like the old Colonel Pyncheon are simply wealthy land speculators with little to no relationship to the land who wish to exploit it for economic gain. Ronald Curran notes the difference between the relations to the land held by Matthew Maule and Colonel Pyncheon, asserting that the Maules held a "natural claim" to the land in contrast to "aristocratic" pretensions.[102] While this may let the Maules off easy, it is clear that they are not invested in violence in the way the Puritans are. These latter landowners—those in the mold of Colonel Pyncheon—receive Hawthorne's strongest censure. Thus Hawthorne's Gothic text, with all of its groaning structures and characters, forcefully advocates the belief that exploitation of the land and its congenial inhabitants is a crime against nature.

While Matthew Maule and Colonel Pyncheon both want the same piece of land, their reasons for wanting it are very different. Matthew Maule considers this plot of land his home and Colonel Pyncheon considers it a bit of real estate, a commodity to be bought and sold at will. Their two very different views of the land are further revealed in their relationship with it. Matthew Maule's dwelling, "a hut, shaggy with thatch" that resembled the bird's-nest description Clifford had assigned to Native American homes, was the first dwelling on the site where the House of the Seven Gables was eventually built.[103] Rather than basing their relation to the land on legal ownership,

Matthew Maule and other squatters based their relation to the land on their cultivation of the land and their close living proximity to the earth. This land is not the Maine territory that the Pyncheons allegedly "bought" from the Native Americans but a plot of uninhabited Salem land.

By making a dubious deal with the sagamores, Colonel Pyncheon's ancestor made a pact that he would condemn in others as a kind of deal with the devil. In the introduction to the *Centenary Edition* of Hawthorne's works, William Charvat points out several parallels between the historical Hawthornes and Pyncheons: "There are analogies between the Pyncheon and Hawthorne ancestors as persecutors of witches. The Hawthornes, like the Pyncheons, had once laid claim to extensive lands in Maine, but for this theme Hawthorne also drew upon the well-known story of General Knox's land patent in that state. There are parallels between Clifford's supposed murder of his uncle and the sensational murder in Salem in 1830 of Captain Joseph White by hirelings of a person who wanted to destroy White's will."[104] Several recent studies have considered the Maine land claims, and one of them has focused especially on the relations between the Salem residents and Maine claims. Bancroft notes this in detail, pointing out the discrepancies between what the whites stated and what the Native Americans understood. Thus, the legal claims may well have represented little more than linguistic subterfuge in the eyes of many Native Americans.

The Pyncheons' claim to the land where they had built their house, like their claim to the Maine lands they were trying to obtain, was a legal claim recorded on paper. But the author draws attention to other types of claims. Based on "impressions often too vaguely founded to be put on paper," the narrator expresses his confidence that guilt has hounded generations of Pyncheons because of their ill-gotten lands and wonders whether the later inheritors were not in fact just as culpable as the harsh Colonel Pyncheon who had committed the deed.[105] Based on their close relationship to the land, squatters like Maule in Salem and Native Americans in the Eastern Lands of Maine saw the land open to them rather than shut off from them because of a legal document. The paper on which the deed is inscribed means little to the narrator; human relations to the land are experienced rather than coerced. While the narrator has no problem making claims based on "impressions" that are not "put on paper," the Pyncheons in his story are only too happy to create impressions *on* paper—deeds for the Native American lands in Maine and deeds for the Maule land. Because of these deeds, the papers that stipulate that the land is theirs, most of the Pyncheons have no problem claiming it as their own regardless of the guilt the narrator suggests they should feel. The Maules and the Native Americans both face the curse of the Pyncheon papers, papers that create legal claims opposed to the natural relations the Maules and the Native Americans have heretofore enjoyed.

By contrasting the Pyncheons' legal claims against the "natural" squatting rights of the Maules, Hawthorne highlights the problematics of landownership in America. The first notion of landownership relies upon official sanctions demanded by the imposing figure of the first Pyncheon who enjoyed no real knowledge of the land, and the second relies on firsthand knowledge of "the lands which they or their fathers had wrested from the wild hand of nature by their own sturdy toil."[106] The Maules' actions toward the land indicate a kind of lived relationship with and attendant cultivation of the land, but the original Pyncheons evince instead a greedy manipulation of land rights.

Indeed, issues of landownership haunt the Maules and the Pyncheons in their fight over property rights in a country that has been taken (often violently) from the Native Americans. Likewise, Colonel Pyncheon enacts violence against Maule—a "natural" squatter who at least is coming to know the land—by lodging legal charges to displace him, thereby bringing Maule's curse on the Pyncheon patriarch. The violence against the land and its occupants brings about a curse not only from the Maules but from nature itself as the land becomes diseased, the well becomes polluted, the animals living there become less productive, and violent death becomes hereditary—passed on by nature from one generation to the next. The cursed land effectively curses those who have brought curses upon it. By presenting nature as an entity that can be wronged (or restored, as Phoebe demonstrates) by human action, Hawthorne highlights the role and significance of Nature as an actuality in a "new" world version of Gothic romance.

And so the male figures attempt to resolve the issue by searching for the missing deed while the females attempt to resolve the issue by making the house a home. Wilson comments on the figures of expedition and domestication as masculine and feminine attempts to tame the unruly haunted house: "It is no coincidence that females in these texts try to use traditional housekeeping tasks to subdue the houses, while the males try to conquer the house through exploratory tactics."[107] In both cases, however, the house itself remains a kind of wilderness, and they finally leave it behind, perhaps to be completely reclaimed by nature.

The fact that the Pyncheons continue to be one of the inheritors of the land, even when the land is apparently restored at the end of *Seven Gables*, suggests that the question of rightful ownership is not simply a question of *who* owns it. By the end of the eighteenth century, the Pyncheon family has itself become divided, and Clifford is sent to prison on a dubious conviction of murdering a relative who has died an apoplectic death that is coming to seem hereditary but only for harsh Pyncheons. The eighteenth century saw the rise of a new dominant view of land—land as property to be claimed as one's own. As such, it could easily fall into the various categories of land as commodity, land as home (the domestic space), or land as gift. While the predominant view of land as commodity ceded some ground the view of land as home, Hawthorne seems to emphasize that the view of land as gift is more admirable. Rather than advocating for property rights of any particular groups, Hawthorne suggests that land should be accepted as a gift, much in the same tenor suggested by the words of the Native Americans in the books Hawthorne had read.

By taking note of the interconnectedness of nature and humans in Hawthorne's *Seven Gables*, we may productively reassess the Gothic rationale of his text. The centrality of landownership is repeatedly emphasized through the history of the plot of earth on which the House is built. The old Indian deed which Judge Pyncheon is seeking reminds readers that the land was first taken from the Native Americans, and the squatting rights of the Maules are overturned by the legal manipulations of the Pyncheons. The surviving Pyncheons at the time of the events of the story are struggling over ownership of the plot of land that is diseased by the presence of the usurping Pyncheons, darkened by the presence of a wronged Maule descendant whose identity is hidden behind the name Holgrave, and unexpectedly brightened by the work of a young woman named Phoebe, who has been distanced from this land until the present moment. The cursed land seems to curse those who have brought curses upon it. This view of nature as an entity that can be wronged or restored by human action provides Hawthorne with the material of a Gothic romance that intermingles the workings of nature and humans to investigate rightful human relations to the land.

The marriage of Phoebe and Holgrave, Pyncheon and Maule, suggests that issues of legal inheritance may best be resolved by a natural union between competing parties who have learned to appreciate and cultivate nature rather than manipulating and controlling nature. Their shared declarations of love resulted in a transfiguration of the earth itself: "The bliss which makes all things true, beautiful, and holy, shone around this youth and maiden. . . . They transfigured the earth, and made it Eden again, and themselves the first two dwellers in it. . . . But how soon the heavy earth-dream settled down again!"[108] The house of Pyncheon and the house of Maule have joined in a classic resolution that resembles the reconciliatory ending of Shakespearean comedy. And this is possible because humans have drawn near to each other and to nature.

In the stern portrait of Colonel Pyncheon, we see a stern Puritan who communicates the "very character" of the Pyncheons that "rendered [the Colonel] so long the evil destiny of his race."[109] The pure bloodlines of the Puritan Pyncheons are wrapped up in some "evil destiny" for that race. A pure race seems destined for evil. Without blood mixture, the Pyncheons cannot expect to thrive. Phoebe and Holgrave must marry, joining the Maules and Pyncheons whose families' competing claims to the land have led to the major wrongdoing recounted by Hawthorne's text—the execution of Matthew Maule under false pretexts for the purpose of taking the land he had taken as his own.

The notion of "manifest destiny," a term coined by the famous newspaper editor John O'Sullivan in the decade before Hawthorne wrote *The House of the Seven Gables*, was much discussed in Hawthorne's time. Since O'Sullivan had printed some of Hawthorne's short stories, Hawthorne knew the man who claimed, in perhaps the clearest and most famous statement of "manifest destiny," that the Anglo-Americans claimed "the right of our manifest destiny to overspread and to possess the whole of the continent which Providence has given us for the development of the great experiment of liberty and federated self-government entrusted to us."[110] Hawthorne was privy to debates about such notions, given his brother-in-law Horace Mann's outspoken resistance to slavery and "manifest destiny" alike. In February 1850, just after *The Scarlet Letter* was published, Mann delivered a speech to the House of Representatives against extending slavery into the territory of New Mexico, suggesting that notions of "manifest destiny" that supported slavery were as bad as the idea of providential favor on an ever-expanding nation that included people whose ethnic groups had practiced infanticide (China) or cannibalism (the South Seas).[111]

The Compromise of 1850 placed much emphasis on race relations, but mostly ignored the Native American situation and focused on the African American situation. While it would take another decade for Hawthorne to speak out against the evil of slavery that he called "a monstrous birth" on America's shores, he does touch upon race issues in *Seven Gables* by alluding to the specter of the disappearing Native Americans.[112] And he speaks of their removal from the East with regret. In *Seven Gables*, Holgrave criticizes the "model conservative" of Colonel Pyncheon, "who, in that very character, rendered himself so long the evil destiny of his race."[113] Far from supporting the Pyncheon declaration of right to the land, Hawthorne critiqued this right and suggests here that this is not a "Manifest Destiny" with the favor of Providence so much as an "Evil Destiny" that depends on a race's treacherous claims of superiority.

The surviving Pyncheons at the time of the events of the story are struggling over ownership of the plot of land that is diseased by the presence of the usurping Pyncheons, darkened by the presence of a wronged Maule whose identity is hidden, and brightened by the work of a young Pyncheon woman who has been distanced from this land until the present moment. The cursed land seems to curse those who have brought curses upon it. For all its contrived and seemingly sinister structures, then, the Gothic romance functions for Hawthorne as a mode of serious work—the work of awaking the national conscience to the wrongs committed against those who do not share a Euro-American identity. Ultimately, *The House of the Seven Gables* suggests, the fraught issue of landownership in America may not ever be resolved entirely, but the operations of the natural world play a part in any resolution and so does a supernatural realm vaguely alluded to through apparently active curses and repeated reference to Providence. The judge's intention of getting the House for himself is undone by his timely death—timely from the viewpoint of almost any of the characters other than the judge himself. And his death, followed closely by the death of his son in foreign lands, recapitulates the issue of landownership, and those about to be wronged by the judge actually inherit his lands. The work of reconstituting land claims—just like the work of reconstituting race—is an unfinished work.

NOTES

1. Hawthorne, *Complete Works*, vol. 3, 14.
2. Shawn Michelle Smith, *American Archives: Gender, Race, and Class in Visual Culture* (Princeton: Princeton University Press, 1999), 50.
3. Hawthorne, *Complete Works*, vol. 3, 368.
4. Robert S. Levine, "Genealogical Fictions: Race in *The House of the Seven Gables* and *Pierre*," in *Hawthorne and Melville: Writing a Relationship*, ed. Jana L. Argersinger and Leland S. Person (Athens: University of Georgia Press, 2008), 232.
5. Levine, "Genealogical Fictions," 232.
6. Hawthorne, *Complete Works*, vol. 3, 14.
7. Hawthorne, *Complete Works*, vol. 9, 107.
8. Hawthorne, *Complete Works*, vol. 3, 18.
9. "race, n.6," *OED Online,* March 2018. Oxford University Press.
10. Hawthorne, *Complete Works*, vol. 3, 19.
11. Hawthorne, *Complete Works*, vol. 3, 19–20.
12. Hawthorne, *Complete Works*, vol. 3, 20–21.
13. Hawthorne, *Complete Works*, vol. 3, 21.
14. Jack G. Voller, *The Supernatural Sublime: The Metaphysics of Terror in Anglo-American Romanticism* (DeKalb: Northern Illinois University Press, 1994), 218.
15. Hawthorne, *Complete Works*, vol. 3, 369.
16. John Ayrton Paris and J.S.M. Fonblanque, *Medical Jurisprudence 3* (London: W. Phillips, 1823), *Google Books*, 275. Hawthorne checked out all three volumes of this book during August and September 1833. See Kesselring, *Hawthorne's Reading*, 188.
17. Paris and Fonblanque, *Medical Jurisprudence,* 276.
18. Paris and Fonblanque, *Medical Jurisprudence,* 273–74.
19. Paris and Fonblanque, *Medical Jurisprudence,* 258, 273.
20. Hawthorne, *Complete Works*, vol. 3, 322.

21. Hawthorne, *Complete Works,* vol. 3, 238–39.
22. Hawthorne, *Complete Works,* vol. 3, 248.
23. Hawthorne, *Complete Works,* vol. 3, 248.
24. Hawthorne, *Complete Works,* vol. 3, 248.
25. Hawthorne, *Complete Works,* vol. 3, 212.
26. Hawthorne, *Complete Works,* vol. 3, 253.
27. Hawthorne, *Complete Works,* vol. 3, 23.
28. Hawthorne, *Complete Works,* vol. 3, 41.
29. Hawthorne, *Complete Works,* vol. 3, 41.
30. Hawthorne, *Complete Works,* vol. 3, 31.
31. Hawthorne, *Complete Works,* vol. 3, 33.
32. Hawthorne, *Complete Works,* vol. 3, 147–48.
33. Hawthorne, *Complete Works,* vol. 3, 21, 29, 35, 152, 248.
34. Hawthorne, *Complete Works,* vol. 3, 40.
35. Smith, *American Archives,* 31.
36. Smith, *American Archives,* 40.
37. Smith, *American Archives,* 41.
38. Levine, "Genealogical Fictions," 235–36.
39. Hawthorne, *Complete Works,* vol. 3, 41.
40. See Reginald Horsman, *Race and Manifest Destiny: The Origins of American Racial Anglo-Saxonism* (Cambridge: Harvard University Press, 1981). Horsman examines the significance of such terms as "race," "extinct," "memory," "blood," and "onward course."
41. Hawthorne, *Complete Works*, vol. 3, 41.
42. "History and Culture," Wampanoag Tribe of Gay Head (Aquinnah), www.wampanoagtribe.net/Pages/Wampanoag_WebDocs/history_culture.
43. Hawthorne, *Complete Works,* vol. 3, 113.
44. John Van Wyhe, "The History of Phrenology on the Web," http://www.historyofphrenology.org.uk/constindex.html.
45. Hawthorne checked Combe's book out at the Salem Athenaeum as early as 1836. See Kesselring, *Hawthorne's Reading,* 178.
46. George Combe, *The Constitution of Man Considered in Relation to External Objects,* 2nd edn (Longman and Company, London, 1835), 209–10.
47. Hawthorne, *Complete Works,* vol. 3, 183–85.
48. Hawthorne, *Complete Works,* vol. 3, 1845.
49. Hawthorne, *Complete Works,* vol. 3, 185.
50. Scott, Sir Walter Scott, *Letters on Demonology and Witchcraft, Addressed to J. G. Lockhart, Esq.* (London: John Murray, 1830), 351. Hawthorne checked this out in October 1837. See Kesselring, "Hawthorne's Reading," 190.
51. Hawthorne, *Complete Works,* vol. 3, 49–50.
52. Nathaniel Hawthorne, "The Duston Family," in *American Magazine of Useful and Entertaining Knowledge* 2, no. 9 (May 1836): 396.
53. Reynolds, *Devils and Rebels: The Making of Hawthorne's Damned Politics*, 203.
54. Thomas Maule, "Truth Held Forth and Maintained: According to the Testimony of the Holy Prophets, Christ and His Apostles Recorded in the Holy

Scriptures," 1695, in *Better That 100 Witches Should Live: The 1696 Acquittal of Thomas Maule of Salem, Massachusetts, on Charges of Seditious Libel and Its Impact on the Development of First Amendment Freedoms*, ed. James Edward Maule (Villanova, PA: Jembook Publishing, 1995). I am grateful to American literary critic and historian Joe B. Fulton for bringing this connection to my attention.

55. Maule, "Truth Held Forth," 432–33.

56. Cotton Mather, *Magnalia Christi Americana; Or, The Ecclesiastical History of New-England, from Its First Planting, in the Year 1620, Unto the Year of Our Lord 1698*, vol. 2 (Hartford: Silas Andrus & Sons, 1853), 644–45.

57. Hawthorne, *Complete Works,* vol. 5, 69.

58. Hawthorne, *Complete Works,* vol. 3, 375.

59. Anna C. Brickhouse, "'I Do Abhor an Indian Story': Hawthorne and the Allegorization of Racial 'Commixture'," *ESQ: A Journal of the American Renaissance* 42, no. 4 (1996), 235.

60. Hawthorne, *Complete Works,* vol. 3, 445.

61. Michael J. Colacurcio, "'Red Man's Grave': Art and Destiny in Hawthorne's 'Main-Street'," *Nathaniel Hawthorne Review* 31, no. 2 (2005): 14.

62. Richard Kopley traces the strong structural parallels between Child's *Hobomok* and Hawthorne's *Scarlet Letter* to suggest that Child's text may well have influenced Hawthorne's; in Kopley's brief reading of Hawthorne's first romance in light of *Hobomok*, he adopts the same distancing technique that is not in *The House of the Seven Gables* by positioning the Maules as parallels for Native Americans. See Kopley, *The Threads of The Scarlet Letter: A Study of Hawthorne's Transformative Art*, 123.

63. Yael Ben-Zvi, "Clinging to One Spot: Hawthorne's Native-Born Settlers," *ESQ: A Journal of the American Renaissance* 52, no. 1–2 (2006): 19.

64. Samuel Gardner Drake, *Indian Biography, Containing the Lives of More Than Two Hundred Indian Chiefs: Also Such Others of That Race as Have Rendered Their Names Conspicuous in the History of North America from Its First Being Known to Europeans to the Present Period. Giving at Large Their Most Celebrated Speeches, Memorable Sayings, Numerous Anecdotes, and a History of Their Wars* (Boston: Josiah Drake, 1832), iv.

65. Drake, *Indian Biography,* 1. These lines of poetry are taken from Charles Sprague's full-length work *An Ode: Pronounced before the Inhabitants of Boston, September the Seventeenth, 1830, at the Bicentennial Celebration of the Settlement of the City* (Boston: John Eastburn, 1830).

66. Drake, *Indian Biography,* 83.

67. Hawthorne, *Complete Works,* vol. 3, 91.

68. Hawthorne, *Complete Works,* vol. 3, 200.

69. Hawthorne, *Complete Works,* vol. 3, 308–9.

70. Mary Hunter Austin, "Regionalism in American Fiction," *The English Journal* 21, no. 2 (1932): 105–6. *JSTOR.*

71. Walter Benn Michaels, "Romance and Real Estate," *The American Renaissance Reconsidered*, ed. Donald Pease (Baltimore: Johns Hopkins University Press, 1985), 159.

72. Hawthorne, *Complete Works,* vol. 3, 15–16.

73. "castle in the air, n." *OED Online,* March 2018. Oxford University Press.

74. Hawthorne, *Complete Works,* vol. 3, 16.

75. Stuart Burrows, *A Familiar Strangeness: American Fiction and the Language of Photography, 1839–1945* (Athens: University of Georgia Press, 2010), 50–51.

76. Robert K. Martin, "Haunted by Jim Crow: Gothic Fictions by Hawthorne and Faulkner," *American Gothic: New Interventions in a National Narrative*, ed. Robert K. Martin and Eric Savoy (Iowa City: University of Iowa Press, 2009), 130.

77. Hawthorne, *Complete Works,* vol. 3, 13, 15.

78. Hawthorne, *Complete Works,* vol. 3, 150.

79. Christine Wilson, "Haunted Habitability: Wilderness and American Haunted House Narratives," in *Popular Ghosts: The Haunted Spaces of Everyday Culture*, ed. María del Pilar Blanco and Esther Peeren (New York: Continuum, 2010), 200.

80. Wilson, "Haunted Habitability," 201–202.

81. Hawthorne, *Complete Works,* vol. 3, 17, 45.

82. Hawthorne, *Complete Works,* vol. 3, 18–19.

83. Hawthorne, *Complete Works,* vol. 3, 19.

84. Hawthorne, *Complete Works,* vol. 3, 24.

85. Hawthorne, *Complete Works,* vol. 3, 24–25.

86. Hawthorne, *Complete Works,* vol. 3, 38.

87. Hawthorne, *Complete Works,* vol. 3, 308.

88. Hawthorne, *Complete Works,* vol. 3, 22–23.

89. Jane Lundblad, *Nathaniel Hawthorne and the Tradition of Gothic Romance* (New York: Haskell House, 1964), 62–65.

90. Hawthorne, *Complete Works,* vol. 3, 14, 18–19.

91. Martin, "Haunted by Jim Crow," 132.

92. Martin, "Haunted by Jim Crow," 132.

93. Michaels, "Romance and Real Estate," 157.

94. Emerson, *Nature and Selected Essays*, 38–39.

95. Hawthorne, *Complete Works,* vol. 3, 32.

96. Hawthorne, *Complete Works,* vol. 3, 14.

97. Hawthorne, *Complete Works,* vol. 3, 82.

98. Hawthorne, *Complete Works,* vol. 3, 374.

99. Hawthorne, *Complete Works,* vol. 3, 36.

100. Hawthorne, *Complete Works,* vol. 3, 32.

101. Hawthorne, *Complete Works,* vol. 3, 32.

102. Ronald T. Curran, "'Yankee Gothic': Hawthorne's 'Castle of Pyncheon,'" *Studies in the Novel* 8 (1976): 76.

103. Hawthorne, *Complete Works,* vol. 3, 19.

104. William Charvat, Introduction. Hawthorne, *Centenary Edition of the Works of Nathaniel Hawthorne,* vol. 2, *The House of the Seven Gables* (Columbus: Ohio State University Press, 1962), xxiii.

105. Hawthorne, *Complete Works,* vol. 3, 34.

106. Hawthorne, *Complete Works,* vol. 3, 33.

107. Wilson, "Haunted Habitability," 204.

108. Hawthorne, *Complete Works,* vol. 3, 363.

109. Hawthorne, *Complete Works,* vol. 3, 373.
110. O'Sullivan's statement was first published in the December 27, 1845, edition of *The New York Morning News.* See Julius W. Pratt, "The Origin of 'Manifest Destiny,'" *The American Historical Review* 32, no. 4 (1927): 796.
111. Horace Mann, *Speech of Mr. Horace Mann, of Mass., on the Subject of Slavery in the Territories, and the Consequences of the Threatened Dissolution of the Union* (Washington, DC: Gideon, 1850), 7.
112. Hawthorne, *Complete Works,* vol. 12, 319.
113. Hawthorne, *Complete Works,* vol. 3, 373.

Chapter 5

Et in Arcadia Ego
Adaptation and Natural Limits in **The Blithedale Romance**

> It is very true that, sometimes, gazing casually around me, out of the midst of my toil, I used to discern a richer picturesqueness in the visible scene of earth and sky. There was, at such moments, a novelty, an unwonted aspect, on the face of Nature, as if she had been taken by surprise and seen at unawares, with no opportunity to put off her real look, and assume the mask with which she mysteriously hides herself from mortals.
>
> —Miles Coverdale in *The Blithedale Romance* by Nathaniel Hawthorne[1]

Nathaniel Hawthorne most jarringly disturbs the pastoral setting of *The Blithedale Romance* with the unexpected and untimely event of death. This is not the hallucinatory death of a beautiful woman Edgar Allan Poe romanticizes in "The Philosophy of Composition."[2] It is an ugly death by suicide or something worse, and we are drawn alongside a narrator-character gaping at the actual rigidity of a horror-struck corpse. By replacing beauty and life and harmony with ugliness and death and confusion in *The Blithedale Romance*, Hawthorne upends the pastoral expectations of nineteenth-century Americans. His work stands as a prophecy of the dissolution of any human experiment in nature that fails to account for the imperfections of human nature. The failure of the pastoral project at Blithedale Farm also suggests that the realities of the nonhuman world cannot be adequately recognized if they are taken as nothing more than human projections of transcendence. Natural consequences follow from actions that ignore natural patterns regardless of what one thinks or wants to think. But even more shockingly perhaps, natural events like death happen even to people who are in tune with nature. At least, such occurrences in nature are shocking to the Transcendentalists Hawthorne places in his story at Blithedale Farm.

The Transcendentalism adopted by the Blithedalers involves "seeing" nature in a way that is expected to change one's way of living. Ralph Waldo Emerson's Transcendentalist creed famously exalted eyesight with his image of himself as a "transparent eye-ball": "Standing on the bare ground,—my head bathed by the blithe air, and uplifted into infinite space,—all mean egotism vanishes. I become a transparent eyeball; I am nothing; I see all; the currents of Universal Being circulate through me; I am part or parcel of God."[3] *The Blithedale Romance* represents a challenge to the certainty of Emerson's interpretive gaze by calling into question the accuracy of such sight by noting the blindness of characters who profess to see. Hawthorne was not the only person to satirize Emerson's statement here. Transcendentalist poet and sketch artist Christopher Cranch famously drew a caricature of this statement that reduced the human to a walking eyeball. (See figure 5.1.)

Analyzing Emerson's words in this passage primarily in linguistic terms, Kenneth Burke has connected the image of an "eye" with the "I" of the text who says "ay" to the transcendence of the beyond. Burke suggests that there is an inherent egotism in such idealist seeing that results in a "transcendental dialectic" that is only one step short of the "out-and out pragmatism" of Henry James. Emerson's essay, Burke claims, "treats of Society in terms of Nature—and it treats of Nature in terms of the Supernatural. Thereby even the discussion of Society in its most realistic aspects becomes transcendentally tinged."[4] While Hawthorne, like Burke, satirizes the egotism of the various Transcendentalist seers in *Blithedale*, he takes the concerns of Transcendentalists seriously rather than dismissing them as Burke does. To ignore the possibility of transcendence is to depend upon the human mind alone, something Hawthorne finds only as reliable as his narrators. That is to say, he finds such an approach to understanding quite inadequate. By foregrounding Miles Coverdale as both narrator and character, Hawthorne especially emphasizes the limited perspective of the narrator in *Blithedale*.

For Coverdale is an unreliable narrator who covers as much as he reveals in his text, and we are left to analyze those moments when he is "taken by surprise and seen at unawares, with no opportunity to put off [his] real look, and assume the mask with which [he] hides" from his audience.[5] While Coverdale uses these words to describe his lack of success in understanding nature, his words ironically alert the reader to attend to Coverdale's accidental expressions of his own nature as well. Coverdale is the epitome of the solipsistic human subject, seeing (or imagining that he sees) the shortsightedness of those around him while assuming his own superior vantage point from which to critique the Blithedale community that ends up disappointing him and other members of the community. Pastoral harmony cannot be achieved by

Figure 5.1 Transparent Eyeball by Christopher Pearce Cranch, c. 1837. Public Domain.

narcissistic participants like Coverdale any more than by the other characters who fall short of the ideal.

Hawthorne's abiding suspicions of Enlightenment empiricism lead him to embrace a romantic paradigm for reality, but his satire of Transcendentalism indicates a continuing philosophical distance from the Transcendentalists as well even as he brings them into his fiction. For while Coverdale is quick to criticize Hollingsworth's egotism, he remains blind to his own egotism. And the end of all too blithe mind-over-matter Transcendentalists like Coverdale is frustration—not only when he is shoveling manure onto the fields but also when he has retreated to his hideouts. Judy Schaaf Anhorn aptly notes that *Blithedale* is the story of "a character in his own Arcadia, a poet seeking spiritual recovery in the green world."[6] The figurative pastoral of poetry has become the literal pastoral of a human subject literally immersed in a natural space on the physical earth with the expectancy that nature will convert him into the best form of himself. Coverdale's initial optimism in the outcome of their pastoral experiment sounds itself in his sanguine response to the "longing proselytes" of Blithedale: "In their view, we were as poetical as Arcadians, besides being as practical as the hardest-fisted husbandman in Massachusetts. We did not, it is true, spend much time in piping to our sheep, or warbling our innocent loves to the sisterhood. But they gave us credit for imbuing the ordinary rustic occupations with a kind of religious poetry, insomuch that our very cow-yards and pigsties were as delightfully fragrant as a flower-garden."[7] When Zenobia tells Coverdale that she doubts he will stay at Blithedale Farm very long, he protests that he wants to stay long enough to allow this life teach to him how to write poetry that is "true, strong, natural, and sweet, as is the life which we are going to lead."[8]

While the pastoral setting of Hawthorne's *Blithedale Romance* is readily apparent, this romance clearly entertains the idea of some kind of actual transcendence occurring within the natural world. This romance, more than Hawthorne's earlier book-length works, provides a world in which Hawthorne can analyze the Transcendentalist purposes of those who attempt to live by natural laws rather than by the constructs of inherited human society. Recounting how he has come to disown the Blithedale community, Coverdale commends the noble aspirations that led to its founding:

> We had left the rusty iron framework of society behind us; we had broken through many hindrances that are powerful enough to keep most people on the weary tread-mill of the established system, even while they feel its irksomeness almost as intolerable as we did. . . . It was our purpose—a generous one, certainly, and absurd, no doubt, in full proportion with its generosity—to give up whatever we had heretofore attained, for the sake of showing mankind the example of a life governed by other than the false and cruel principles, on which human society has all along been based.[9]

Natural law, rather than unnatural human convention, was to be the code of the new community. Earlier, discussing domestic labor, Coverdale had delineated the "artificial life," or "the life of degenerated mortals," as something less natural than "the life of Paradise."[10] Coverdale's habit of thinking in starkly oppositional dichotomies about the relation between civilization and nature is challenged by the narrative as a whole, but at first his erroneous binary way of thinking appears to be correct—and it seems to characterize the community's thinking, not just Coverdale's. But such thinking—together with the harsh realities of a nature that is not a mere reflection of the human will—contributes to the failure of the Blithedale project.

In the opening scene of his narrative, Hawthorne's narrator-character Miles Coverdale most clearly identifies his own personal reasons for joining the Blithedalers and initially embracing their vision of reform. "[P]uffing out a final whiff of cigar-smoke," he remembers, "I quitted my cosey [sic] pair of bachelor-rooms—with a good fire burning in the grate, and a closet right at hand, where there was still a bottle or two in the champagne-basket, and a residuum of claret in a box,—quitted, I say, these comfortable quarters, and plunged into the heart of the pitiless snow-storm, in quest of a better life."[11] Immediately getting literally immersed in the elements of nature in a snow-storm, Coverdale creates a fitting picture of the human in nature. Reformation of the world according to nature is a noble goal that Coverdale initially appreciates. When Zenobia asks him why he has come to Blithedale Farm, Coverdale declares that his purpose in joining the Transcendentalists is to learn how to write poetry "that shall have the notes of wild birds twittering through it, or a strain like the wind-anthems in the woods, as the case may be."[12] Such a unity with nature that allows one to live a natural life from which may flow the most natural poetry possible is Coverdale's goal, and Blithedale Farm is the means to that end.

As in Hawthorne's earlier romances, the view of nature advanced here is inflected by scientific and religious conceptions of the world. Especially in the voices of Zenobia and Hollingsworth, we hear the suggestions of competing scientific ideas about human physicality and adaptation. Coverdale's reflections on the human-nature relationship typically focus more theoretically than scientifically on the way humans are affected by our environment, but he records the other views as well. When coming face to face with actual death at Blithedale, Coverdale turns to religious language to understand the human situation in the natural world—following not the lightly spiritual language of Zenobia but instead the heavier religious tones of Hollingsworth. Death imposes such absolute limits on human action within the natural world that even such an irresolute man as Coverdale must recognize that he is bound to such limitations by his status as a natural being. Hawthorne's intimations concerning natural adaptations and limitations in *Blithedale* emphasize the contingent status of human existence within the biosphere by raising the specter of death as a challenge to short-sighted views of the natural world that fail to account for the totality of human and nonhuman existence.

TESTING NATURAL CORRESPONDENCES

In *Blithedale*, the Transcendentalist community takes on the project of reforming the world by living according to natural laws informed by spiritual connections between humans and nature. As Coverdale explains, the project at Blithedale Farm was a kind of spiritual undertaking: "As the basis of our institution, we purposed to offer up the earnest toil of our bodies, as a prayer no less than an effort for the advancement of our race."[13] At first, the Blithedalers throw themselves enthusiastically into this combined exercise of body, mind, and soul. In his most direct comment on nature's lessons, Coverdale remarks about the change of lifestyle required to be able to work in the fields. As he recovers from an illness contracted through his lack of readiness for the demands of laboring in the soil and rejoins his fellow Blithedalers who are seeking an "enlightened culture of the soil," Coverdale exclaims: "In my new enthusiasm, man looked strong and stately,—and woman, oh how beautiful!—and the earth a green garden, blossoming with many-colored delights! Thus Nature, whose laws I had broken in various artificial ways, comported herself to me as a strict but loving mother, who uses the rod upon her little boy for his naughtiness, and then gives him a smile, a kiss, and some pretty playthings to console the urchin for her severity."[14] Nature's laws must be respected, and humans have a place within the natural world that they must recognize rather than arrogantly assuming a position of superiority.

Transcendentalists generally and Emerson in particular adopted a correspondence theory of nature, the idea that outward and inward forms—like nature and human nature—are parallel structures. For Emerson, mind, matter, and spirit correspond fully: "Every natural fact is a symbol of some spiritual fact. Every appearance in nature corresponds to some state of the mind."[15] The correspondence theory of nature, as espoused by American Transcendentalists, is expressed most poetically in the words of Christopher Pearse Cranch's poem "Correspondences":

All things in nature are beautiful types to the soul that can read them;
Nothing exists upon earth, but for unspeakable ends,
Every object that speaks to the senses was meant for the spirit;
Nature is but a scroll; God's handwriting thereon.
. . .
Now with infinite pains we here and there spell out a letter,

> Here and there will the sense feebly shine through the dark.
> When we perceive the light that breaks through the visible symbol,
> What exultation is ours! *We* the discovery have made!
> Yet is the meaning the same as when Adam lived sinless in Eden,
> Only long hidden it slept, and now again is revealed.[16]

For the most part, Hawthorne seems to agree with the Transcendentalists that attending to nature should effect a reformation of the world by bringing it back to its natural patterns. For Hawthorne as for the Transcendentalists, nature and humanity, nature and spirit, tend to correspond. However, the outcomes of *Blithedale* suggests that correspondence by itself does not fully account for the reality of nature. While Hawthorne comes close espousing a correspondence theory of nature, death undermines the sufficiency of such a view to fully account for the world in which we find ourselves. In *Blithedale*, Hawthorne illustrates the limits of this perspective in resolving the dilemmas that rise even for humans who act according to nature.

The Transcendentalists at Blithedale expected that nature itself would provide the space needed to test theories of correspondence. As David Van Leer has noted, the idea of the universe as an "infinite space" appears in the writing of both Hawthorne and Emerson. Van Leer suggests that this term may be "specifically Transcendental," and it is certainly the case that Romantic and Transcendentalist writers in America and abroad do show a liking for the term. The philosopher John Locke and others also use the term.[17] In fact, a quick survey of the philosophical and literary magazines of the time show that the idea of "infinite space" was current in nineteenth-century intellectual circles both within and outside of America. German writers such as Immanuel Kant and English writers like Samuel Taylor Coleridge—both highly influential on the American Transcendentalists—discuss "infinite space" in relation to transcendence (Kant in *The Critique of Pure Reason*)[18] and as a reality that exists beyond the realm of human perception itself (Coleridge in *Biographia Literaria*).[19] Although these ideas of "infinite space" as a modern philosophic field of sorts may have influenced both Emerson and Hawthorne, they both draw on the term primarily as a descriptor of the universe as a vast space in which humans find themselves and in which they must search for human (or any) significance within a larger reality.

In *Blithedale*, Coverdale meditates on "infinite space" in his hermitage and again when he is about to leave the Transcendentalist community and return to the city. From his treetop perch, which he alternately calls his "hermitage" and his "observatory," Coverdale looks out "not for starry investigations, but for those sublunary matters in which lay a lore as infinite as that of the planets."[20] Thus, the local scene serves as a microcosm of the universe. As he prepares to leave Blithedale, Coverdale reflects further on the position of humans in the universe, marking out his skepticism of common Transcendentalist views of this topic:

> It was impossible, situated as we were, not to imbibe the idea that everything in nature and human existence was fluid, or fast becoming so; that the crust of the Earth in many places was broken, and its whole surface portentously upheaving; that it was a day of crisis, and that we ourselves were in the critical vortex. Our great globe floated in the atmosphere of infinite space like an unsubstantial bubble. No sagacious man will long retain his sagacity, if he live exclusively among reformers and progressive people, without periodically returning into the settled system of things, to correct himself by a new observation from that old stand-point.[21]

The "infinite space" seems about to engulf Coverdale, but he suspects that this engulfment is merely a trick of the mind rather than reality. Ironically, it is while he is in a community surrounded by nature that Coverdale feels he must get away so that he can grasp reality again. Perhaps like the philosophies of Kant and Coleridge—both of whom had a great influence on the Transcendentalists—the Transcendentalist community seemed unreal to Coverdale. Even though he may have understood the "infinite space" in which humans find themselves in the universe, Coverdale's pensive desire to establish an "original relation" to that world is not matched with actions and passions that matched that desire. The very idea of "infinite space," it may be, is not well suited to action; its vastness is too overwhelming. The universe must be considered in relation to something, and Emerson advocated humanity as the center of the relationship. Hawthorne, however, treats humanity—primarily in the person of Coverdale—as too fickle and too short-sighted to be a reliable source for ascertaining the reality of nature and being.

Despite initial enchantment with Transcendentalist ideals, Coverdale ultimately finds this community based on Transcendentalism lacking. His aghast exclamations upon witnessing Westervelt's coldness toward Zenobia expresses an awareness of the limits of nature in guiding humans aright. "Nature thrusts some of us into the world miserably incomplete on the emotional side, with hardly any sensibilities except what pertain to us as animals," Coverdale exclaims. "No passion, save of the senses; no holy tenderness, nor the delicacy that results from this."[22] Zenobia deserves so much more than a cold machine like Westervelt, and Coverdale seems to hope he will fit the bill. Despite Coverdale's recognition of Westervelt's shortcomings, his hope that he himself can displace Westervelt in Zenobia's life becomes myopic as he focuses on himself rather than remembering the reasons he has been aghast at Westervelt's apparent indifference to what Coverdale first (and most accurately) sees as Zenobia's natural right of independence from the demands of a domineering man. Coverdale, like the materialist Westervelt, overlooks any natural rights she may have as he begins to fancy Zenobia for himself.

Coverdale and his companions at Blithedale Farm move from confidence in their ability to see the correspondences between nature and humans to an increasing awareness that the better life is not to be had for a song. It takes hard work. While Emerson depicts a farm as a beautiful and moral thing, Hawthorne emphasizes that it is also an external reality in which and with which the farmer must work. In *Nature*, Emerson claims that "every natural process is a version of a moral sentence. The moral law lies at the centre of nature and radiates to the circumference. It is the pith and marrow of every substance, every relation, and every process. All things with which we deal, preach to us. What is a farm but a mute gospel?"[23] Blithedale Farm, however, proves to be not only "mute" but it also ultimately lacks the "good news" necessary to any gospel. It is a place of disappointment and death that lacks both resurrection and redemption, at least in the scope of Coverdale's narrative.

Coverdale's problematic, unreliable voice partially obscures Hawthorne's evaluation of Transcendentalist idealism in *Blithedale*, but it acutely illustrates the difficulty of living an idealist life. Human subjectivity quickly skews the pursuit of idealism in any form. Like Poe's unreliable narrators, Coverdale continually defends his actions to readers with the dubious object of persuading us to take his side. The harder he tries, however, the more suspicious his readers often grow. When Zenobia smiles and shuts her curtain upon realizing that Coverdale is watching her through the window, for example, he hastily informs the reader that Zenobia should have recognized his highly artistic and therefore noble reasons for observing her. Of all people, Coverdale exclaims, she ought to have appreciated his "endeavor—by generous sympathies, by delicate intuitions, by taking note of things too slight for record, and by bringing my human spirit into manifold accordance with the companions whom God assigned me—to learn the secret which was hidden even from themselves."[24]

The project at Blithedale, Coverdale avers, represents in the final analysis little more than an "exploded scheme for beginning the life of Paradise anew."[25] Before her death, Zenobia tells Coverdale that she too has lost faith in the Transcendentalist community: "Of all varieties of mock-life, we have surely blundered into the very emptiest mockery in our effort to establish the one true system. I have done with it; and Blithedale must find another. . . It was, indeed, a foolish dream! Yet it gave us some pleasant summer days, and bright hopes, while they lasted."[26] In the preface of *The Blithedale Romance*, Hawthorne similarly calls his experience at Brook Farm "certainly the most romantic episode of [my] own life,—essentially a daydream, and yet a fact,—and thus offering an available foothold between fiction and reality."[27] That *The Blithedale Romance* resembles an "episode" of Hawthorne's own life marks its difference from his two previous romances. In the introductory preface of his earlier romance *The Scarlet Letter*, Hawthorne had also recalled his time in Transcendentalist communities first at the Brook Farm commune and then in the pastoral town of Concord where he had daily interactions with other Transcendentalists. His recollection, he writes, occurs "[a]fter my fellowship of toil and impracticable schemes with the dreamy brethren of Brook Farm; after living for three years within the subtile [*sic*] influence of an intellect like Emerson's; after those wild, free days on the Assabeth, indulging fantastic speculations, beside our fire of fallen boughs, with Ellery Channing; after talking with Thoreau about pine-trees and Indian relics, in his hermitage at Walden."[28] Although this passage seems to depreciate the Transcendentalists, indicating as it does Hawthorne's conviction that the Transcendentalists were dreamers full of "impracticable schemes," Hawthorne is himself a dreamer. And he adopts the Transcendentalist love of the natural environment even while critiquing their implicit claims of unadulterated spiritual perspicacity in tune with the natural world.

UTOPIAN DREAMS AND THEORIES OF PHYSICAL ADAPTATION

In *The Blithedale Romance*, Coverdale gives us a utopian Transcendentalist community in which "the many tongues of Nature whispered mysteries, and seemed to ask only a little stronger puff of wind to speak out the solution of its riddle."[29] In this place, nature can effect change and does indeed accomplish some measure of change. Soon after arriving at Blithedale, Coverdale declares that they have come to Blithedale to live as if in Paradise. Pointing out the snowdrift outside the window, however, Zenobia says, "We shall find some difficulty in adopting the paradisiacal system, for at least a month to come. . . . As for the garb of Eden,' added she, shivering playfully, 'I shall not assume it till after May-day!'"[30] This, of course, sets Coverdale's voyeuristic blood astir, and he imagines her in the place of Eve appearing naked before Adam. When the residents of the farm are choosing a name, various names are proposed, including "Sunny Glimpse," "The Oasis," "Sahara," and "Utopia." This latter name is suggested by Coverdale but "was unanimously scouted down, and the proposer very harshly maltreated, as if he had intended a latent satire."[31] Yet clearly, *The Blithedale Romance* does serve as a satire of a utopian pastoral society attempting to live in harmony with each other and their natural environment.

At first, Coverdale declares, there were indeed moments when he would "discern a richer picturesqueness in the visible scene of earth and sky," times when he could observe "an unwonted aspect, on the face of Nature, as if she had been taken by surprise and seen at unawares, with no opportunity to put off her real look, and assume the mask with which she mysteriously hides herself from mortals."[32] The frequent observations of a life close to nature produce at least moments when nature reveals itself. But almost as soon as they arrive on the farm, Coverdale realizes that their idealism will be put to the test. Silas Foster, the only experienced farmer in residence, tells them they must get pigs at the market to sustain their project. Coverdale, faced with the demands of nature, responds in disbelief: "Pigs! Good heavens, had we come out from among the swinish multitude, for this?"[33] When Silas adds that they must get a head start on the vegetables for the market and that it would take three "city folks" to do the work of "one common field-hand," the relation of humans to the natural world takes on a new meaning.

The Blithedalers' noble enterprise of leaving human constructs behind becomes further complicated when Silas tells them they will have "to compete with the market-gardeners round Boston" to make their living. Coverdale reflects, "It struck me as rather odd, that one of the first questions raised, after our separation from the greedy, struggling, self-seeking world, should relate to the possibility of getting the advantage over the outside barbarians in their own field of labor. But, to own the truth, I very soon became sensible that, as regarded society as [sic] large, we stood in a position of new hostility, rather than new brotherhood."[34] A farm seems little better than the city after all, despite their closeness to nature away from the artificial constraints of city life. After the initial shock of the real jutting up against the ideal, however, the ominous foreshadowings of the dissolution of the Blithedale project give way again at least awhile to the spirit of optimism in which the project was begun.

Hawthorne's actual experience as a member of this Transcendentalist community makes his pastoral not simply an imaginative work with illusory literary coloring but a commentary on humans' relationship with the rest of the natural world in light of observations and living experiments that have actually been conducted. As Hawthorne admits in the preface, this story represents "a faint and not very faithful shadowing of BROOK FARM, in Roxbury, which (now a little more than ten years ago) was occupied and cultivated by a company of socialists."[35] Brook Farm and its fictionalized counterpart Blithedale were not the only examples of social experimentation with a more natural life than that of industrializing society at large. Religious groups such as the celibate Shaker villagers, the communitarian Harmonists, the pietistic Amana Colonists, and the free-love Christian Communists of Oneida all created self-sustaining communities closely connected with nature and the means of production. Less religious communities based upon self-sustaining economies in tune with the natural environment were also formed—the economic reformers of New Harmony, Indiana, the Abolitionist reformers of Nashoba, Tennessee, and the shareholding Fourierists proposing to live in immense phalansteries surrounded by extensive grounds and gardens. The Transcendentalists too founded communities beginning with a small group that settled briefly on a short-lived experimental farm they called Fruitlands before Brook Farm was established in 1841, a decade before Hawthorne sat down to write *Blithedale*. As different as these various communities were, they all shared an aversion for what Coverdale in *The Blithedale Romance* calls "the greedy, struggling, self-seeking world" of an urbanizing, industrializing nation.[36]

In *Blithedale*, Hawthorne offers several explicit references to nineteenth-century pastoral models of self-sustaining communities close to nature. This list includes buildings, administrative groups, jobs, and economic systems such as the Pantisocracy first proposed for life in the New World by famous British poets Samuel Taylor Coleridge and Robert Southey. In an 1851 entry in his American notebooks, Hawthorne indicated his reading of Pantisocracy as a partial inspiration for the story that would show up in *The Blithedale Romance* the following year: "Coleridge's 'Pantisocracy'—in connection with the subject of communities."[37] At the very end of the eighteenth century, Coleridge and his fellow poet Robert Southey planned to begin a kind of utopian community in America. In his study of "romantic Indians," Tim Fulford outlines Coleridge's project thus: "Pantisocracy, as Coleridge named it, would be a realization of the just society and natural life about which the philosophers William Godwin and Jean Jacques Rousseau had written. Dedicated to agriculture and literature, the Pantisocrats would live in equality, peace, and harmony, like the Indians among whom they would settle (or, at least, like the Indians portrayed by Rousseau and Raynal)."[38]

In *Blithedale*, Native Americans show up with characters from old world literature in a masque that occurs in the midst of the woods. But Blithedale Farm is most like Coleridge's projected Pantisocracy by being "dedicated to agriculture and literature." Hawthorne emphasizes the effect of literature on the aspirations of the natural community which spends part of its time working the soil and another part of its time engaged in intellectual pursuits in the attempt to merge the two. While he is sick, Coverdale "read interminably in Mr. Emerson's Essays, 'The Dial,' Carlyle's works, George Sand's romances (lent me by Zenobia), and other books which one or another of the brethren or sisterhood had brought with them."[39] As the literary organ of the larger Transcendentalist intelligentsia, *The Dial* was edited by Fuller, Emerson, and George Ripley. Fuller and Emerson only visited Brook Farm, but George Ripley along with his wife Sophia were the chief masterminds of that Transcendentalist project.

Hawthorne also mentions the Phalanstery, or Phalanx, a building design planned by the French scientist-philosopher Jean-Baptiste Joseph Fourier and brought to America by political philosopher Albert Brisbane. The term "Association" was sometimes used for any of these groups, but is especially associated with the Phalansteries and (in Hawthorne's book) with the Transcendentalists at Brook Farm. But the Transcendentalists are more often referred to as the community, which was shaped something like Shaker villages or Amana colonies. The Transcendentalists often started their communities in large old farmhouses. Brook Farm—and its fictional counterpart Blithedale—transitioned from a Transcendentalist community to a Fourierist one but without ever building the projected Phalanstery.

Another important model of a self-sustaining community that was highly influential in England was the cottage industry, a cozy system of localized production and distribution of goods. According to Nigel Goose, the number of cottage industries increased dramatically between the years 1840 and 1850; in towns like Bedfordshire some of these industries increased by more than six times the original amount.[40] American readers like Hawthorne were familiar with the concept of the cottage economy outlined by William Cobbett's 1822 book *Cottage Economy*. Describing the good life that he thinks within reach of the vast majority, Cobbett reminds us that *economy* "means, *management,* and nothing more," but that the term "is generally applied to the affairs of a house and family, where affairs are an object of the greatest importance, whether as relating to individuals or to a nation." Further, he adds, "for a family to be happy, they must be well supplied with *food* and *raiment*. To live well, to enjoy all things that make life pleasant, is the right of every man who constantly uses his strength judiciously and lawfully."[41] And he sets out to give instruction on how to provide for oneself and one's family by means of a cottage economy that brings the production of goods back to one's visible surroundings—to one's home environment. Such a cottage economy, he insists is good for the individuals engaged in it as well as for the nation whose citizens can depend upon a healthy economy not subject to the vicissitudes of the more unsettled capitalist economy of a developing American society.

Hawthorne's reading of Cobbett's book likely influenced his conception of Blithedale Farm as a place where, as Coverdale says, "The bond of our Community was such, that the members had the privilege of building cottages for their own residence within our precincts, thus laying a hearth-stone and fencing in a home private and peculiar to all desirable extent, while yet the inhabitants should continue to share the advantages of an associated life."[42] The ideal is to create a cottage community with shared duties and pleasures that still allowed space for individual development and culture. Coverdale is eager to move out of the farmhouse they are sharing at the moment, telling Hollingsworth, "I do long for the cottages to be built, that the creeping plants may begin to run over them, and the moss to gather on the walls, and the trees—which we will set out—to cover them with a breadth of shadow."[43] He is ready for the newness to wear off, ready to settle into a comfortable life at Blithedale at peace with nature and with like-minded neighbors ready to participate in something like a cottage economy.

In the eco-agrarian prophet Wendell Berry we have something like a contemporary advocate of cottage industries. "A person who undertakes to grow a garden at home, by practices that will preserve and not exploit the economy of the soil, has set his mind decisively against what is wrong with us," Berry declares. "He is making vital contact with the soil and the weather on which his life depends."[44] Coverdale finds the effect of such a relation with the natural world liberating at first. And he entertains the idea that human closeness to nature may have good effects not only on the humans but also on the natural world. He feels himself part of an "enlightened culture of the soil" when he walks outside after recovering from an illness to witness the other members of the community cheerfully engaged in various agricultural tasks around the farm.[45] At such a moment, he finds it easy to believe that their more natural arrangement with the physical earth "had begun to produce an effect upon the material world and its climate."[46] Coverdale's intuitions here are borne out by our contemporary experience, now that ecological studies have exposed the deep interconnections between human and nonhuman nature.

The Blithedalers are excited to live close to nature in the expectation that it will reveal natural patterns for humans to adopt and follow. But their language strongly suggests that they are also curious whether the natural world might reform their human bodies into more healthy shapes than city life has done. And so they engage with theories of physicality and adaptation. Shortly before he realizes that Hollingsworth has other designs for the community, Coverdale exults that future generations "will have a great public hall, in which your portrait, and mine, and twenty other faces that are living now, shall be hung up; and as for me, I will be painted in my shirtsleeves, and with the sleeves rolled up, to show my muscular development. What stories will be rife among them about our mighty strength . . . though our posterity will really be far stronger than ourselves, after several generations of a simple, natural, and active life."[47] Here in the country away from the stifling buildings and stale air, tinged perhaps with whiffs of industrial smoke, humans could hope to develop naturally once again by working with nature. Coverdale seems unable to differentiate between more promising facets of scientific discovery and pseudoscientific theories prevalent in nineteenth-century America, entertaining notions of potential benefits without committing strongly to any scientific theory. Hawthorne registers a more critical attitude in Hollingsworth's retort: "You seem . . . to be trying [to see] how much nonsense you can pour out in a breath."[48]

By predicting that their "posterity will really be far stronger," Coverdale alludes to nineteenth-century scientific theories about environmental influences on the body. In an appraisal of Charles Lyell's 1832 book on geology printed in one of the multiple volumes of *The Museum of Foreign Literature and Science* that Hawthorne checked out of the Salem Athenaeum in 1836, the reviewer pauses to rail against "the most stupid and ridiculous" Lamarckian theory of evolutionary change.[49] The French naturalist Jean-Baptiste Lamarck was known for his advancement of the theory of acquired characteristics—inherited traits acquired by the parent and passed on to the child born after the acquisition of said trait—as an evolutionary trait. Although Charles Darwin would not introduce his theory of natural selection as the evolutionary mechanism whereby biological lifeforms are shaped until several decades after Lyell's book was published, the term "transmutation" was used to refer to principles of essential change in life forms during this period. The reviewer of Lyell's work observes that mummified dogs, cats, and bulls from the ancient Egyptian period "were in every respect conformable to the species of those different animals now living, although they have been carried by man to every climate, and force to adapt themselves to circumstances very different from those by which they were surrounded in Egypt thirty centuries ago. These are the facts that seem decisive against the visions of Lamarck, and those who, like him, have been advocates for the accidental transmutation of every species of animal from its original."[50] He goes on to praise Lyell for his opposition to Lamarck's ideas at the time: "Mr. Lyell mentions several interesting facts," he declares, "which show that mere modifications in the individual, do not transmute the whole species."[51] Hawthorne's access to the review of Lyell's work and other reviews and articles like it gave him the mix of scientific terminology that is sprinkled throughout *Blithedale*. And while *evolution* was not yet a term in vogue, evolutionary ideas are certainly being discussed in Hawthorne's reading materials. The fact that these terms also show up in his writing indicate Hawthorne's attention to the idea of biological change even though he does not make any direct statements about it. Whether or not biological changes in human bodies could be affected by one's interaction with the environment is clearly indicated in muscular development, as Coverdale notes above. Permanent biological changes in a species—in the Blithedalers' human descendants—is something Coverdale predicts (to the derision of Hollingsworth) but has not yet observed.

For Hollingsworth, adaptation is a response to one's bodily activity within the natural order. The old farmer Silas Foster, Hollingsworth tells Coverdale, is what he will become if he continues working as a farmer: "[he] is your prototype, with his palm of sole-leather, and his joints of rusty iron . . . and his brain of . . . Savoy cabbage."[52] As the prototype of the "farmer," Silas Foster is an example of what Coverdale could become—part animal, part mechanism, part vegetable. He mentions no likelihood of becoming an artist, a poet, as Coverdale is hoping. But Hollingsworth is being facetious, scoffing Fourierist ideas, with his reference to the cabbage—a sign of *concord* in Fourier's scheme of living in harmony with the universe as well as a reminder of Fourier's theory of the consciousness of plants.[53] Hollingsworth is also mocking the idea of transmutation, as is shown by his next comment about Coverdale's coming physical alterations: "Your physical man will be transmuted into salt beef and fried pork, at the rate, I should imagine, of a pound and a half a day; that being about the average which we find necessary in the kitchen."[54] Although it is highly unlikely that Hollingsworth really expects Coverdale's physical form to take the shape of what he is eating, he poses cutting-edge scientific theories as miracles of sorts in order to persuade Coverdale to sign on to his brand-new method of reforming prisoners. Using new, little-tested theories of nature as metaphors for his own aims, Hollingsworth invites Coverdale to join him in taking the "great black ugliness of sin . . . out of a thousand human hearts . . . [and] spend our lives in an experiment of transmuting it into virtue!"[55] Hollingsworth is convinced that his experimental method of criminal reform will be his great contribution to society. Using scientific terms of the day to make an argument about his supposedly noble aims, Hollingsworth does not fail to impress, but Coverdale does not adopt his theory in the end. Hollingsworth's implantation of his own vision keeps him from learning from nature as well—he desires a reformatory more than he desires to learn from nature.

Zenobia also applies theories of adaptation to the world around them, suggesting that the gender roles prescribed by social custom may be upset in the end. At Blithedale, situated as they are beyond the strictures of society, gender roles might be eliminated or at least made more natural. In her study of "the savage in the house," Lydia Fisher characterizes Zenobia as a specimen of "unprocessed womanhood, released from the conventions of marital ownership and domestic motherhood."[56] While Zenobia initially claims to be content with the customary "feminine occupations," she clarifies that she is only satisfied with such an arrangement "for the present. By and by, perhaps," she adds, "when our individual adaptations begin to develop themselves, it may be that some of us, who wear the petticoat, will go afield, and leave the weaker brethren to take our places in the kitchen."[57] Her suggestion that their newfound freedom from social customs will result in as yet unseen "adaptations" could be taken as a comment about developing one's talents. Given Hawthorne's attention to environmental effects, however, along with his use of a word prevalent in biological theories of the time, he is likely referring to physical development—at the very least, the development of muscles that would allow stronger woman to take the place of "weaker brethren" who could stay inside.

Zenobia is also a woman of natural beauty and presence. Fisher calls Zenobia "an outlier of appealing, savage nobility," at first preferred by Coverdale as a figure of "healthy, unfettered, and organic womanhood."[58] While Coverdale finds her erotic and sexually appealing, he also finds her power of personhood too much for his ultimately mild-mannered ways. But Priscilla has long been fascinating as well, despite her apparent frailty when she is first introduced. Coverdale and Zenobia both describe her in natural metaphors that are sometimes organic enough to conjure images of literal growth and physical development. "As I first saw her," Coverdale notes, "she had reminded me of plants that one sometimes observes doing their best to vegetate among the bricks of an enclosed court, where there is scanty soil, and never any sunshine. At present, although with no approach to bloom, there were indications that the girl had human blood in her veins."[59] The blood in her veins gives her a different kind of vitality than the plants even though her physical frailty makes her sometimes seem more spirit than animal. "She is one of those delicate, nervous young creatures, not uncommon in New England," Westervelt tells Coverdale, "and whom I suppose to have become what we find them by the gradual refining away of the physical system among your women. Some philosophers choose to glorify this habit of body by terming it spiritual; but, in my opinion, it is rather the effect of unwholesome food, bad air, lack of out-door exercise, and neglect of bathing . . . all resulting in a kind of hereditary dyspepsia."[60] For a cynical materialist like Westervelt, Priscilla's wispiness is a sign of poor health, perhaps a sign of bad blood she has inherited, rather than a sign of an enhanced spiritual sensitivity.

The wispiness of Priscilla, much like her father Old Moodie in whom "the throb of the soul's life [was] too faint" is remedied in part by her time in nature.[61] Set free at Blithedale Farm, she regains her health and grows more naturally than she had in her heretofore cooped-up life: "So unformed, vague, and without substance, as she had come to us, it seemed as if we could see Nature shaping out a woman before our very eyes, and yet had only a more reverential sense of the mystery of a woman's soul and frame. Yesterday, her cheek was pale,—to-day, it had a bloom."[62] Priscilla is in earnest without becoming driven like Hollingsworth. In this sense, she benefits most from being in nature despite being less intellectual than her friends. The longer she is outdoors in nature, the healthier and the more animal-like Priscilla becomes. Botanical figures of speech turn into zoological ones. When Coverdale finds her out with Zenobia one May morning, he watches her running about and remarks to Zenobia, "She is the very picture of the New England spring; subdued in tint, and rather cool, but with a capacity of sunshine, and bringing us a few Alpine blossoms. . . . The best type of her is one of those anemones." Zenobia remarks on Priscilla's improved health but notes her "wildness" as well as the animation of her once-frail physique. "Why, as we strolled the woods together," exclaims Zenobia, "I could hardly keep her from scrambling up the trees, like a squirrel. She has never before known what it is to live in the free air, and so it intoxicates her." She pronounces it almost ludicrous "to see a creature so happy—especially a feminine creature."[63] We are reminded again of the gendered world of human society and of Zenobia's hope that at least some of that gendering can be extinguished by a life lived in rhythm with nature.

Attuned to at least some of the recent scientific innovations in biological theory, Coverdale is well situated at Blithedale to test theories of bodily development—but only if he continues long enough to see change over time. Mesmerism, which he describes as the new science, offers a shortcut of sorts, having an immediate impact on the human body. But the effect is not permanent. Another "new science" Coverdale uses to make sense of the varying shapes of the human body is the pseudoscience of phrenology. In keeping with nineteenth-century theories about the relationship between the size and shape of the forehead as a measure of the size and capacity of the brain, Coverdale points out numerous phrenological details as he observes the nature of people around him. He remarks, for example, that many of the women who attend the public exhibitions of mesmerism are "stern in feature, with marked foreheads, and a very definite line of eyebrow; a type of womanhood in which a bold intellectual development seems to be keeping pace with the progressive delicacy of the physical constitution."[64] Earlier, while waiting for Old Moodie at a bar in the city, Coverdale—ever the people-watcher—notices a young man with "a good forehead, with a particularly large development just above the eyebrow; fine intellectual gifts, no doubt, which he had educated to this profitable end" of running a good business as a barkeeper.[65] His comments about phrenology, today considered a pseudoscience like mesmerism, illustrate the exploratory attitude of his quasi-scientific comments. Like the other characters at Blithedale, however, Coverdale uses scientific comments that are often more facetious than serious. It is as if such observations may or may not offer insights into the human condition, but Coverdale is too lazy or incompetent to put his ideas to the test long enough to discover their degree of veracity.

DEATH AND THE LIMITS OF IDEALISM

The shocking scene of Zenobia's death in nature—a classic scene of death by water—provides the most striking depiction of death in Hawthorne's work. The scene of the catastrophe elicits contradictory responses in the edgy Coverdale and effectively silences Hollingsworth who only grunts a few responses in the entire remainder of the romance. Coverdale, on the other hand, becomes excessively loquacious in the scenes that follow, despite his initial comment that to describe Zenobia's death well would be "a sin and shame" since it is "the ugliest" death imaginable. But he gives a description nonetheless, emphasizing the natural imagery surrounding her death—her bodily reaction to water and death. "Her wet garments swathed limbs of terrible inflexibility. She was the marble image of a death-agony. Her arms had grown rigid in the act of struggling, and were bent before her with clenched hands; her knees, too, were bent, and—thank God for it!—in the attitude of prayer."[66] But then he continues his incantation of terror, "Ah, that rigidity! It is impossible to bear the terror of it. It seemed . . . as if her body must keep the same position in the coffin, and that her skeleton would keep it in the grave; and that when Zenobia rose at the day of judgment, it would be in just the same attitude as now!"[67] In his reflection on the grotesque scene of Zenobia's death, Coverdale draws attention to the intrusion of death in this seemingly idyllic scene.

When Zenobia's nature shuts down—when she becomes intermixed with the watery elements of nature in the drowning incident—Coverdale tells Westervelt that Zenobia committed suicide because of a broken heart. Westervelt shakes his head and scoffs, "her heart had a manifold adaptation; her constitution an infinite buoyancy, which . . . would have borne her upward triumphantly for twenty years to come."[68] If Westervelt is right, the secrets of Zenobia's life that Coverdale is constantly seeking to discover have given her heart extra strength. However, Westervelt almost immediately calls her heart a "troublesome organ," contradicting his declaration of its "manifold adaptation." Maybe she has physical heart problems, broken down by the heavy strains she faced. Maybe she has a physically strong heart, reconstituted in response to the hardships she faced. Coverdale also admits that Zenobia had a "diversified capacity" in her nature that was lost when she died—when her body quit working. Whatever the case, Coverdale decides in the end that the woman's "sphere" was, in Zenobia's case, "narrower than her development required."[69]

After her death and burial, Coverdale stands pensively at the mound marking Zenobia's grave to reflect: "The grass grew all the better, on that little parallelogram of pasture-land, for the decay of the beautiful woman who slept beneath. How Nature seems to love us! And how readily, nevertheless, without a sigh or complaint, she converts us to a meaner purpose, when her highest one—that of a conscious intellectual life and sensibility—has been untimely balked! While Zenobia lived," Coverdale adds, "Nature was proud of her, and directed all eyes upon that radiant presence, as her fairest handiwork. Zenobia perished . . . [Nature] adopts the calamity at once into her system, and is just as well pleased, for aught we can see, with the tuft of ranker vegetation that grew out of Zenobia's heart, as with all the beauty which has bequeathed us no earthly representative except in this crop of weeds."[70] In this passage, we see the human body adapting to life and death, to possibility and disintegration, to rich development as a human and to transformation into fertilizer for the soil in which it is buried. The human body is a member of the natural world regardless of how it is reconstituted. In the face of such awfully materialist imagery, Coverdale can only shudder and look for something that seems more real than the incomprehensibility of absolute dissolution of her personhood. Even here in a beautiful world where a community gathered to work with the grain of nature, the ugliness of death has forced the members of the community to face one of the hard realities of nature as well as her more pleasant ones.

Before being faced with the awful reality of Zenobia's corpse, Coverdale had been able to idealize death. Speaking of death in poetic tones, he had mused blithely:

> Would it not be well, even before we have absolute need of it, to fix upon a spot for a cemetery? Let us choose the rudest, roughest, most uncultivable spot, for Death's garden-ground; and Death shall teach us to beautify it, grave by grave. By our sweet, calm way of dying, and the airy elegance out of which we will shape our funeral rites, and the cheerful allegories which we will model into tombstones, the final scene shall lose its terrors; so that hereafter it may be happiness to live, and bliss to die. None of us must die young. Yet, should Providence ordain it so, the event shall not be sorrowful, but affect us with a tender, delicious, only half-melancholy, and almost smiling pathos![71]

To Coverdale's suggestion that death itself can be smoothed over into a beautiful part of the idealized pastoral life of bliss without heartache, love without sorrow, pleasantries without pains, Hollingsworth retorts, "That is to say . . . you will die like a Heathen, as you certainly live like one."[72] But Zenobia's actual death is far from a "sweet, calm way of dying," and there are no "cheerful allegories" that crown death with "a tender, delicious, only half-melancholy, and almost smiling pathos!" Nobody is smiling. Death is not delicious. The "final scene" had all "its terrors" for Coverdale as he helped fish her body from the water. Coverdale's dream of a beautiful death is mere fantasy.

By juxtaposing pleasant pastoral scenes with the awful image of Zenobia's death, Hawthorne undercuts the Transcendentalist idealism of the community with a note of grim realism. In a study of the early reception of Hawthorne's works, Edwin Cady finds Hawthorne's work a touchstone in early critical debates between idealists and realists who studied Hawthorne's works with attention to "the still current problem of the nature of reality" and to the "central" question of "the literary or the philosophical battles over ideality."[73]

At Blithedale Farm, Transcendentalist illusions are no longer possible when faced with Zenobia's awful death. Like Hawthorne's friend Margaret Fuller, Zenobia believed that natural laws were different than the assumptions of the patriarchal structure of nineteenth-century American society and that attention to these natural laws would lead to greater freedom and opportunity for women. But her death in nature cuts short her experiment—her attempt to find out if her hypothesis about women's development is correct. As in his earlier American romances, Hawthorne adopts the theme of death in a pastoral setting, or *Et in Arcadia Ego*, a phrase made familiar by Renaissance painter Nicolas Poussin, whose painting was famous in the nineteenth century and whose paintings by that name were well known to the eighteenth- and nineteenth-century literati. (See figure 5.2.)

Art historian Erwin Panofsky has traced the changing meanings associated with *Et in Arcadia Ego*, pointing out that the difference of meaning suggested by Poussin's final painting of that name and earlier such paintings. While "the modern reader" of the mid-twentieth century had interpreted the words to mean something like "I, too, was born, or lived, with the shepherds in Arcady," as suggested by the later painting, earlier paintings suggest that "death is even in Arcadia."[74] This is especially apparent if Poussin's painting is compared to the painting upon which he is thought to have based his first

Figure 5.2 Et in Arcadia Ego by Nicolas Poussin, 1637. Public Domain.

work, another painting with the same title by Giovanni Francesco Barbieri, better known as Guercino. (See figure 5.3.)

In Guercino's painting, the famous death's head *memento mori* reminder of death places the emphasis even more strongly on death as an active part of even the most idealized pastoral life. Arianne Baggerman and Rudolf Dekker similarly place Poussin's *Et in Arcadia Ego* in contrast with the message it gave when placed on Rousseau's tomb. As Baggerman and Rudolf put it, Rousseau's emphasis on a lost youth is a new treatment of Arcadia and reflects his sense of being "as uprooted as Adam after the Fall, and while writing his memoirs he became homesick for the lost paradise of his youth." Such treatment of Arcadian and Edenic legends as restoration to youth referred to them as "an ideal state of nature that had been lost to them as adults."[75] Coverdale invokes Arcadia to color his picture of pastoral life that is (alas!) past. But Coverdale also invokes Arcadia to emphasize the unescapable reality of death's entrance even into a pastoral landscape. Tony Tanner notices the same subtext in *Blithedale*, noting that the "green mound"

Figure 5.3 Et in Arcadia Ego by Guercino (Giovanni Francesco Barbieri), 1618. Public Domain.

suggests a grave: "And it is this and all that it implies—call it mortality, call it mutability—which Coverdale has to face, and his text, if it can, absorb. ET IN ARCADIA EGO."[76]

Hawthorne's difference from Emersonian Transcencentalism becomes apparent when studied against Emerson's proclamation of the incontrovertible power of the spirit over the material world: "As fast as you conform your life to the pure idea in your mind, that will unfold its great proportions. A correspondent revolution in things will attend the influx of the spirit. So fast will disagreeable appearances, swine, spiders, snakes, pests, mad-houses, prisons, enemies, vanish; they are temporary and shall be no more seen."[77] In *The Scarlet Letter*, Hawthorne rejects this scheme of mind and spirit over matter by planting a prison as the central focus of the first scene of a new world Utopia. In *The House of the Seven Gables*, he indulges Emerson's ideas about the erasure of "disagreeable appearances" by having Phoebe drive out the spiders and pests that have begun to infest the Pyncheon house and by removing the enemy Judge Jaffrey through a death that nobody mourns. But in *The Blithedale Romance*, such appearances return with a vengeance: swine, toil, and a kind of madness create disillusionment in Coverdale, whom Hawthorne presents as an unreliable narrator like many of Poe's nervous narrators. And like Poe's narrators, particularly in "The Tell-Tale Heart," Coverdale may be covering his own complicity in Zenobia's death. Coverdale's guilt may be caused by a direct murder—a possibility advanced by Louise De Salvo and others—or indirectly in the way that Hollingsworth is blamed and calls himself a murderer for his part in Zenobia's disillusionment with life.[78] Or he may be "covering" something else—perhaps the secret that he was in love with Priscilla as he tells us in a last-ditch effort to make us believe his cause was worthy after all. Or—as Lauren Berlant argues—he may be "covering" his voyeuristic desires for Zenobia—making us believe that all his looking was just as philosophically motivated as the "looking" for a new land with utopian ideals that he and his fellow Blithedalers espoused.[79]

For Hawthorne, nature can terrify as well as inspire. The presence of death changes Coverdale's otherwise blithe narrative into something utterly different from the light comedy it seemed at first to be. *Blithedale* suggests that Emersonian idealism was not sustainable in the long term and offered only a temporary reprieve from the questions of life rather than the comprehensive answer about the meaning of life that it initially seemed to promise. Indeed, death obliterates the power of the eyeball as well as the blithe hopes of those who immerse themselves in the natural world with expectations of ultimate purification or enlightenment. Coverdale's "too much sympathy" and Hollingsworth's "overplus" of purpose similarly resulted in disillusionment and estrangement instead of the all-encompassing harmony they desired.[80] Despite all their excesses, however, there seems to be one thing the Blithedalers do not have enough—a sincere desire to learn from the natural order rather than implanting their own ideas in nature. Saying you want to learn from nature is not the same thing as allowing nature to teach you on its own terms.

Coverdale's tone of disillusionment also clouds the import of Hawthorne's narrative. What is clear in *Blithedale* is nature's ability to show humans their limitations; although Transcendentalists' attempts to know the world are limited in scope by their own shortsightedness, these attempts are not without value. The occasional glimpses of nature the Blithedalers experience counterbalance their more solipsistic impositions onto nature. Even if Coverdale's interpretations are sometimes self-defensive and sometimes self-contradictory, *Blithedale* does illustrate the lessons of the natural order. Even Coverdale learns from nature to be less presumptuous—a lesson his companion Hollingsworth learns to an even greater degree as his goals are transformed by nature's rebuke of his monomaniacal obsession to build a "natural" reformatory for criminals. Nature, for Hawthorne, has the power of restoring one's natural vitality. And that may be enough—at least for the sensibility of a noncommittal person like Coverdale.

AN OPEN CONCLUSION

Coverdale's pessimism suggests Hawthorne's own growing conviction that romance had seen its day in America. Almost prophetically in the face of the coming Civil War, *The Blithedale Romance* predicts that the Transcendentalists' reliance on natural law to reform society would fail, in part, because "seeing" nature can be merely a narcissistic reflection of one's own impure gaze. The selfishness of human nature often leads observers in *The Blithedale Romance* to develop tunnel vision rather than accurate sight. For Hawthorne, humans in nature discover more fully the inextricable nature of material and spiritual being. In *The Blithedale Romance*, mere observance results in solipsist sight that keeps people from actually seeing the natural order. The failure of sight even in nature demonstrates Hawthorne's critique of Emersonian optimism about the prospects of Americans' ability to live according to a natural order. Reform must begin not with mere observation but with an active, long-term commitment to finding the human place in the natural order by finding ways to return to nature. Without such commitment, even the most focused seeing may become diseased and counter to reality. The reformation experienced by the Blithedalers is much more limited than they expect, but most of those seeking natural reform are themselves reformed by nature. Hawthorne intimates that, even if learning from nature does not immediately reform society, periodic returns to the natural order may point humans toward a better life—but more likely on a small scale than a grandiose one.

In *The Blithedale Romance*, as in *The Scarlet Letter*, Hawthorne gives us a pastoral vision that ultimately fails to deliver on its promises. Hawthorne investigates the place of humans in the universe by considering the possibilities of nature and the divine as sites of reality in which humans are participants. The American situation, Hawthorne suggests, offers a new place not only in space and time but also in the philosophical tradition of Western civilization in which to ask age-old questions. How can humans live in harmony with the world around them, and what does the Natural world reveal—if anything—about a divinely ordered world where all parts work together in harmony? While Hawthorne's texts announce that such a vision is fraying, that paradise has again been lost in American history, he also finds the space within America's history for exemplars who have at least reached toward such harmony. Recounting the story of his involvement at Blithedale, he looks back with pride at his effort to contribute to societal reform by establishing a life outside of the artificial constraints of the city: "Whatever else I may repent of, therefore, let it be reckoned neither among my sins nor follies, that I once had faith and force enough to form generous hopes of the world's destiny—yes!—and to do what in me lay for their accomplishment; even to the extent of quitting a warm fireside, flinging away a freshly lighted cigar, and travelling far beyond the strike of city clocks, through a drifting snowstorm."[81] That he still claims such affinity with the idea, if not the practice, even after seeing it fail, suggests that Coverdale may sense some value in the experiment—a value that he cannot put into words.

Like many people living at a distance from nature today, Coverdale and his associates have come from residences where they feel cut off from the natural world. Going out into nature seems to reestablish—if only for a moment—our connection to the natural world. By returning to nature periodically, Coverdale demonstrates (even if he does not himself learn) that the disintegration of the Blithedale community does not mean the natural world has nothing to teach humanity. As Zenobia tells him, he must be "in earnest" if he expects to be at home in nature—or in the city, for that matter.[82] And when they first move to Bithedale Farm, the Blithedalers' "going out" is not a temporary thing. They aim to live close to nature, hoping to learn from it in order to achieve greater harmony. By the middle of the nineteenth century, the industrializing world had already begun pushing people away from the sources of their food, from the source of the fabrics they wore, and from a self-sustaining way of life. Those who joined together at Blithedale, Coverdale tells us, were there "in quest of a better life."[83] Rather than knuckle down under wage slavery and be tied to a specialized job they didn't like, they wanted to form a community where people were able to interact naturally and happily with each other. In *Blithedale*, we find that even well-planned communities designed for harmonious human-human interaction and human-environment interplay can fail. Perhaps a thriving human community in touch with the natural world is not simply a matter of economy, of arrangement. Perhaps such a benevolent community that depends upon the good will of others is ripe for abuse. But even more significantly, perhaps it does not well-equipped to address human limitations that lead them to ultimate ends of disillusionment and death.

As in other pastoral romances, Nathaniel Hawthorne's *Blithedale Romance* is charged with erotic, ecological, and spiritual tones. Human gender and sexuality are as much part of the experiment in nature as are agriculture and domesticity. The entrance of death into the pastoral colony at Blithedale Farm, however, draws attention not only to the failure of a projected agrarian utopia but also to the natural limits of humanity. Such failure to recognize limits, in Hawthorne's reckoning, is not an anomaly that plagued the Blithedalers only but is something endemic to human nature—an indication of the insufficiency of any human vision for attaining a perfect state of being. Unmet desires in the community, not a lack of sustainability planning, are the cause of failure. As Hawthorne's characters discover, how we actually interact with our societies and environment bears greater ecological and spiritual significance than what we say about them. America was in need of a new vision—one that was based upon more than untested platitudes of harmony with nature that left many people outside the community. For America was and is a dream that involves men and women of many classes, races, and sociopolitical backgrounds. Today we are again in need of a new vision of our interactions with the natural world to counteract the damage we inflict upon the environment by our wasteful use of natural resources. Working toward such a healthy interaction would in turn make the planet healthier and help us to rediscover our natural rhythms with all of the creatures of the earth, human and nonhuman.

NOTES

1. Hawthorne, *Complete Works,* vol. 5, 394.
2. In Zenobia's death, Hawthorne in facts seems to be demonstrating that there is nothing more ugly than the death of a beautiful woman. This directly contradicts Poe's famous statement that "the death, then, of a beautiful woman is, unquestionably, the most poetical topic in the whole world. See "The Philosophy of Composition," in *Poe: Essays and Reviews,* ed. Gary Richard Thompson (New York: The Library of America, 1984), 19.
3. Emerson, *Nature and Selected Essays,* 39.
4. Kenneth Burke, "I, Eye, Ay: Emerson's Early Essay on 'Nature': Thoughts on the Machinery of Transcendence," *The Sewanee Review* 74, no. 4 (1966): 882–83.

5. Hawthorne, *Complete Works*, vol. 5, 394.
6. Judy Schaaf Anhorn, "'Gifted Simplicity of Vision': Pastoral Expectations in The Blithedale Romance," *ESQ: A Journal of the American Renaissance* 28, no. 3 (1982): 137.
7. Hawthorne, *Complete Works*, vol. 5, 412–13.
8. Hawthorne, *Complete Works*, vol. 5, 336.
9. Hawthorne, *Complete Works*, vol. 5, 341–42.
10. Hawthorne, *Complete Works*, vol. 5, 339.
11. Hawthorne, *Complete Works*, vol. 5, 331.
12. Hawthorne, *Complete Works*, vol. 5, 336.
13. Hawthorne, *Complete Works*, vol. 5, 342.
14. Hawthorne, *Complete Works*, vol. 5, 389.
15. Emerson, *Nature and Selected Essays*, 49.
16. Christopher Pearse Cranch, *Poems* (Philadelphia: Carey and Hart, 1844), lines 1–4, 11–16.
17. Van Leer, "Hester's Labyrinth: Transcendental Rhetoric in Puritan Boston," 62.
18. Immanuel Kant, *Critique of Pure Reason*, ed. Patricia Kitcher, trans. Werner S. Pluhar (Indianapolis: Hackett Publishing, 1996), 458.
19. Samuel Taylor Coleridge, *Biographia Literaria, or, Biographical Sketches of My Literary Life and Opinions*, ed. James Engell and W. Jackson Bate (Princeton: Princeton University Press, 1985), 200.
20. Hawthorne, *Complete Works*, vol. 5, 432–33.
21. Hawthorne, *Complete Works*, vol. 5, 480.
22. Hawthorne, *Complete Works*, vol. 5, 436.
23. Emerson, *Nature and Selected Essays*, 59.
24. Hawthorne, *Complete Works*, vol. 5, 502.
25. Hawthorne, *Complete Works*, vol. 5, 330.
26. Hawthorne, *Complete Works*, vol. 5, 576–77.
27. Hawthorne, *Complete Works*, vol. 5, 322.
28. Hawthorne, *Complete Works*, vol. 5, 43.
29. Hawthorne, *Complete Works*, vol. 5, 432.
30. Hawthorne, *Complete Works*, vol. 5, 339.
31. Hawthorne, *Complete Works*, vol. 5, 361–62.
32. Hawthorne, *Complete Works*, vol. 5, 394.
33. Hawthorne, *Complete Works*, vol. 5, 343
34. Hawthorne, *Complete Works*, vol. 5, 343.
35. Hawthorne, *Complete Works*, vol. 5, 321.
36. Hawthorne, *Complete Works*, vol. 5, 343.
37. Hawthorne, *Centenary Edition*, vol. 8, 310.
38. Tim Fulford, *Romantic Indians: Native Americans, British Literature, and Transatlantic Culture, 1756–1830* (New York: Oxford University Press, 2006), 120.
39. Hawthorne, *Complete Works*, vol. 5, 379.
40. Nigel Goose, "Cottage Industry, Migration, and Marriage in Nineteenth-Century England," *The Economic History Review* 61, no. 4 (2008): 798–800.

41. William Cobbet, *Cottage Economy: Containing Information Relative to the Brewing of Beer, Making of Bread, Keeping of Cows, Pigs, Bees, Ewes, Goats, Poultry and Rabbits, and Relative to Other Matters Deemed Useful in the Conducting of the Affairs of a Labourer's Family* (London: C. Clement, 1822), 1–2.

42. Hawthorne, *Complete Works*, vol. 5, 410–11.

43. Hawthorne, *Complete Works*, vol. 5, 468.

44. Wendell Berry, *A Continuous Harmony: Essays Cultural and Agricultural* (Berkeley: Counterpoint, 2012), 80–81.

45. Hawthorne, *Complete Works*, vol. 5, 389.

46. Hawthorne, *Complete Works*, vol. 5, 389.

47. Hawthorne, *Complete Works*, vol. 5, 467.

48. Hawthorne, *Complete Works*, vol. 5, 467.

49. From the *Monthly Review,* Review of "Principles of Geology," in *The Museum of Foreign Literature and Science,* vol. 20 (June 1832): 597. For Hawthorne's use of this and other volumes of *The Museum,* see Kesselring, *Hawthorne's Reading,* 187.

50. Review of "Principles of Geology," 598.

51. Review of "Principles of Geology," 599.

52. Hawthorne, *Complete Works,* vol. 5, 395.

53. Honoré de Balzac's 1846 story "The Unconscious Mummers," a sculptor gone mad with Fourier's ideas creates an allegorical sculpture of Harmony, a woman with six breasts and symbols of "brotherhood" and agricultural peaceful living: "At her feet, besides, I have put an enormous Savoy cabbage, the Master's symbol of Concord. Oh, it is not Fourier's least claim to our veneration that he revived the association of plants and ideas; every detail in creation is linked to the rest by its significance as part of a whole." In *The Unconscious Mummers (Les Comediens Sans Le Savoir) and Other Stories,* trans. Ellen Marriage (New York: Macmillan, 1901), 45.

54. Hawthorne, *Complete Works,* vol. 5, 395.

55. Hawthorne, *Complete Works,* vol. 5, 472.

56. Lydia Fisher, "The Savage in the House," *Arizona Quarterly: A Journal of American, Literature, Culture, and Theory* 64, no. 1 (Spring 2008): 60.

57. Hawthorne, *Complete Works,* vol. 5, 338.

58. Fisher, "The Savage in the House," 62.

59. Hawthorne, *Complete Works,* vol. 5, 377.

60. Hawthorne, *Complete Works,* vol. 5, 429.

61. Hawthorne, *Complete Works,* vol. 5, 524.

62. Hawthorne, *Complete Works,* vol. 5, 402.

63. Hawthorne, *Complete Works,* vol. 5, 386–87.

64. Hawthorne, *Complete Works,* vol. 5, 543.

65. Hawthorne, *Complete Works,* vol. 5, 520.

66. Hawthorne, *Complete Works,* vol. 5, 586.

67. Hawthorne, *Complete Works,* vol. 5, 586.

68. Hawthorne, *Complete Works,* vol. 5, 591.

69. Hawthorne, *Complete Works,* vol. 5, 356.

70. Hawthorne, *Complete Works,* vol. 5, 595–96.

71. Hawthorne, *Complete Works,* vol. 5, 468.

72. Hawthorne, *Complete Works,* vol. 5, 468.

73. Edwin H. Cady, "The Wizard Hand: Hawthorne, 1864–1900," in *Hawthorne Centenary Essays*, ed. Roy Harvey Pearce (Columbus: Ohio State University Press, 1964), 324.

74. Erwin Panofsky, *Meaning in the Visual Arts: Papers in and on Art History* (Garden City, NY: Doubleday Anchor, 1955), 295.

75. Arianne Baggerman and Rudolf Dekker, *Child of the Enlightenment: Revolutionary Europe Reflected in a Boyhood Diary*, trans. Diane Webb (Boston: Brill, 2009), 210, 212.

76. Tony Tanner, Introduction to *The Blithedale Romance* (New York: Oxford University Press, 1999), xii.

77. Emerson, *Nature and Selected Essays,* 81.

78. Louise De Salvo, *Nathaniel Hawthorne* (Atlantic Highlands, NJ: Humanities Press, 1987), 118–20.

79. See Lauren Berlant, "Fantasies of Utopia in *The Blithedale Romance*," *American Literary History* 1, no. 1 (Spring 1989): 30–62. Berlant argues their experiment involves a repression of history and—for Coverdale—an epistemology based upon sexuality, making their vision of utopia little more than a delusion.

80. Hawthorne, *Complete Works,* vol. 5, 495, 598.

81. Hawthorne, *Complete Works,* vol. 5, 332.

82. Hawthorne, *Complete Works,* vol. 5, 397.

83. Hawthorne, *Complete Works,* vol. 5, 331.

Chapter 6

Exploring the Ruins of the Human Animal in *The Marble Faun*

> Nature needed, and still needs, this beautiful creature; standing betwixt man and animal, sympathizing with each, comprehending the speech of either race, and interpreting the whole existence of one to the other. What a pity that he has forever vanished from the hard and dusty paths of life."
>
> —Kenyon in *The Marble Faun*[1]

The last romance Hawthorne completed, *The Marble Faun*, has sometimes been treated as a travel guide for nineteenth-century American tourists in Italy. But it is no mere guidebook. Martin Kevorkian has recently attempted "a recovery of what may be sacrificed in hasty dismissals of *The Marble Faun*," claiming that it facilitates "a meditative encounter with Nature." Kevorkian acknowledges that Hawthorne does not say exactly what may be learned from nature but notes that Hawthorne "does hint, in *The Marble Faun*, that Nature may itself be a victim of human violence, and that the traces of that violence may be read in the human-altered face of Nature."[2] Kevorkian argues further that Hawthorne is interested in physical reality not just an abstraction, delineating Hawthorne's critique of violence in terms of environmental destruction and human persecution—two types of violence caused by self-centered attitudes of those who have little room for anyone or anything they perceive as obstacles to their power. Before Kevorkian, one of the few scholars to take nature seriously in *The Marble Faun* was Dorothy Waples, who posed the question of whether *The Marble Faun* most represents a tale of "nature caught in the snare of guilt" or as "nature improved by a share of guilt."[3] While Waples clearly recognizes the relationship between nature and human activity at play in this text, she turns to a consideration of the religious implications of Hawthorne's text without closely examining his keen investigation of humanity's imbrication in and difference from the natural world as a whole.

Judy Schaaf Anhorn examines *The Marble Faun* as a formal work of pastoral exile and return that illustrates Hawthorne's own "pastoral hope of recovery in return" from Italy to his home in America.[4] Hawthorne does indeed hope for a return, for numerous returns, but the return he emphasizes in *The Marble Faun* is not a return from nature to court or civilization—as in traditional pastoral—but a return from the city of Rome to a home close to nature. Like his character Donatello, Hawthorne himself leaves his home close to nature in Concord, Massachusetts, to enter the old cities of Europe for a time. When Donatello returns to his home in nature—to his castle in the countryside surrounding Florence—a partial sense of natural harmony is renewed as Donatello reestablishes some of his connection to the natural world.

Jennifer Mason has more recently and directly resisted the common scholarly assumption that Hawthorne was not interested in the natural world by drawing attention to Hawthorne's descriptions of pets such as dogs and cats. Such respect for "companion species," Mason argues, provides an impetus for Hawthorne's repeated comparisons of Donatello to dogs. According to popular nineteenth-century French naturalist Georges-Louis Leclerc, the Count of Buffon, dogs share at least some elements of human psychology. Mason links Buffon's descriptions of dogs to the Hawthorne's descriptions of the "animal" character of Donatello: "Donatello's physical body, certainly, is patterned on Praxiteles' sculpture of the 'wild' faun, but it would be difficult to find a more accurate description of Donatello's psychological traits than those that nineteenth-century Americans—following Buffon—ascribed to the dog."[5]

With the notable exceptions just mentioned, scholars have routinely dismissed or overlooked the significance of nature in *The Marble Faun*. In some ways, the lack of scholarly attention to nature in *The Marble Faun* is not all that surprising. Given the book's catalogue of art galleries, sculptures, museums, cathedrals, and other artistic wonders of Rome, there is no shortage of scholarly discussion on the role of art in *The Marble Faun*. This book certainly does investigate art's function in the formation and representation of human society. However, art in *The Marble Faun* is examined not only in Italian art galleries but also in Hawthorne's reflections on the relations between art and nature, and most particularly in the human-animal, historical-mythical character of Donatello. A count whose castle is situated in the pastoral scenery near Florence rather than Rome, Hawthorne's Donatello is rumored to be a faun with mystical abilities to understand the chatter of animals, the chirping of birds, the sounds on the breeze, and the movement of the flowers and trees. The historical Donatello, on the other hand, was an Italian sculptor who preceded Michelangelo and served as a bridge between medieval and Renaissance art. Deanna Fernie claims that the historical Donatello serves Hawthorne's purposes because he "represents an artistic culture still essentially in its beginnings, and by extension . . . more reflective of the nascent project of American art than the maturity of a Michelangelo."[6] While Fernie develops her ideas about Hawthorne with regard to nationality, the idea that art began as a response to nature and as a working out of human's natural abilities is at the root of Hawthorne's exploration of old world art and nature.

Because Hawthorne's use of nature terminology so often works as metaphoric language, it is often assumed to be *only* metaphoric. Especially in *The Marble Faun*, however, the metaphors are often also literal truths. And who better to emblematize this doubleness of metaphor and literal meaning than Donatello, a real-life person who seems like a famous statue and who also seems like a mythic personage? Donatello is a real person in nineteenth-century Italy, but he is also a representative of prehistoric personhood whose mixed pedigree shows how difficult and probably unnecessary it is to establish pure bloodlines into antiquity. By examining the animal nature of humans in light of emerging nineteenth-century questions of scientific racism and timeless legends of human origins, Hawthorne focuses on the biological nature of humans as well as potential limits to our biological capacity for existence and extinction. The malarial atmosphere and the rubbish in the courtyards of Rome raise the specters of disease and even possible extinction, further intimating biological limits on human existence. Yet by restoring our sympathies with nature, Hawthorne suggests, we can hope to enjoy our lives on earth and leave behind a world worth passing on to our progeny.

Recapitulating pagan mythology alongside the Garden of Eden and other prehistorical accounts of human origins, *The Marble Faun* draws readers into "a period when man's affinity with nature was more strict, and his fellowship with every living thing more intimate and dear."[7] Nathaniel Hawthorne's interest in the mythic figure of the faun reflects his growing conviction that a greater "affinity with nature" and a closer sense of "fellowship" with the creatures of the biosphere were needed in the nineteenth century. His story serves as a cautionary tale that "[e]very crime destroys more Edens than our own!"[8] Even the gardens of the earth that we inhabit today can be damaged by our violence, bringing about bitter consequences and ever further estrangement from our original "affinity with nature." Like his earlier romances, *The Marble Faun* shows Hawthorne's interest in how humans participate in the natural world. But in this romance, Hawthorne also demonstrates his conflicted fascination with alternative accounts of human origins and potential extinction within the natural order—particularly for those who insist upon pure bloodlines, on the one hand, and for those who ignore natural and spiritual laws, on the other.

When Donatello murders the man haunting Miriam's footsteps, he joins the human community of sinners, but he also loses his connection with animals, birds, the wind, the water, and the rhythms of nature. As Kevorkian notes, Donatello's impulses of violence reenact the biblical story of the Fall in *The Marble Faun* by breaking Donatello's concord with nature. This fallenness, emphasized by the old man's literal fall over the cliff from which Donatello pushes him, is part of what it means to be human. What humans have in common is sin. The artfulness of Miriam's look and Donatello's action have led to the demise of another person as well as to their own moral downfalls. While Donatello's loss of naturalness is accompanied by a gain of artfulness, it comes at the cost of a crime against another natural being—violence that violates and terminates the material existence of a natural body. But artfulness may also be redemptive, Hawthorne suggests, particularly for those who receive this story as a cautionary tale that calls for acts of penance by violent people and those who plot violence wittingly or unwittingly.

Hawthorne's romance does not answer the questions it raises despite the conclusion he adds later in response to readers' demands for more answers. But the story strongly suggests that modern culture has lost a primary form of knowledge, a prior way of life in which mythological creatures are somehow real, in which humans are as innocent as the rest of nature, in which an earthly paradise of some sort exists, in which humans and nature are simultaneously mixed and pure. Something is wrong with humans, and something is wrong with nature. How to right these wrongs remains an open question for Hawthorne. And how exactly to account for the violence and evil that brings harm and disturbs the harmony of humans and nature remains a conundrum for Kenyon. For Hilda, of course, a religious answer will do—hope for grace will not go as an unanswered prayer. The other characters do not share her high degree of confidence in ultimate justice and harmony. The appearance and subsequent imprisonment of someone like Donatello further develop the sense of something being wrong with the world.

THE ANIMAL NATURE OF HUMANS

In the brief opening chapter of *The Marble Faun*, Hawthorne reflects on the artistic vision behind the sculpture of the Faun of Praxiteles. As the four major characters browse through the sculpture garden of the Roman Capitol, their conversation shifts the focus from the titular sculpture to Donatello, the only member of the party who is not an American tourist. Donatello is the spitting image of the sculpture—or he might be if he were wearing only a lion-skin cape. (See figure 6.1.)

Exploring the Ruins of the Human Animal in The Marble Faun

Figure 6.1 Capitoline Faun, by Praxiteles, Fourth Century, Exemplar from the Capitoline Museums. Public Domain.

Identifying the sculpture's apparent "animal nature" as the "most essential part of the Faun's composition, Hawthorne designates it a "sportive and frisky thing, in marble" that is "[n]either man nor animal, and yet no monster, but a being in whom both races meet, on friendly ground."[9] This choice of words suggests some disagreement with Linnaeus's classification of satyrs and fauns and other such mythological beings as a distinct group called *homo monstrosus*.[10] Donatello is pronounced "no monster" despite being between species, or "races." Hawthorne's reflection on the faun in this passage indicates further that his fascination with this mythic creature is strongly linked to its close relationship with nature: "All the pleasantness of sylvan life, all the genial and happy characteristics of creatures that dwell in woods and fields, will seem to be mingled and kneaded into one substance, along with the kindred qualities of the human soul. Trees, grass, flowers, woodland streamlets, cattle, deer, and unsophisticated man."[11] As the representative of a mythic Arcadian past before decay and evil brought destruction to the world, both the marble faun of Praxiteles' statue and the living faun Donatello are in tune with the natural world in a way that moderns only dream of being.

Hilda remarks that the main difference between Donatello and the sculpture is in their facial expressions, which tell her "that the Faun dwelt in woods and fields, and consorted with his like; whereas, Donatello has known cities a little, and such people as ourselves."[12] Her statement suggests that Donatello is not quite the noble savage so touted in literature of this period but is instead a quasi-mythical creature at home with his animal nature in a way that humans rarely are. Like nonhuman animals, Donatello rarely has the "impulse to express himself copiously in words. His usual modes of demonstration were by the natural language of gesture, the instinctive movement of his agile frame, and the unconscious play of his features, which, within a limited range of thought and emotion, could speak volumes in a moment."[13] His animalistic body language is more expressive than his words, and he seems to understand intuitively much more than he has learned how to talk about. "He gave Miriam the idea of a being not precisely man, nor yet a child," the narrator notes, "but, in a high and beautiful sense, an animal,—a creature in a state of development less than what mankind has attained, yet the more perfect within itself for that very deficiency."[14] He is a human animal at home with his nature even though his verbal language skills are underdeveloped. In contemporary parlance, he might be classed as someone with a learning disability.

Hawthorne avoids directly taking a position on the scientific controversies that sometimes embroiled the reading public during the nineteenth century by comparing Donatello to a dog rather than an orangutan, the animal thought to be most similar to humans. Mason suggests that Hawthorne may avoid comparing Donatello with orangutans in order to avoid making any seeming statement of support for emerging theories of evolutionary development. But she also notes that while "Donatello's physical body, certainly, is patterned on Praxiteles' sculpture," Hawthorne follows nineteenth-century American scientific writers who describe "psychological traits ... ascribed to the dog."[15] Hawthorne's reading of Cuvier may also have led him to dissociate the orang-utan from humans because, according to Cuvier, the orangutan's "reputed ... resemblance to Man" has been "exaggerated" by individuals who were relying on test cases based on external features of young orangutans before "the muzzle becomes much more prominent." And comparing the intelligence of the orangutan to other animals, Cuvier claims it is "not very much surpassing that of the Dog."[16] When orangutans do show up, it is with "faces that would have been human, but for their enormous noses" in the company of "a whole host of absurd figures" of the carnival, including clowns and humans with heads of other animals including dog-headed humans.[17] The narrator here echoes Cuvier's distinction between the noses of humans and the muzzles of grown orangutans.

Donatello's animal nature is also emphasized as he is compared to dogs throughout Hawthorne's story, whether a pet dog, a spaniel, a bull-dog, a greyhound, or simply a hound.[18] When walking through the woods with Miriam, his actions are like those of an excited dog out on a stroll with its human companion. He runs in front of Miriam, then pauses to watch in excitement as she catches up with him. The narrator describes Donatello's devotion to Miriam as a kind of puppy love: "Donatello was as gentle and docile as a pet spaniel; as playful, too, in his general disposition, or saddening with his mistress's variable mood like that or any other kindly animal which has the faculty of bestowing its sympathies more completely than men or women can ever do."[19]

The excitement of Donatello's animal spirits is disturbed, however, by the presence of the old man who haunts Miriam's steps, and his natural exuberance turns spontaneously into "animal rage."[20] When his "animal rage" spills into action, Donatello's "tiger-like fury" takes over even as Miriam urges calm.[21] Eventually, his unresolved animal rage leads him to kill, and the act of killing effects a transformation in his very nature. The narrator describes the subsequent absence of Donatello's "fine, fresh glow of animal spirits," an absence that alarms Kenyon, who then wonders if they have been merely "eclipsed" or if they have become "utterly extinct."[22] Miriam too notices the change and feels chagrined to find a seemingly cultured man in place of "the wild boy, the thing of sportive, animal nature, the sylvan Faun."[23] Donatello's act of violence puts him at odds with nature not only in Rome but also with his home in the Apennines where he feels as if he has lost his connection with his ancestral family and can no longer "live their healthy life of animal spirits, in their sympathy with nature, and brotherhood with all that breathed about them."[24] In Donatello's act of murder, we have a reenactment of the Edenic fall by which a once-innocent person in tune with his surroundings falls from that state of innocence and harmony.

Hawthorne was both a cat man and a dog man, enjoying the company of either, although his love of cats seems to come first—as evidenced by mentions of the family cat Beelzebub in his letters home while a student at Bowdoin College in Maine. Mason notes that Hawthorne and his wife got a cat named Pigwiggen soon after setting up house in Concord and remarks upon Hawthorne's sense of companionship with Leo, their Newfoundland dog (56–57). While Mason has certainly done the most to draw attention to Hawthorne's pets as companion species, Paul Auster has also recently published a section of Hawthorne's notebooks called *Twenty Days with Julian & Little Bunny*.[25] Although Auster primarily notes the relationship between Hawthorne and his young son who were alone in the Berkshires for three weeks, he also remarks briefly upon Hawthorne's comments on the natural world and his changing perception of the pet rabbit. "The diary includes many keenly written passages about the shifting light of the landscape," Auster notes, adding as a parenthesis, "few novelists looked at nature as attentively as Hawthorne did" and then focusing on Hawthorne's increasing interest in the life of the bunny: "a handful of droll and increasingly sympathetic descriptions of Hindlegs, the pet rabbit."[26] In a letter to her mother, Sophia wrote of the material he put together that it includes "a charming history of poor little Bunny, who died the morning of the day we returned."[27] This delightful little book, written as an account of his adventures while she was on a three-week trip away with their two daughters, shows Hawthorne's interest in the pet bunny as a kind of companion for himself and his young son during this time.

Comparing Donatello to a pet—a dog—rather than a primate also allows Hawthorne to focus on the companionship that can be enjoyed between humans and intelligent nonhuman animals. Responding to theories of dogs' higher degree of intelligence than most animals, along with his observations of their sense of companionship with humans, Hawthorne offers a doggish human in the form of Donatello to help us learn how to regain such sympathies. In her argument for pets as companion species of humans, Donna Harraway postulates that "communication across irreducible difference is what matters" to our success as a species.[28] If so, our existence and well-being is contingent upon the existence and well-being of companion species such as the dog. It stands to reason, then, that people with dog-like characteristics, like Donatello, can contribute to our success as a species. Kenyon also finds an unlikely companion species in a "buffalo-calf" that begins "to make an acquaintance with him," jogging along and frisking about alongside him as he walks the Italian countryside not far outside the city. Kenyon feels whole again "in body and soul" through the combination of "this natural intercourse with a rude and healthy form of animal life" and the sunshine and the breeze, which work together to make him "happy with mere life."[29]

In the brief conclusion that Hawthorne adds to *The Marble Faun* after his first readers thought his romance left too many mysteries unresolved, he claims that "the story and the characters . . . bear, of course, a certain relation to human nature and human life" but that those who inquire "how Cuvier would have classified poor Donatello, or . . . whether he had furry ears or no," must consider *The Marble Faun* "to that extent, a failure."[30] It is not written as a scientific treatise. He adds, regarding the question of Donatello's faun-like ears, "[o]n that point, at all events, there shall be not one word of explanation."[31] There is no actual description of Donatello's ears in Hawthorne's text; they are always hidden beneath the mop of hair that grows over his ears. But we do find plenty of clues in Hawthorne's romance to show that he was indeed thinking about the human-animal status of Donatello. *Transformation*, the British title of *The Marble Faun*, directly suggests Hawthorne's interest in biological classifications, taking a form of Jean-Baptiste Lamarck's term *transformisme* (which Lamarck used to describe his own developing theory of evolution, or, as it was then called, the transmutation of species). But, though he alludes to both Lamarck and Cuvier, biologists who took different sides in public debates on the issues regarding the origins and development of human life in the years preceding Darwin's *On the Origin of Species*, Hawthorne refuses to commit to either. Hawthorne had not read Darwin's work by this time, given the fact that *The Marble Faun* was sent to the printer for proof-texts, only days before the release of Darwin's paradigm-shifting book on November 24, 1859.[32] But it is clear that Hawthorne was very interested in his milieu's questions about human origins and human relationships with the rest of the biological world.

Cuvier's fame as the first naturalist to include extinct animals within his classification system may also have contributed to Hawthorne's thinking about the animal nature of humans. According to the editors of the 1840 edition of Cuvier's *Animal Kingdom* (produced eight years after Cuvier's death), Cuvier's work "brought the extinct species into their proper situations in the living catalogue, and enabled every discoverer of a new animal, or part of an animal, instantly to connect it with its proper tribe or family."[33] By focusing on an "extinct" creature that served as a missing link between humans and nonhuman animals, Hawthorne plays with these nineteenth-century questions about human origins but avoids direct statements that engage scientific controversies of the time. Donatello's human-animal status is both emphasized and destabilized by the nineteenth-century uncertainty about the relationship between humans and other animal species.

As some critics have pointed out, Hawthorne's comparison of Donatello to a nonhuman animal also bears racial implications. Blythe Anne Tellefsen follows Nancy Bentley in situating Donatello and Miriam as figures identified to some extent with the African American community.[34] Citing David Walker's 1829 *Appeal to the Coloured Citizens of the World* for decrying "the *insupportable insult*" of the ruling class who told slaves "that they were not of the *human family*" because blacks were in line with animals and whites were not, Paul Outka draws attention to the common "conflation of slaves with domesticated animals."[35] Donatello's connection to African Americans is underscored by Hawthorne's later comment in an essay that fugitive slaves seem "akin to the fauns and rustic deities of olden times" in their apparent natural kinship with the world around them.[36] In the context of Hawthorne's writing, it is important to remember that historically race could mean anything from different family lines to different species of plants and animals.[37]

Mason also raises the specter of race, assuming that "the depiction of Donatello depicts a belief in fixed racial qualities," yet wondering, "how are we to make sense of his subsequent transformation?"[38] As Mason points out, the change in Donatello's nature—while uncertain in its depiction of the lines between species and races—provides support for the viability of racial mixture. Hawthorne's association of Donatello with the mixed-blood Miriam further suggests that this romance was taking up the issue of race relations that was dominating the political atmosphere of antebellum America. Miriam is described as a woman of uncertain origin but is rumored to be "the offspring of a Southern American planter . . . [with] one burning drop of African blood in her veins" who had fled from her parental plantation.[39] Because of the common expectation that mixed-blood children follow the condition of their mothers (not of their white slaveholding fathers), Miriam could likely have been claimed as a slave if it was true that she was of African descent. Given the provenance of the Fugitive Slave Law at the time of Hawthorne's writing, a woman like Miriam would not have been safe anywhere in America if she was in fact a fugitive slave.

Given the racial markers in *The Marble Faun* and Hawthorne's aversion to violence, however, it is rather starling to see that Donatello's inclusion as a human being comes as a result of his own act of violence. Is violence then inevitable? Or is it only inevitable in certain situations—such as when some people are excluded from the human communities where they live? Or is Hawthorne's simply attempting to write a contemporary story of how humans are corrupted by moving from the natural state but that such movement might be desirable because it results in one's inclusion in the broader experience of human community? In any case, violence brings evil to an uncorrupted state of natural innocence. And it brings a solidarity with others that has been missing up to that point. The direness of Donatello's actions, for example, draws him into Miriam's confidence. Yet when Kenyon suggests that this is an example of "the fortunate fall," Hilda adamantly protests. And readers are left wondering what to think about the effects of violence on humanity and nature. Is Hawthorne hinting that violence will happen if blacks are present but not included in the human community of the United States? Even more horrifying to one of Hawthorne's pacifist bent, is he suggesting that blacks themselves must violently achieve their membership in that community? The unsettling conversation between Hilda and Kenyon remains unresolved despite Hilda's loud pronouncement and Kenyon's seeming compliance.

In his consideration of some of these questions, again through the guise of fauns in Italy, Kenyon claims that fauns in the past "must really have existed. Nature needed, and still needs, this beautiful creature, standing betwixt man and animal, sympathizing with each, comprehending the speech of either race, and interpreting the whole existence of one to the other. What a pity that he has forever vanished."[40] Here his voice drops to a melodramatic whisper to suggest that Donatello may actually be that missing link—previously thought to be extinct—between human and nonhuman animals. The divisions we make between human races, like the divisions we make between humans and the earth and all that is in it, represent a loss in our human nature even if we gain in human culture. Hawthorne's evasive style of fiction allows him to speculate about such matters without directing challenging or advocating particular positions. But at the end of *The Marble Faun*, it is clear that more than one potential option remains: Hilda's hope, Kenyon's skeptical half-hope, Miriam's melancholy, and Donatello's despair. Miriam has her freedom but seemingly in exile. Whether or not Donatello can be lifted from his prison cell and from his despair has yet to be seen. In the American corollary of this situation—are slaves only to be free in exile? Can they hope for freedom and acceptance into the circle of the human community that has thrust them out?

ESCAPING THE SOIL AND ATMOSPHERE OF RUIN

Like the animal nature of humans, the soil and atmosphere are less than fully healthy. In Rome is "the native soil of ruin" as well as that one "final charm . . . bestowed by the malaria." Here is "ancient dust, the mouldiness of Rome, the dead atmosphere . . . the hard pavements, the smell of ruin and decaying generations."[41] How malaria spread was uncertain in Hawthorne's time, but the narrator suggests that it has something to do with the "dead atmosphere" as well as its "ancient dust" and its "mouldiness." The idea that dead bodies and moldy buildings contributed to this infection indicates that Hawthorne was concerned with the human impact on the environment as well as the environment's effects on humans. With our attention now drawn to "the nervous and unwholesome atmosphere of Rome," the narrator refers ominously to possible murderers and lunatics and other "vagabonds" roaming the city.[42] Such seediness in this area of the city is enough to dampen the spirits of most people, but not Hilda's. In the high tower where she sits painting, Hilda escapes the foul smells below. But she descends and passes through the "squalid entrance-way" of the city, a place where the "unfragrant atmosphere" and "the rubbish of the courtyard" assail her senses of smell and sight.[43] And in "the corrupted atmosphere of the city beneath," Hilda exposes herself to whatever sicknesses may lurk in its corners but seemingly without harm.[44]

This heavy emphasis on the unhealthy atmosphere of Rome was personal for Hawthorne, whose sixteen-year-old daughter Una contracted malaria while the family was in Rome. In the notebook entry when he realizes that she has contracted the infamous Roman Fever (malaria), Hawthorne rails at "the unamiableness of the outside atmosphere," which has just been made even worse by a season of "ugly, hopeless clouds, chill, shivering winds, drizzle, and now and then pouring rain, much more than enough."[45] He mentions his hopeless desire for "the sunshine of the New Jerusalem" in this state, adding, "It is extremely soul-crushing, this remorseless gray, with its icy heart."[46] Una comes close to dying during her four-month illness, which adds to his black mood in Rome. When they can finally leave behind "the languor of the Roman atmosphere" in their journey north along the "exceedingly refreshing" seashore whose "sight and fragrance" is so "exceedingly refreshing," Hawthorne notes that Una "revived visibly." His relief is almost palpable when he notes that the next morning as they reach the Tuscan region of northern Italy that Una already "shows herself so strong" that they could go traveling along the northern Italian landscape or simply relax to enjoy the enlivening influence of the seashore.[47] The influences of the atmosphere on the human body serve as reminders of the vital connection between human and the elements of nature.

Unlike the personal notes in his notebook, however, Hawthorne's romance maintains its focus on the characters grappling with their own dearth of natural and spiritual health, which took them to the healthy air of the Italian countryside away from Rome and to the holy sites within the city of Rome. For throughout the book, we continue to see numerous mentions of this "poison in the atmosphere."[48] And yet we also see Hilda pausing prayerfully before religious paintings that speak of the salvation of one's soul. The narrator suggests that she is cognizant of her soul's "need and hunger for a spiritual revelation" if she is to be spiritually as well as physically whole, and thus it is that she feels "a vast and weary longing" to see again a painting she has seen before, Sodoma's sixteenth-century fresco titled "Christ Bound to the Column." Here, the narrator remarks, she found an image of "the Son of God . . . in a state so profoundly pitiful" yet simultaneously "rescued from it . . . by nothing less than a miracle." Suffering and death itself are being deposed, suggesting the hope that even death is not the awful end of nature as it might seem.[49] This was certainly Hilda's hope though the ever-cynical Kenyon casts doubt on her religious hope for redemption and speaks of Eden as something forever lost. The connections to a lost Garden of Eden that his characters make in *The Marble Faun*—like his own wish for "the sunshine of the New Jerusalem" while Una was battling the malaria during chilly months in Rome—suggest Hawthorne's hope (however shrouded in mystery) that nature and spirit might be redeemed someday.

In *The Marble Faun*, however, that redeemed state is clearly not realized. Miriam tells Donatello that he should be afraid of "the air that we breathe" because "it is full of malaria," a far cry from the healthy "Arcadian environment of vine-yards, fig-trees, and olive-orchards" that flourish at the site of Donatello's home.[50] The poor herdsmen are pitied as "poor serfs, having little to eat and nothing but the malaria to breathe."[51] The "deaths of myriads, have corrupted all the soil, creating an influence that makes the air deadly to human lungs."[52] Hawthorne's firsthand knowledge of malaria clarifies his almost vicious excoriation of the seemingly beautiful atmosphere that hides a malignant illness. The contaminated soil and atmosphere of Rome contrasted sharply with the Apennines where Donatello's home was located in Florence, the capitol of Tuscany. The atmosphere there was still nourishing, and they could still enjoy it if they left Rome to do so. In our time as well as Hawthorne's, a return to a healthier atmosphere is crucial to our existence and our coexistence with other members of the natural world of the twenty-first century.

When Hawthorne describes Hilda's walk through the dangerous parts of the city, he may well be alluding to the invisible presence of bacteria, which nineteenth-century scientists called "animalcules." While abroad, Hawthorne continued to pay attention to the *American Journal of Science and the Arts*.[53] One article that appeared during his time abroad addresses "In the Theory of Spontaneous Generation," with Professor Milne Edwards speaking at the Academy of Sciences at Paris, declaiming the possibility of spontaneous generation and espousing instead the idea that "animalcules were derived from germs of extreme minuteness, which were spread every where in nature, and floating up as fine dust in the atmosphere, settled on all bodies to develop only where the conditions of air, water and organic decomposition favored."[54] "Animalcules" was a term that encompassed a large variety of bacteria, protozoa, and similar microscopic lifeforms. While Hawthorne doesn't use their scientific name, he refers to dust and decay in terms that invoke such conditions—most often in relation to the development of "the Roman fever."

Hilda continues to walk through the foul atmosphere of the city, seemingly without any repercussions. If she is indeed Saint Hilda, as she has been called, perhaps her sanctity gives her this immunity. But Hilda is less than saintly in her lack of recognition of the conditions of the people in the city. "With respect to whatever was evil, foul, and ugly, in this populous and corrupt city, she trod as if invisible," the narrator says admiringly before adding a less admiring note, "and not only so, but blind. She was altogether unconscious of anything wicked that went along the same pathway."[55] She eventually finds herself, however, in "the foulest and ugliest part of Rome. In that vicinity lies the Ghetto, where thousands of Jews are crowded into a narrow compass, and lead a close, unclean, and multitudinous life, resembling that of maggots when they over-populate a decaying cheese."[56] The ghetto is a breeding ground for poverty, uncleanliness, and all of their related diseases. Hawthorne does not tell us why these ghettos exist, but he emphasizes the excessive crowding and lack of hygiene that contribute to its unhealthy atmosphere. The invisibility of the animalcules (or bacteria) that create infections, like the invisibility of the fly eggs that give birth to maggots crawling around on decayed cheese, also contributes their unhealthiness. The Jews stuffed into these crannies could only expect outbreaks of deathly illnesses in such unclean spaces. It is interesting that Hilda would pass through this area designated for Jews, yet Miriam, who is also rumored to be "the daughter and heiress of a great Jewish banker," is not to be found in this space.[57] As she does throughout the novel, Miriam subverts the unjust ordering of society and shapes her own spaces of existence in the world. Hilda, however, simply seems oblivious to the injustices as well as the environmental blight caused by these injustices.

Even in the seemingly healthy space atop the lovely Pincian Hill, where the natural beauty is guarded by soldiers, the appearance of health is deceptive. Ironically, this place is thought to be restorative: "Here sits . . . the consumptive girl, whose friends have brought her, for cure, to a climate that instils poison into its very purest breath."[58] In front of them and below them, they see mountains and water and trees and the slow "advance of vegetation" in a land whose gradual change of season allows "time to dwell upon each opening beauty, and to enjoy the budding leaf, the tender green, the sweet youth and freshness of the year."[59] The high places above or outside the city—like Hilda's tower—are thought to be more healthy, but this is not always the case. When the characters ascend the hill to the Coliseum in the moonlight, the atmosphere seems more wholesome. There Hawthorne's characters are "able to catch the evanescent fragrance that floats in the atmosphere of life above the heads of the ordinary crowd."[60] But even this is no guarantee, as we see by the narrator's comments about the deceptive Pincian Hill.

Before his Fall, Donatello tires of the unnaturalness of Rome—its "hard pavements" and "smell of ruin and decaying generations" and everything else that settles over him "like a cloud which had darkened over him without his knowing how densely."[61] Rome is festering, it seems, "nothing but a heap of broken rubbish" with the current city built atop "thirty feet of soil" that covers the old city "like the dead corpse of a giant."[62] In this ancient city, the "dust of all those years" has compounded the musty smell of death and its attendant infections.[63] And after committing murder, Donatello is no longer immune to the infection of the city in at least a symbolic rendering of the relationship between human wrongdoing and environmental malaise. When Miriam finds Donatello "shaking as with the cold fit of the Roman fever," she takes him to "the quiet shade and sunshine of that delightful retreat" at the gardens at the Villa Medici.[64] So Rome has some healthy spaces embedded within it to counteract the influence of a poisoned environment. Nonetheless, the ever "morbid" Kenyon supposes that there is in Rome "a contagious element, rising fog-like . . . and brooding over the dead and half-rotten city, as nowhere else on earth."[65] Kenyon tries to cheer Donatello by reminding him, "This languid Roman atmosphere is not the airy wine that you were accustomed to breathe at home. . . . We shall both be the better for some deep draughts of the mountain-breezes."[66] And it is refreshing even if it does not convert them back to the kind of harmony with nature that a mythic faun would have enjoyed.

Donatello's connection with nature is not only with the biosphere of all living things on earth but also with the soil and the atmosphere that mark the boundaries of biological existence. At his home in Florence, Donatello is alive to "the rich soil, so long uncultivated and untrodden . . . lapsed into nearly its primeval state of wilderness . . . now overgrown with tangled and riotous vegetation," but reminding his visitors of the Golden Age touted by poets.[67] According to the legend surrounding Donatello's heritage, their beginning could be traced all the way back to the prehistoric era of human history: "In those delicious times, when deities and demi-gods appeared familiarly on earth, mingling with its inhabitants as friend with friend,—when nymphs, satyrs, and the whole train of classic faith or fable, hardly took pains to hide themselves in the primeval woods,—at that auspicious period, the lineage of Monte Beni had its rise" among people in close communion with the earth "not altogether human, yet partaking so largely of the gentlest human qualities."[68] Even before visiting Donatello's home in the Florentine countryside, Kenyon had tried to convince Hilda that Donatello, like the fauns from "their Arcadian haunts of yore," had developed within a unique "external environment."[69] Passing on the legendary story of Donatello's ancestry, Kenyon exclaims, "Why, my dear Hilda, he is a Tuscan born, of an old, noble race in that part of Italy; and he has a moss-grown tower among the Apennines, where he and his forefathers have dwelt, under their own vines and fig-trees, from an unknown antiquity."[70] Hawthorne's reach back into ancient myths in order to imagine a human in harmony with the natural world suggests a belief or hope that such a unity must have existed at one time even if we do not enjoy such harmony in the modern world.

When Donatello is reunited with the nonhuman natural world in his home in the Apennine Mountains near Florence, the union is striking for the other characters to witness. "He drank in the natural influences of the scene" and soon became wildly active, running "races with himself along the gleam and shadow of the wood-paths." A Tarzan of the Tuscan forests, Donatello jumps to grab a branch and swings freely through the air "as if he had flown . . . through the air" and then stops to become a literal tree-hugger, embracing the tree as if it were a nymph.[71] "Then, in order to bring himself closer to the genial earth, with which his kindred instincts linked him so strongly, he threw himself at full length on the turf, and pressed down his lips, kissing the violets and daisies, which kissed him back again."[72] And he becomes one with the creatures as well as the plants, as "green and blue lizards . . . scrupled not to scramble over him, with their small feet . . . the birds alighted on the nearest twigs and sang," all seeming as if they "recognized him . . . as something akin to themselves; or else they fancied that he was rooted and grew there."[73] His harmony with nature is wide ranging and quite literal. But Donatello also offers a warning that, had he heeded it, he could have retained his healthy connection with nature. He retells an old tale of the "spring of delicious water" animating the fountain of his Florentine home, telling his auditors that the water spirit started to avoid the man who came to wash there because "[t]he guilty man had polluted the pure water."[74] Nature could not remain in communion with one whose violence could break out against it. With such descriptions, Hawthorne builds the sense of connection between human and nonhuman nature. Human wrongdoing is again seen as the cause of environmental distress. Although Hawthorne does not trace the development of such a cause-effect relationship, he continues to hint of such a connection throughout *The Marble Faun*.

RESTORING THE LOST SYMPATHIES
AND INSTINCTS OF NATURE

In the person of Donatello, Hawthorne depicts sympathies *of* nature and sympathies *with* nature that humans seem to have lost. In "Some Principles of Animal Psychology," an address read by D.F. Weinland at the American Association in Baltimore in May 1858 and published in *The American*

Journal of Science and the Arts, a journal Hawthorne had before him in Italy, the relationship between plants and animals were discussed in terms that correlate with the concerns of *The Marble Faun*: "The true difference between plants and animals consists in this, that animals have a consciousness of an outer world, while plants have none."[75] Observations of dogs, Weinland argues, demonstrate their consciousness of an outer world by tracing "sympathetic motions" within dogs that correspond to the activities of other dogs or humans. Perhaps more surprisingly, he finds in creatures such as lizards as well as monkeys a proliferation of organs for "sympathetic motions" despite a wide variety of "different anatomical features."[76] When we first meet Donatello, he seems to have only a small degree of consciousness but an abundance of sympathetic motions. Before he commits murder, Donatello possesses such limited consciousness that he has very little recollection of his past existence and even finds it hard to remember the passing of time. After his murder, his fall into humanity, his sense of consciousness rapidly expands.

In Donatello, before the murder, we find sympathy "of a livelier kind" as he gets excited by the natural scenery. "Donatello's sympathies" with the natural world make him unique, the narrator argues, as do his strong links "(and by no monstrous chain) with what we call the inferior tribes of being, whose simplicity, mingled with his human intelligence, might partly restore what man has lost of the divine!"[77] Thus, Donatello offers an example of simplicity, intelligence, and natural sympathy for humans who have lost their instinctive connections to nature and the divine. The restorative air breathed through this scene of Donatello's union with nature is described in atomistic terms: "[T]hese wild pets of nature dreaded him no more in his buoyant life than if a mound of soil and grass and flowers had long since covered his dead body, converting it back to the sympathies from which human existence had estranged it."[78] The elements of the human body are elements of the natural environment and the body can be literally converted into "a mound of soil and grass and flowers" or converted by a recovered sympathy with nature.

After he commits murder and returns with Kenyon to his home in the Apennines, Donatello hopes to reestablish his communication with the natural world. In this physical space of trees and birds and animals and mountain streams, Donatello "was believed to possess gifts by which he could associate himself with the wild things of the forests, and with the fowls of the air, and could feel a sympathy even with the trees, among which it was his joy to dwell."[79] When Kenyon hears the wordless sounds that come from Donatello in his attempt to recover his link to nature again, Kenyon feels a strange thrill of the interconnectivity of all of nature. Donatello, on the other hand, is majorly frustrated by his inability to commune with the natural world anymore. The experience, however, is enough to inspire Kenyon with a vague perception of what aligning one's sympathies with nature might have brought about in a prelinguistic world: "In this bright dialect—broad as the sympathies of Nature—the human brother might have spoken to his inarticulate brotherhood that prowl the woods, or soar upon the wing, and have been intelligible to such extent as to win their confidence."[80] If humans could only learn again how to "associate with the wild things" and to "feel sympathy" with them, Kenyon supposes, we could expect to find a radical reinvigoration of our natural selves.

Besides the figure of Donatello, women in *The Marble Faun* seem to be more in touch with natural sympathies than are men—at least men like Kenyon. Miriam exhibits her strong natural sympathies, for example, by making sketches with "a force and variety of imaginative sympathies."[81] And her sympathies are shaped by her hope for "a fresher and better world."[82] And in Hilda's paintings, we are told, lay "all the warmth and richness of a woman's sympathy," paintings made by "this guiding light of sympathy."[83] Kenyon notices that Hilda "is abundantly capable of sympathy, and delights to receive it."[84] She responds to the doves that brought her "what sympathy they could, and uttering soft, tender, and complaining sounds, deep in their bosoms, which soothed the girl more than a distincter utterance might. And sometimes Hilda moaned quietly among the doves, teaching her voice to accord with theirs, and thus finding a temporary relief."[85] Like Donatello, Hilda seems able to communicate with the animals because her sympathies are so well aligned with them.

Hawthorne's emphasis on the necessity of natural sympathies is closely linked to his deliberations on natural instincts. But while Donatello's instincts lead him to the close connection with nature that he enjoys at first, it is also his instincts—"one of those instinctive, unreasoning antipathies which the lower animals sometimes display"—that incline him toward enmity with the man shadowing Miriam.[86] And after he pushes the old man over the cliff while Miriam watches, Donatello and Miriam are "instinctively" drawn together into a "new sympathy" with each other's precarious knowledge and situation.[87] When discussing how to go about righting the wrong of murdering the old man, Miriam declares that Donatello's guilt makes him act as his own judge and claims that "earthly justice" is not to be hoped for. But Donatello dismisses her claims with his own: "I have no head for argument, but only a sense, an impulse, an instinct, I believe, which sometimes leads me right."[88] On the question of whether or not to turn himself in to the Roman authorities, Miriam is clearly opposed. She does not expect justice through legal means. Donatello is not so sure. Perhaps facing justice for his crime of murder is the natural thing to do. At least his instinct seems to be telling him so.

Like Donatello, Hilda's instincts seem to serve her well sometimes. But Kenyon questions the adequacy of Hilda's instincts from time to time. When he is bothered by their ignorance of Miriam's origins, for example, he asks if Hilda's "delicate instincts" lead her to trust or distrust Miriam. Hilda, for her part, declares that their love for each other does not require more knowledge. "I love her dearly . . . and trust her most entirely," Hilda retorts finally when Kenyon continues to press her on questions of Miriam's origins.[89] For Hilda, national origins and racial origins are not as important as the sense of sisterhood she shares with Miriam. For her part, Miriam's "insatiable instinct" also disposes her toward "friendship, love, and intimate communion."[90]

The solidarity of sisterhood, like the solidarity of shared crime, offers an example of Cuvier's comment that human instinct is most developed as a "disposition to mutual existence." Cuvier further suggests that humans' "disposition to mutual existence" is the only trait of humans "resembling instinct."[91] In most other animals, he has identified instinct as "a supplement for intelligence" and an aid in the "preservation, in a proper degree, of each species."[92] Human intelligence and instinct, being inversely proportional to each other, make the recovery of an innocent state of nature more difficult. A person cannot very well lose his or her intelligence, but perhaps it is possible to regain one's natural instincts. At least, this seems to be what the narrator hopes. All of Hawthorne's characters have instincts, but Donatello's instincts are most developed and Kenyon's are least developed. Donatello learns that unchecked instincts can lead to crimes against nature (such as murder), and Kenyon learns that instincts would help him to become a more natural man. Hilda, having her instincts trained to her religious principles, remains fiercely defensive of them. Miriam distrusts human instincts because she has seen the miscarriage of justice.

Kenyon also learns to hear and trust his own instincts a bit more at the end when he reflects on Donatello's nature: "Faun or not, he had a genial nature, which, had the rest of mankind been in accordance with it, would have made earth a paradise to our poor friend."[93] According to Kenyon, Donatello's loss of his status as an unfallen natural creature represents a loss for "the rest of mankind." Kenyon seems to speak more truly perhaps than he knows. Rather than the "genial" nature of a faun in tune with the natural world, we are left with a nervous man who does not quite know how to deal with the guilt caused by his disruption of the natural order through an act of violence. Donatello's newly proven status of being fully human interferes with his ability to commune with the natural world, but it leads to his separation from the human world as well since he must flee if he is to escape being punished for his crime. He has interfered with the rhythms of human nature as well as with the rhythms of nonhuman nature.

Instincts as well as natural sympathies are more present in Donatello's animal nature than in the nature of the other characters. This suggests Hawthorne's belief that instincts are morally neutral, conditioned by environmental influences. Kenyon remarks that the Emperor Vespasian fostered a following "from the people whose bloody instincts he pampered."[94] The emperor knew how to cultivate certain instincts for his own ends, and the people generally supported him for doing so. While Donatello lived in a harmonious natural setting, his instincts led him to a deep communion with nature and humans in that environment. But when Donatello went to Rome and saw the man stalking Miriam, his instincts responded to that environment with an attempt to right the wrongs he saw in the poisonous atmosphere of the city. Hawthorne's study of Donatello thus indicates his recognition of environmental influences on humans as well as human influences on the environment.

CONFLICTED VIEWS OF ART, NATURE, AND RACE

Hilda's presence in the novel has often been a mystery to readers, who find her saintly attitudes cloying and simplistic, not worthy of a writer like Hawthorne. But Hilda plays a vital role in the end. It is her insistence that no determinants seal one's fate that pries this work loose from tight grip of the nineteenth-century racism that surrounds this work. Hawthorne's preface appears a kind of inside joke to readers who think he will not address political issues. "No author, without a trial," he writes, "can conceive of the difficulty of writing a romance about a country where there is no shadow, no antiquity, no mystery, no picturesque and gloomy wrong, nor anything but a commonplace prosperity, in broad and simple daylight, as is happily the case with my dear native land."[95] The irony could not be stronger for anyone who hears the drumbeats of the approaching Civil War, as Hawthorne's first readers surely did. Hawthorne's letters indicate that these drumbeats of war were already being heard in Europe as well as America by this time, so there certainly is more to this preface than meets the eye. The beautiful image of America that Hawthorne claims to espouse in the statement in his preface is clearly marred by the presence of slavery in the United States during the nineteenth century. And while Hawthorne's earlier works focus on the dark undercurrents created by his persecuting Puritan ancestors, the dark undercurrents of *The Marble Faun* are surely related to issues of race and the inevitable approach of the American Civil War.

Hawthorne is not outspoken on the question of slavery. He is skeptical, however, of the Abolitionists' typical approach to the issue, critiquing Emerson and other abolitionists to task for "breathing war," which has led Hawthorne scholars such as Brenda Wineapple to assume that Hawthorne "failed to sympathize with any nonwhite population" even though it is no secret that he "despised the slave trade, which implicated both North and South."[96] My analysis of *The Marble Faun*, like my earlier reassessment of *The House of the Seven Gables*, offers a reconsideration of Hawthorne's sympathy for nonwhites both inside and outside of national borders. One of Hawthorne's contemporary critics was his sister-in-law Elizabeth Peabody, who criticized him multiple times for not voicing support for the Abolitionist cause. Hawthorne's responses were typically mild, but when Peabody criticized Hawthorne and Sophia for what she considered their ambivalence on the slavery issue, Sophia wrote back in indignation: "We wonder what you can mean, as we both feel quite innocent, and hate the evil [slavery] quite as much as you do."[97] At the risk of sounding hyperbolic, I think it vital to Hawthorne's romance to read it as a cautionary tale about America's national sin rather than simply as a travelogue of the experience of Americans in Italy. Why else would he so dramatically refigure the Fall from a state of original goodness as when the faun (representative of man in a prelapsarian state) causes the monk to fall over the cliff and is immediately afterward struck by guilt and shame? The story does examine Americans and mixed-race individuals trying to find their place in the world, but it is a world that has already been sullied by a sense of fallenness.

Responding to the prelapsarian goodness of Donatello before the Fall, Miriam exclaims, "Nature and Art are just at one sometimes."[98] In these words, Hawthorne embeds the relationship between nature and art that he finds at the root of all human nature: humans are natural artists, and doing art is the result of humans developing naturally. The environment ("nature") and human culture ("art") are not too far removed from each other to prevent the reestablishment of a balance of sorts. While art—or artfulness—may lead to downfall, an artistic vision may also work to redeem some degree of what has been lost in the broken relationship between humans and nature. This view of the role of artist gives art a role in righting the wrongs caused by violence within the natural world—whether the violence of racism or the violence that exploits nonhuman nature. In the character of Donatello, art and nature are situated slowly but surely as poles of human identity that must be maintained in healthy tension in order for humans to live in harmony with themselves and the rest of the physical world. Hawthorne's Donatello is a "natural" work of art as myth is turned toward nature, and creatures in a state of nature meet humans who have paradoxically been both corrupted and fulfilled by human arts. With Donatello, we may hope that we have not wholly lost the natural instinct "which sometimes leads [us] right."[99]

Despite Hawthorne's sympathetic presentation of Donatello in race-conscious terminology, Tellefsen concludes that Hawthorne's vision for America and race in *The Marble Faun* precludes the presence of African Americans in America's future.[100] Kenyon's prophecy "that such men must change their nature, or else perish" seems to lean in that direction, comparing them as he does to "antediluvian creatures, that required, as the condition of their existence, a more summer-like atmosphere than ours."[101] One idea for resolving the issue of slavery was the Liberia colonization movement, which proposed resettling freed slaves in Liberia, an African country known for its year-round tropical climate. While colonization proceeded and a Liberian independence movement was largely accomplished by freed America slaves, it had fallen into disfavor by the time of Hawthorne's writing with many Abolitionists considering it almost as abhorrent as slavery since it was dependent upon displacement of peoples rather than immediate emancipation.[102]

Given the fact that Donatello has apparently succeeded in "changing his nature," however, Kenyon may simply be musing among possibilities rather than articulating a stance. Hilda, for her part, declares, "I will not accept your moral!"[103] And Kenyon is quick to offer another possibility by turning his attention to Donatello's ability to adapt—it may be, he says, that Donatello has been "developing a thousand high capabilities, moral and intellectual, which we never should have dreamed of asking for, within the scanty compass of the Donatello whom we knew."[104] In the increasingly racist climate of nineteenth-century America, Frederick Douglass had certainly surprised many white Americans by showing an intelligence that many whites— whether or not deliberately racist—had come to think blacks did not or could not have. Kenyon has earlier pointed out that Donatello has the "germs of faculties that have heretofore slept" and that these faculties have been brought to life by "the intermixture of his former simplicity with a new intelligence. But he is bewildered with the revelations that each day brings."[105] So *The Marble Faun* sounds at least an ambiguous note that perhaps the assumptions of white Americans about the future of black Americans needs to be reexamined. Perhaps African Americans' circumstances have simply not allowed for the development of their capacities. Or perhaps their capacities have been seriously underrated.

Hawthorne's attention to race in *The Marble Faun* is also hinted by Donatello's imprisonment at the end as well as in Miriam's subversive underground activity and escape to freedom. By assigning the crime of murder to Donatello and making Miriam an accomplice of sorts, Hawthorne supplies a plausible scenario for why both of them would fear losing their freedom. In the conclusion Kenyon ruefully reports that Donatello has been imprisoned for his crime in a secret dungeon.[106] He has been apprehended, he is in chains, languishing somewhere in prison, much like the runaway slave who has been apprehended. But the ending of the final chapter before the conclusion has been added offers a more hopeful possibility: "But Hilda had a hopeful soul, and saw sunlight on the mountain-tops."[107] Maybe, like the escaped Miriam, he would one day have his freedom. If one of the rumors about Miriam is true, she has already escaped previously—leaving behind the slavery enjoined upon her by he "one-drop" rule of African American identity in the slave-holding South.

Hawthorne's pastoral setting in Italy draws upon inherited myths and religious stories to explore the interrelations between humans and nature in *The Marble Faun*. This promulgates yet another variation on the pastoral themes that characterize all of his romances. Nature is a teacher, and humans have lost a vital quality by becoming estranged from nature. In an "original" pastoral state, such as the Golden Age Donatello is said to descend from, humans lived close to a natural environment brimming with life and happiness.[108] Fauns did not build cities that stamped out large swaths of the natural world, and they retained a closer connection to the natural world as well as a healthier existence. In the ruins of Rome in the nineteenth century, however, the foul air is not only depressing but a potential cause of disease. Nature can be harmed by humans, who can in turn be harmed by nature.

The Marble Faun is a lament for the humans' loss of connectivity with nature but offers tentative hope for restoration of this deteriorated relationship by advocating a refreshment of natural sympathies that have been cultivated out of human experience. When Donatello experiences his so-called fortunate fall, he is no longer innocent and his experience makes him part of the human family but not all is as fortunate as it may seem. He loses his ability to converse with nature, and he no longer hears from the birds and the trees, the animals and the fountain—losing, in effect, part of his original nature. Hawthorne's emphasis on the ruins underscores that this story is not simply a search for human origins but an exploration of the possibility of human extinction. In an earlier apocalyptic short story "The New Adam and Eve," Hawthorne more directly imagines a future world in which the physical earth is oblivious to the extinction of humanity.[109] By resurrecting the figure of the vanished species of the faun, even if such a being never actually existed as Linnaeus supposed it did, Hawthorne draws attention to the temporality of species as well as a loss in the reciprocal connection between the human species and the environment.

NOTES

1. Hawthorne, *Complete Works*, vol. 6, 27.
2. Martin Kevorkian, "Reading the Bloody 'Face of Nature': The Persecution of Religion in Hawthorne's *The Marble Faun*," *Contagion: Journal of Violence, Mimesis, and Culture* 13 (2006): 140.

3. Dorothy Waples, "Suggestions for Interpreting *The Marble Faun*," *American Literature* 13, no. 3 (November 1941): 225.

4. Judy Schaaf Anhorn, "Pastoral Exile and *The Marble Faun*," *Nineteenth-Century Literature* 43, no. 1 (June 1988): 28.

5. Mason, *Civilized Creatures: Urban Animals, Sentimental Culture, and American Literature, 1850-1900*, 67.

6. Deanna Fernie, *Hawthorne, Sculpture, and the Question of American Art* (New York: Routledge, 2016), 226.

7. Hawthorne, *Complete Works,* vol. 6, 25.

8. Hawthorne, *Complete Works,* vol. 6, 247.

9. Hawthorne, *Complete Works,* vol. 6, 25.

10. Hawthorne was perusing Linnaeus's work as early as in 1830, when he checked out *A General System of Nature* from the Salem Athenaeum. See Kesselring, *Hawthorne's Reading*, 185.

11. Hawthorne, *Complete Works,* vol. 6, 25.

12. Hawthorne, *Complete Works,* vol. 6, 22.

13. Hawthorne, *Complete Works,* vol. 6, 97.

14. Hawthorne, *Complete Works,* vol. 6, 98.

15. Mason, "Civilized Creatures," 67.

16. George Cuvier, *Cuvier's Animal Kingdom, Arranged According to Its Organization; Forming the Basis for a Natural History of Animals, and An Introduction to Comparative Anatomy*, ed. Edward Blyth et al. (London: W.S. Orr and Company, 1840), 55.

17. Hawthorne, *Complete Works,* vol. 6, 504.

18. Hawthorne, *Complete Works,* vol. 6, 28, 33, 59, 102, 158, 170, 177, 186, 201.

19. Hawthorne, *Complete Works,* vol. 6, 59.

20. Hawthorne, *Complete Works,* vol. 6, 104, 112, 177.

21. Hawthorne, *Complete Works,* vol. 6, 176.

22. Hawthorne, *Complete Works,* vol. 6, 213.

23. Hawthorne, *Complete Works,* vol. 6, 367.

24. Hawthorne, *Complete Works,* vol. 6, 277.

25. Paul Auster, Introduction to *Twenty Days with Julian & Little Bunny By Papa*, ed. Nathaniel Hawthorne (New York: New York Review of Books, 2003), xxviii–xxix. Auster was apparently unaware that this work was privately published in 1904, claiming his own 2003 publication as the first time it was individually published as its own book and pointing back to Julian Hawthorne's excerpts in the biography of *Nathaniel Hawthorne and His Wife* (1884) as well as its full inclusion in Randall Stewart's publication of Hawthorne's *American Notebooks* in 1932.

26. Auster, Introduction to *Twenty Days,* xli.

27. In Auster, Introduction to *Twenty Days,* xxvi.

28. Donna Harraway, *The Companion Species Manifesto: Dogs, People, and Significant Otherness* (Chicago: Prickly Paradigm Press, 2003), 49.

29. Hawthorne, *Complete Works,* vol. 6, 477–78.

30. Hawthorne, *Complete Works,* vol. 6, 522–23.

31. Hawthorne, *Complete Works,* vol. 6, 527.

32. Fredson Bowers, "Textual Introduction" in *Centenary Edition of the Works of Nathaniel Hawthorne,* vol. 4. *The Marble Faun,* ed. Nathaniel Hawthorne (Columbus: Ohio State University Press, 1968), lxxxv.

33. In Cuvier, *Animal Kingdom,* iii.

34. Blythe Ann Tellefsen, "'The Case with My Dear Native Land': Nathaniel Hawthorne's Vision of America in *The Marble Faun,*" *Nineteenth-Century Literature* 54, no. 4 (March 2000).

35. Paul Outka, *Race and Nature: From Transcendentalism to the Harlem Renaissance* (New York: Palgrave Macmillan, 2008), 55.

36. Hawthorne, *Complete Works,* vol. 12, 319.

37. See "race, n.6," *OED Online,* March 2018. Oxford University Press.

38. Mason, "Civilized Creatures," 61.

39. Hawthorne, *Complete Works,* vol. 6, 38.

40. Hawthorne, *Complete Works,* vol. 6, 27.

41. Hawthorne, *Complete Works,* vol. 6, 97–98.

42. Hawthorne, *Complete Works,* vol. 6, 51–52.

43. Hawthorne, *Complete Works,* vol. 6, 53.

44. Hawthorne, *Complete Works,* vol. 6, 71.

45. Hawthorne, *Complete Works,* vol. 10, 486.

46. Hawthorne, *Complete Works,* vol. 10, 486.

47. Hawthorne, *Complete Works,* vol. 10, 507–508.

48. Hawthorne, *Complete Works,* vol. 6, 116, 123, 315.

49. Hawthorne, *Complete Works,* vol. 6, 387–88.

50. Hawthorne, *Complete Works,* vol. 6, 101.

51. Hawthorne, *Complete Works,* vol. 6, 109.

52. Hawthorne, *Complete Works,* vol. 6, 112.

53. See Hawthorne, *Complete Works,* vol. 8, 358. Hawthorne writes, "I saw Silliman's Journal on one of the desks, being the only trace of American science, or American learning or ability in any department, which I discovered in the University of Oxford."

54. Milne Edwards, "On Spontaneous Generation," (1859), 402. In Benjamin Silliman et al., *The American Journal of Science and the Arts* 27 (May 1859), https://www.biodiversitylibrary.org/item/113458#page/1/mode/1up.

55. Hawthorne, *Complete Works,* vol. 6, 440.

56. Hawthorne, *Complete Works,* vol. 6, 441.

57. Hawthorne, *Complete Works,* vol. 6, 38.

58. Hawthorne, *Complete Works,* vol. 6, 125.

59. Hawthorne, *Complete Works,* vol. 6, 125.

60. Hawthorne, *Complete Works,* vol. 6, 184–85.

61. Hawthorne, *Complete Works,* vol. 6, 93.

62. Hawthorne, *Complete Works,* vol. 6, 134–35.

63. Hawthorne, *Complete Works,* vol. 6, 135.

64. Hawthorne, *Complete Works,* vol. 6, 229.

65. Hawthorne, *Complete Works,* vol. 6, 468.

66. Hawthorne, *Complete Works,* vol. 6, 212.

67. Hawthorne, *Complete Works,* vol. 6, 267.
68. Hawthorne, *Complete Works,* vol. 6, 269.
69. Hawthorne, *Complete Works,* vol. 6, 126.
70. Hawthorne, *Complete Works,* vol. 6, 127.
71. Hawthorne, *Complete Works,* vol. 6, 93.
72. Hawthorne, *Complete Works,* vol. 6, 94.
73. Hawthorne, *Complete Works,* vol. 6, 94.
74. Hawthorne, *Complete Works,* vol. 6, 284.
75. D.F. Weinland, "Some Principles of Animal Psychology" (1859), 1. In Silliman, *American Journal* (May 1859).
76. Weinland, "Animal Psychology," 3–4.
77. Hawthorne, *Complete Works,* vol. 6, 90.
78. Hawthorne, *Complete Works,* vol. 6, 94.
79. Hawthorne, *Complete Works,* vol. 6, 271.
80. Hawthorne, *Complete Works,* vol. 6, 286–87.
81. Hawthorne, *Complete Works,* vol. 6, 63.
82. Hawthorne, *Complete Works,* vol. 6, 145.
83. Hawthorne, *Complete Works,* vol. 6, 74.
84. Hawthorne, *Complete Works,* vol. 6, 147.
85. Hawthorne, *Complete Works,* vol. 6, 379.
86. Hawthorne, *Complete Works,* vol. 6, 52.
87. Hawthorne, *Complete Works,* vol. 6, 205.
88. Hawthorne, *Complete Works,* vol. 6, 490.
89. Hawthorne, *Complete Works,* vol. 6, 133.
90. Hawthorne, *Complete Works,* vol. 6, 138–39.
91. Cuvier, *Animal Kingdom,* 48.
92. Cuvier, *Animal Kingdom,* 31.
93. Hawthorne, *Complete Works,* vol. 6, 519.
94. Hawthorne, *Complete Works,* vol. 6, 185.
95. Hawthorne, *Complete Works,* vol. 6, 15.
96. Brenda Wineapple, *Hawthorne: A Life* (New York: Random House, 2004), 188.
97. See Bruce Ronda, *Elizabeth Palmer Peabody: A Reformer on Her Own Terms* (Cambridge, MA: Harvard University Press, 1999), 264. Ronda outlines the interchange between Elizabeth, her sister, and Hawthorne, emphasizing that Hawthorne was opposed to slavery but also uneasy with Abolitionists' approach to the issue.
98. Hawthorne, *Complete Works,* vol. 6, 29.
99. Hawthorne, *Complete Works,* vol. 6, 190.
100. Tellefsen, "The Case," 472–73.
101. Hawthorne, *Complete Works,* vol. 6, 519.
102. See "African American Mosaic: Colonization," *Library of Congress,* https://www.loc.gov/exhibits/african/afam002.html.
103. Hawthorne, *Complete Works,* vol. 6, 519.
104. Hawthorne, *Complete Works,* vol. 6, 519.

105. Hawthorne, *Complete Works,* vol. 6, 326.
106. Hawthorne, *Complete Works,* vol. 6, 526.
107. Hawthorne, *Complete Works,* vol. 6, 522.
108. Hawthorne, *Complete Works,* vol. 6, 269.
109. Hawthorne, *Complete Works,* vol. 6, 519.

Chapter 7

Postscript

Hawthorne's Unfinished Romances

> Man's finest workmanship, the closer you observe it, the more imperfections it shows; as in a piece of polished steel a microscope will discover a rough surface. Whereas, what may look coarse and rough in Nature's workmanship will show an infinitely minute perfection, the closer you look into it. The reason of the minute superiority of Nature's work over man's is, that the former works from the innermost germ, while the latter works merely superficially.
>
> —Nathaniel Hawthorne, *American Notebooks*, October 7, 1837[1]

So what do we make of Hawthorne's attention to the natural world? If we see him seriously engaging the concepts of nature that were prevalent with the thinkers and writers around him, his natural metaphors take on a deeper meaning. They are no longer simply metaphors but patterns built into the fabric of the universe that we ignore at our own peril. Hawthorne even entertains the idea that myths may have had more connection to prehistoric reality than we are accustomed to thinking. It may well be that some of our natural metaphors come from realities of nature that once were known by experience. Even today, there is no denying that scientific understandings of the prehistoric world continue to be reshaped as we learn and relearn the realities of our past. As we continue to imagine futures that we may influence by our actions, the open-ended finales of Hawthorne's romances extend the possibility of hopeful futures that can only be realized if we learn how not to repeat the sins of the foregoing generations.

When I began this intense focus of Hawthorne's work from an ecological perspective, I expected to focus primarily on the wilderness trope that informs some of his most well-known works (e.g., "Young Goodman Brown"). I was not expecting to become immersed in a world of medicine, biology, geology, race, and environmental influences. While wilderness did indeed play a significant part in my analysis, as expected, so did Paradise. The American geography offered the Puritans a new world that they sometimes referred to as a New Eden before fearing it as a wilderness to be tamed. In the nineteenth century, the sins of the fathers came down to haunt descendants of the Puritans like Hawthorne who was troubled by the potential wrongdoing implicit in white ownership of American lands. But the gifts of the land—whether herbs that might bring medical healing or the forgotten rhythms of nature that might refresh the human soul or the animals and a variety of lifeforms that remind us that we share the globe with other creatures—were not simply for utilitarian consumption. We participate in a natural fellowship or communion with the rest of nature. As members of the human race, those who insist upon purity of bloodlines can choose to perpetrate violence or to adapt to a changed world.

I was also interested to find out what Hawthorne's reading choices revealed about his thinking while writing. I knew some of his sources, such as the pastoral and Gothic romances he had read since childhood, but I wanted to see if other readings gave additional clues about Hawthorne's understanding of nature. I had heard the rumors of Hawthorne's racism and was interested to see how it compared to other racisms of the nineteenth century. I was fascinated by the high number of scientific books on his reading lists. Yet I did not expect issues of race to be as strongly connected to nature or as complexly woven throughout his romances as I found them to be. Nor did I expect his approach to the natural world to represent as much of engagement with science as it apparently is. It is my hope that my findings represent only the beginning of a recovery of Hawthorne's attention to the natural world as a reality with which we are so thoroughly imbricated.

While it is difficult to draw any conclusions from Hawthorne's romances that he left unfinished at the end of his life, they do suggest that he was continually reworking his earlier ideas about nature to respond to a world where the saying that "all men are created equal" might apply to the natural rights of nonwhite races and to women as well as to white men. All of these unfinished works in some way investigate the mixed heritage of Americans who have inherited much from the British and the Native Americans and now possibly from black Americans as well. The outcome of the Civil War would determine how such a mixed heritage would play out in American life, but Hawthorne did not live to see the outcome of the Civil War.

Some of Hawthorne's unfinished manuscripts also involve a search for a natural elixir that might bring not only temporary health but permanent health and physical immortality. Hawthorne expressed his frustration with these manuscripts, but it is hard to know which parts frustrated him most and which parts he considered essential to the future. Unfortunately no Elixir of Life was found in time to restore Hawthorne's health, and he died of undiagnosed medical causes a couple of months before his sixtieth birthday. Had he lived to see the end of the American Civil War, perhaps he would have put his pen to use addressing race issues more directly than he does in his completed fiction. But it was almost a year after Hawthorne's death that Robert E. Lee surrendered, Lincoln was assassinated, and the brand-new president Andrew Johnson declared the war ended.

In *Septimius Felton*, the most complete of the unfinished manuscripts that Hawthorne wrote, we are introduced to a mixed-race figure in the title character. Despite bearing the name of a Roman emperor, Septimius had English blood and Native American blood. Set in the early days of the Revolutionary War rather than the real-time early days of the Civil War, *Septimius Felton* represents one of Hawthorne's attempts to address national issues by invoking a historical corollary that allows him some authorial distance from the political issues at hand. The historical mixture of Native American and English blood was perhaps a less volatile subject than the mixture of African American and European American blood during the Civil War era when Hawthorne was writing.

Since this is a lesser-known work of Hawthorne, a brief overview is in order. Septimius Felton is an orphan raised by a crusty old aunt of his who was said to be descended from chieftains of an unnamed Native American tribe. But the women of the white community where Septimius and his Aunt Keziah live do not consider her one of them: "In their view, she was a dram-drinking, pipe-smoking, cross-grained old maid and, as some thought, a witch; and, at any rate, with too much of the Indian blood in her to be of much use."[2] For her part, Aunt Keziah prefers her Native American background to the conventional lives women are expected to live in the white community. As she tells Septimius, "If you could be an Indian, methinks it would be better than this tame life we lead."[3] And she is especially disenchanted with the life of a white woman.

On her deathbed, Aunt Keziah tells Septimius, "Oh, Seppy, how I hate the thought of the dull life women lead! A white woman's life is so dull! Thank Heaven, I'm done with it! If I'm ever to live again, may I be whole Indian, please my Maker!"[4] As she approaches death's door, Aunt Keziah mutters of her daydreams of witch meetings in the woods, mentioning deacons and mothers and "an Indian" and "a nigger" at the meeting, before adding, "they all have equal rights and privileges at a witch meeting . . . Oh dear me! But I'm a Christian woman and no witch; but those must have been gallant times!"[5] Ironically, it is at her dream of a witch meeting that she does not have to worry about being treated as one of the community. And neither do Native Americans and African Americans. Her dream is better than the reality so far available to her in the European American community. How exactly Hawthorne planned to work out the details of this romance is not clear, but what is clear is that he was imagining a world in which mixed-race identities would be worthy of consideration.

Aunt Keziah is also knowledgeable about medicinal herbs of the American forests. Charles Swann suggests that Hawthorne was shaping a contrast between "Indian matriarchy" as a part of nature and "Puritan patriarchy" as a part of culture.[6] Given the prominence of Aunt Keziah and her emphasis on the constraints placed upon a white woman, this seems likely. Hawthorne clearly has these ideas on his mind at the time of his writing, and his attention to nature and human nature seems about to gain a fresh wind. But he is also ill, and the Civil War is weighing heavily on his mind. In a letter dated August 3, 1862, Hawthorne writes, "I doubt whether I ever again have spirits and vigor and tranquility to produce another Romance. Since my return from England, my health has not been so good as formerly, and this terrible war will not let us think of anything but itself."[7] In his biography of Hawthorne, Arlin Turner finds that Hawthorne's life-ending symptoms indicate that he most likely suffered from cancer, which ultimately resulted in an aggressive, and fatal, brain tumor.[8] No Elixir of Life was found in time to stop Hawthorne's death.

During this difficult period before his death, Hawthorne also has the violence of war on his mind. Apologizing to a British friend in 1863 for not responding to his last letter, Hawthorne writes, "When society is about to be overturned from its foundations, the courtesies of life must needs be a little damaged in advance of the general ruin."[9] In a letter to her son a few weeks before Hawthorne's death, Horace Mann's mother relates a conversation with Hawthorne's wife: "Sophia told me yesterday that his malady was partly mental—that he *agonizes* about the country, and cannot possibly write in his peculiar vein while everything is in limbo. He has that sort of imagination which realizes things put as they are, and all the uncertainty and suffering are daguerrotyped [sic] in him. . . . We shall have it all bye and bye in books, for he always puts himself into his books; he cannot help it."[10] Unfortunately, Hawthorne's illness kills him before the end of the Civil War and before he is able to write another book, so we do not have the type of postwar book Mrs. Mann and others expected. What we have instead are drafts of the American Claimant and Elixir of Life manuscripts.

For these last attempts to create an Elixir of Life romance, Hawthorne claims as his impetus a legend Thoreau has told him of a man who lived in Hawthorne's house in Concord, a man who believed he would never die.[11] Hawthorne's interest in the Elixir of Life is not new, however. In a number of his earlier short stories, Hawthorne has already written tales about the search for the Elixir of Life. In an ironic twist of fate, Hawthorne wrote his friend and college classmate Longfellow about the Elixir of Life manuscripts in January 1864, four months before he died, telling him, "As is always the case, I have a notion that this last book would be my best; and full of wisdom about life and death—and yet it will be no deadly disappointment if I am compelled to drop it."[12] Since he did not finish any of these novels before his death, however, none of these books became his best. And yet, within their pages, we find a glimpse of his cumulative artistic vision and his attempts to address more directly some of those issues that he had only indirectly addressed before. But he has not clearly settled into a plan for this future. Though he laments the ravages of war, Hawthorne also abhors slavery and praises the invigorating effects of wartime valor: this mixed sentiment about human life and death enters into his final attempts at a romance during this time.

Despite his inability to finish a romance during these last years, Hawthorne does write and publish a few essays and sketches. Hawthorne sees the Civil War, like preceding large-scale wars, as a time when civilization's foundations are shaken. Traditional assumptions and practices face the risk of dissolution, bringing notions of nature and identity into focus once more. In the satirical pacifist essay "Chiefly About War Matters," we find telling snippets of Hawthorne's thoughts about human nature, race, and the environment. In this essay, Hawthorne mentions meeting Lincoln and then turns to battlefields of the American environment that has been violated by the war:

> [T]the war has done a great deal of enduring mischief, by causing the devastation of great tracts of woodland scenery, in which this part of Virginia would appear to have been very rich. Around all the encampments, and everywhere along the road, we saw the bare sites of what had evidently been tracts of hard-wood forest, indicated by the unsightly stumps of well-grown trees, not smoothly felled by regular axe-men, but hacked, haggled, and unevenly amputated, as by a sword, or other miserable tool, in an unskillful hand. Fifty years will not repair this desolation! An army destroys everything before and around it, even to the very grass . . . [N]ot a blade of grass is allowed to grow.[13]

The devastation will leave a long-lasting disfigurement on the American landscape as well as in the depleted population. So human concerns are not the only concerns Hawthorne considers. By doing such long-term damage, our armies bring about "desolation" upon the literal landscape of America.

But the human interest in the battlefield scenes are also apparent to Hawthorne. The fugitive slaves he sees excite his sympathy, and he picks up on the thoughts about race that have informed his romances. Only here he addresses the issue directly, admiring the naturalness of the band of black soldiers even while using racialized language:

> They were unlike the specimens of their race whom we are accustomed to see at the North, and, in my judgment, were far more agreeable. So rudely were they attired,—as if their garb had grown upon them spontaneously,—so picturesquely natural in manners, and wearing such a crust of primeval simplicity which is quite polished away from the northern black man . . . akin to the fauns and rustic deities of olden times. . . . I felt most kindly towards these poor fugitives, but knew not precisely what to wish in their behalf. . . . For the sake of the manhood which is latent in them, I would not have turned them back; but . . . [they] must henceforth fight a hard battle with the world, on very unequal terms.[14]

Despite his desire for their freedom, Hawthorne is not naïve enough to think that they will have it easy when they have been emancipated. Instead, he recognizes that they still have "a hard battle" ahead of them and that they will likely have to fight "on very unequal terms." Given the full century of Jim Crow segregationist policies that followed the end of the Civil War, Hawthorne unfortunately was right.

Given the fresh encounter with Hawthorne's writings that I advocate in this book, I have included many passages of Hawthorne's writing for rereading. In seeing Hawthorne's statements about nature to be really *about* nature (and not simply a symbolic mask for something else), I hope other readers will come away from this reconsideration of Hawthorne's work with a deeper understanding of the ways Hawthorne engages the world from the vantage point of the artist-author. For readers not accustomed to thinking of Hawthorne's writing in terms of nature and material reality, a notebook entry he wrote in 1837 may be instructive: "Nature's workmanship will show an infinitely minute perfection" that allows for infinite study "the closer you look into it . . . [Nature] works from the innermost germ."[15] While Hawthorne's texts sometimes raise more questions than they answer, I hope we may see the end of claims that Hawthorne was an exception among the Concord writers—the one writer among them who didn't care about the world of nature. For when we read his work with a recognition of the way he engages nineteenth-century issues of race, adaptation, and environment, it becomes nigh impossible to place his work outside the flow of nature writing.

Whatever else we may draw from Hawthorne's works, several implications for human flourishing are clear. Our fulfillment as humans has something to do with our relationship with the natural world. Our existence as members of a larger material and spiritual world require us to continuously seek out the most meaningful purposes of our life. Medical science, biology, and geology offer clues to our existence as material creatures. Religion, myth, and history offer clues to our existence as spiritual creatures. The presence of moral and physical evils inherent in the human condition require us to think carefully about our assumptions rather than offering too blithe answers to difficult problems.

Our origins as creatures of nature demand an investigation of this natural world of which we are part. But our ending, our extinction—either individually or as a species—also deserves our careful attention. Death poses the ultimate challenge for medical science, and Hawthorne's fascination with stories of the fabled Elixir of Life shows his interest in what medical science may never be able to accomplish—the immortality of the body. The hard reality of death also calls into question Transcendentalist idealism and Emerson's confidence in his ability to see all by troubling the expectation of tranquility with the intrusion of death. For Hawthorne, nature is a necessary but not sufficient teacher since death halts the work of nature that is our human body or at least transforms it into fertilizer for more life. But if individual humans are immortal, as Hawthorne hopes, our death and bodily disintegration does not mark the end for us even if it ends our participation in earthly nature as we know it. So while Hawthorne's skepticism of Transcendentalist ideals is apparent throughout his writing, he does share some of their beliefs. For Hawthorne, as for the Transcendentalists, nature is both material and spiritual. Humans are part of the natural order and should find their place in that natural order, recovering a harmony with nature that has faded in the dust and machinery of the modern world.

NOTES

1. Hawthorne, *Complete Works,* vol. 9, 97.
2. Hawthorne, *The Complete Works of Nathaniel Hawthorne,* vol. 11, *The Dolliver Romance, Fanshawe, and Septimius Felton, with an Appendix Containing The Ancestral Footprint.* Riverside Edition (Boston: Houghton Mifflin, 1883), 361.
3. Hawthorne, *Complete Works,* vol. 11, 359.
4. Hawthorne, *Complete Works,* vol. 11, 359.
5. Hawthorne, *Complete Works,* vol. 11, 358.
6. Charles Swann, *Nathaniel Hawthorne: Tradition and Revolution* (New York: Cambridge University Press, 1991), 69.
7. Hawthorne, *Centenary Edition of the Works of Nathaniel Hawthorne,* vol. 18, *The Letters, 1857–1864,* ed. William Charvat et al. (Columbus: Ohio State University Press, 1987), 468.
8. Arlin Turner, *Nathaniel Hawthorne: A Biography* (New York: Oxford University Press, 1980), 391.
9. Hawthorne, *Centenary Edition,* vol. 18, 543.
10. MS *Antioch* in Hawthorne, *Centenary Edition,* vol. 18, 653.
11. Hawthorne, *Centenary Edition of the Works of Nathaniel Hawthorne,* vol. 13, *The Elixir of Life Manuscripts: Septimius Felton, Septimius Norton, The Dolliver*

Romance, ed. William Charvat et al. (Columbus: Ohio State University Press, 1977), 557.
    12. Hawthorne, *Centenary Edition,* vol. 18, 640.
    13. Hawthorne, *Complete Works,* vol. 12, 317–18.
    14. Hawthorne, *Complete Works,* vol. 12, 318–19.
    15. Hawthorne, *Complete Works,* vol. 9, 97.

Bibliography

Abel, Darrel. *The Moral Picturesque: Studies in Hawthorne's Fiction.* West Lafayette, IN: Purdue University Press, 1988.

"African American Mosaic: Colonization." *Library of Congress.* https://www.loc.gov/exhibits/african/afam002.html.

Anhorn, Judy Schaaf. "'Gifted Simplicity of Vision': Pastoral Expectations in The Blithedale Romance." *ESQ: A Journal of the American Renaissance* 28, no. 3 (1982): 135–53.

———. "Pastoral Exile and *The Marble Faun.*" *Nineteenth-Century Literature* 43, no. 1 (June 1988): 24–41.

Amundson, Ron. *The Changing Role of the Embryo in Evolutionary Thought: Roots of Evo-Devo.* New York: Cambridge University Press, 2005.

Armbruster, Karla and Kathleen R. Wallace. *Beyond Nature Writing: Expanding the Boundaries of Ecocriticism.* Charlottesville: University of Virginia Press, 2001.

Auster, Paul. Introduction. *Twenty Days with Julian & Little Bunny By Papa*, edited by Nathaniel Hawthorne. New York: New York Review of Books, 2003.

[Austin], Mary Hunter. "Regionalism in American Fiction." *The English Journal* 21, no. 2, (1932): 97–107.

Autrey, Max L. "'My Kinsman Major Molineux': Hawthorne's Allegory of the Urban Movement." *College Literature* 12, no. 3 (Fall 1985): 211–21.

Baggerman, Arianne and Rudolf Dekker. *Child of the Enlightenment: Revolutionary Europe Reflected in a Boyhood Diary*, translated by Diane Webb. Boston: Brill, 2009.

Bakhtin, Mikhail. *The Dialogic Imagination: Four Essays,* edited by Michael Holquist, translated by Caryl Emerson and Michael Holquist. Austin: University of Texas Press, 1981.

Balzac, Honoré de. *The Unconscious Mummers (Les Comediens Sans Le Savoir) and Other Stories*, translated by Ellen Marriage. New York: Macmillan, 1901.

Bate, Jonathan. *Romantic Ecology: Wordsworth and the Environmental Tradition.* London: Routledge, 1991.

Baym, Nina. *The Scarlet Letter: A Reading*. Boston: Twayne, 1986.
Bedell, Rebecca. *The Anatomy of Nature: Geology and American Landscape Painting, 1825-1875*. Princeton: Princeton University Press, 2001.
Bell, Michael Davitt. *Hawthorne and the Historical Romance of New England*. Princeton: Princeton University Press, 1971.
Bell, Millicent. *Hawthorne and the Real: Bicentennial Essays*, edited by Millicent Bell. Columbus: Ohio State University Press, 2005.
Ben-Zvi, Yael. "Clinging to One Spot: Hawthorne's Native-Born Settlers." *ESQ: A Journal of the American Renaissance* 52, no. 1–2 (2006): 17–44.
Bercovitch, Sacvan. *The American Jeremiad*. Madison: University of Wisconsin Press, 1978.
Bergland, Renée L. *Maria Mitchell and the Sexing of Science: An Astronomer among the American Romantics*. Boston: Beacon Press, 2008.
Berkeley, David. "Allegory." In *A Dictionary of Biblical Tradition in English Literature*, edited by David L. Jeffrey. Grand Rapids: William B. Eerdman's Publishing, 1992.
Berlant, Lauren. "Fantasies of Utopia in *The Blithedale Romance*." *American Literary History* 1, no. 1 (Spring 1989): 30–62.
Berry, Wendell. *A Continuous Harmony: Essays Cultural and Agricultural*. Berkeley: Counterpoint, 2012.
Blair, Hugh. *An Abridgement of Lectures on Rhetoric*. Boston: Thomas & Andrews, 1803. Archive.org.
Boudreau, Kristin. *Sympathy in American Literature: American Sentiments from Jefferson to the Jameses*. Gainesville: University Press of Florida, 2002.
Bowdoin College. *Laws of Bowdoin College*. Hallowell, ME: Goodale, 1817.
Bowers, Fredson. "Textual Introduction." *Centenary Edition of the Works of Nathaniel Hawthorne*, vol. 4. *The Marble Faun*, edited by Nathaniel Hawthorne. Columbus: Ohio State University Press, 1968.
Bradstreet, Anne. "Contemplations." *The Works of Anne Bradstreet in Prose and Verse*, edited by John Harvard Ellis. Charlestown: Cutter, 1867.
Brickhouse, Anna C. "'I Do Abhor an Indian Story': Hawthorne and the Allegorization of Racial 'Commixture'." *ESQ: A Journal of the American Renaissance* 42, no. 4 (1996): 233–53.
Brodhead, Richard H. *The School of Hawthorne*. New York: Oxford University Press, 1986.
Bryant, William Cullen. "A Forest Hymn." *Yale Book of American Verse*, edited by Thomas R. Lounsbury, 1912. www.bartleby.com/102/18.html.
Buell, Lawrence. "American Pastoral Ideology Reappraised." *American Literary History* 1 (1989): 1–29.
———. *The Environmental Imagination: Thoreau, Nature Writing, and the Formation of American Culture*. Cambridge, MA: Belknap Press, 1995.
———. *The Future of Environmental Criticism*. Malden, PA: Blackwell, 2005.
Burke, Kenneth. "I, Eye, Ay: Emerson's Early Essay on 'Nature': Thoughts on the Machinery of Transcendence." *The Sewanee Review* 74, no. 4 (1966): 875–95.
Burrows, Stuart. *A Familiar Strangeness: American Fiction and the Language of Photography, 1839-1945*. Athens: University of Georgia Press, 2010.

Butler, Martin. "Introduction." In *Cymbeline*, by William Shakespeare. New York: Cambridge University Press, 2005.

Cady, Edwin H. "The Wizard Hand: Hawthorne, 1864-1900." In *Hawthorne Centenary Essays*, edited by Roy Harvey Pearce, 317–34. Columbus: Ohio State University Press, 1964.

"castle in the air, n." *OED Online*. March 2018. Oxford University Press.

Charvat, William. "Introduction." In *Centenary Edition of the Works of Nathaniel Hawthorne*, vol. 2. *The House of the Seven Gables*, edited by Nathaniel Hawthorne. Columbus: Ohio State University Press, 1962–.

Cleaveland, Parker. *An Elementary Treatise on Mineralogy and Geology, Designed for the Use of Pupils, – For Persons, Attending Lectures on These Subjects, – and as a Companion for Travellers in the United States of America*, vol. 1, 2nd ed. Boston: Cummings and Hilliard, 1822.

Cobbet, William. *Cottage Economy: Containing Information Relative to the Brewing of Beer, Making of Bread, Keeping of Cows, Pigs, Bees, Ewes, Goats, Poultry and Rabbits, and Relative to Other Matters Deemed Useful in the Conducting of the Affairs of a Labourer's Family*. London: C. Clement, 1822.

Coleridge, Samuel Taylor. *Biographia Literaria, or, Biographical Sketches of My Literary Life and Opinions*, edited by James Engell and W. Jackson Bate. Princeton: Princeton University Press, 1985.

Cook, Reginald. "The Forest of Goodman Brown's Night: A Reading of Hawthorne's "Young Goodman Brown." *The New England Quarterly* 43, no. 3 (September 1970): 473–81.

Colacurcio, Michael J. *The Province of Piety: Moral History in Hawthorne's Early Tales*. Durham: Duke University Press, 1995.

———. "'Red Man's Grave': Art and Destiny in Hawthorne's 'Main-Street'." *Nathaniel Hawthorne Review* 31, no. 2 (2005): 1–18.

Combe, George. *The Constitution of Man Considered in Relation to External Objects*, 2nd ed. Longman and Company, London, 1835.

Cranch, Christopher Pearse. "Correspondences." *The Dial* 1, no. 3 (January 1841). *Google Books*.

Crews, Frederick. *The Sins of the Fathers: Hawthorne's Psychological Themes*. Berkeley: University of California Press, 1989.

Cronon, William. *Uncommon Ground: Rethinking the Human Place in Nature*. New York: Norton, 1996.

Curran, Ronald T. "'Yankee Gothic': Hawthorne's 'Castle of Pyncheon.'" *Studies in the Novel* 8 (1976): 69–80.

Cuvier, George. *Cuvier's Animal Kingdom, Arranged According to Its Organization; Forming the Basis for a Natural History of Animals, and An Introduction to Comparative Anatomy*, edited by Edward Blyth et al. London: W.S. Orr and Company, 1840.

Danforth, Samuel. "A Brief Recognition of New-England's Errand into the Wilderness: An Online Electronic Text Edition." 1670. Edited by Paul Royster, *Digital Commons,* University of Nebraska-Lincoln, UNL Libraries, 2006.

Daniel, Janice B. "'Apples of the Thoughts and Fancies': Nature as Narrator in *The Scarlet Letter*." *American Transcendental Quarterly* 7, no. 4 (1993): 307–20.

Decker, George. *The American Historical Romance*. New York: Cambridge University Press, 1987.
De Salvo, Louise. *Nathaniel Hawthorne*. Atlantic Highlands, NJ: Humanities Press, 1987.
Drake, Samuel Gardner. *Indian Biography, Containing the Lives of More Than Two Hundred Indian Chiefs: Also Such Others of That Race as Have Rendered Their Names Conspicuous in the History of North America from Its First Being Known to Europeans to the Present Period. Giving at Large Their Most Celebrated Speeches, Memorable Sayings, Numerous Anecdotes, and a History of Their Wars*. Boston: Josiah Drake, 1832.
Edwards Milne. In Benjamin Silliman et al., *The American Journal of Science and the Arts*, vol. 27 (May 1859). https://www.biodiversitylibrary.org/bibliography/44570#/summary.
Eigner, Edwin M. "The Bad Tradition and the Romance of Man." In *Robert Louis Stevenson and the Romantic Tradition*, edited by Edwin M. Eigner. Princeton: Princeton University Press, 1966.
Emerson, Ralph Waldo. *The Journals and Miscellaneous Notebooks of Ralph Waldo Emerson, vol. 11. 1848-1851*, edited by A.W. Plumstead, William H. Gilman, and Ruth H. Bennett. Cambridge, MA: Belknap Press, 1975.
———. *Nature and Selected Essays*, edited by Larzer Ziff. New York: Penguin, 2003.
Empson, William. *Some Versions of Pastoral*. New York: New Directions, 1974.
"Fairyland Pond." *The Walden Woods Project*. The Thoreau Institute at Walden Woods. www.walden.org/property/fairyland-pond.
Felt, Joseph Barlow. *The Annals of Salem: From Its First Settlement*. Salem, MA: Ives, 1827.
Fernie, Deanna. *Hawthorne, Sculpture, and the Question of American Art*. New York: Routledge, 2016.
Fisher, Lydia. "The Savage in the House." *Arizona Quarterly: A Journal of American, Literature, Culture, and Theory* 64, no. 1 (2008): 49–75.
Flynn, Kelly M. "Nathaniel Hawthorne Had a Farm: Artists and Laborers in The Blithedale Romance." In *Reading the Earth: New Directions in the Study of Literature and Environment*, edited by Michael P. Branch et al. Moscow: University of Idaho Press, 1998.
Fulford, Tim. *Romantic Indians: Native Americans, British Literature, and Transatlantic Culture, 1756-1830*. New York: Oxford University Press, 2006.
Fuller, Margaret. Review of *Mosses from an Old Manse*, by Nathaniel Hawthorne. In *Nathaniel Hawthorne: The Contemporary Reviews*, edited by John L. Idol, Jr. and Buford Jones. New York: Cambridge University Press, 1994.
———. *Summer on the Lakes, in 1843*. Urbana: University of Illinois Press, 1991.
Gatta, John. *Making Nature Sacred: Literature, Religion, and Environment in America from the Puritans to the Present*. New York: Oxford University Press, 2004.
Glotfelty, Cheryl. Introduction. "Literary Studies in an Age of Environmental Crisis." In *The Ecocriticism Reader: Landmarks in Literary Ecology*, edited by Cheryl Glotfelty and Harold Fromm, xv–xxxvii. Athens: University of Georgia Press, 1996.

Goose, Nigel. "Cottage Industry, Migration, and Marriage in Nineteenth-Century England." *The Economic History Review* 61, no. 4 (2008): 798–819.

Harraway, Donna. *The Companion Species Manifesto: Dogs, People, and Significant Otherness*. Chicago: Prickly Paradigm Press, 2003.

Hawthorne, Julian. *Hawthorne Reading: An Essay*. Cleveland: Rowfant Club, 1902.

Hawthorne, Nathaniel. *The Centenary Edition of the Works of Nathaniel Hawthorne*, vol. 8. *The American Notebooks*, edited by William Charvat et al. Columbus: Ohio State University Press, 1972.

———. *The Centenary Edition of the Works of Nathaniel Hawthorne*, vol. 13. *The Elixir of Life Manuscripts: Septimius Felton, Septimius Norton, The Dolliver Romance*, edited by William Charvat et al. Columbus: Ohio State University Press, 1977.

———. *The Centenary Edition of the Works of Nathaniel Hawthorne*, vol. 15. *The Letters, 1813-1843*, edited by William Charvat et al. Columbus: Ohio State University Press, 1984.

———. *The Centenary Edition of the Works of Nathaniel Hawthorne*, vol. 16. *The Letters, 1843-1853*, edited by William Charvat et al. Columbus: Ohio State University Press, 1985.

———. *The Centenary Edition of the Works of Nathaniel Hawthorne*, vol. 17. *The Letters, 1853-1856*, edited by William Charvat et al. Columbus: Ohio State University Press, 1987.

———. *The Centenary Edition of the Works of Nathaniel Hawthorne*, vol. 18. *The Letters, 1857-1864*, edited by William Charvat et al. Columbus: Ohio State University Press, 1987.

———. *The Complete Works of Nathaniel Hawthorne*, 13 vols., with Introductory Notes by George Parsons Lathrop. Riverside Edition. Boston: Houghton Mifflin, 1882–1883.

———. "The Duston Family." *American Magazine of Useful and Entertaining Knowledge* 2, no. 9 (May 1836): 395–97.

"History and Culture." Wampanoag Tribe of Gay Head (Aquinnah). www.wampanoagtribe.net/Pages/Wampanoag_WebDocs/history_culture.

Horrocks, Sam. "Planting out after *Blithedale:* Transcendental Agrarianism and Ecocritical Economy." *Resilience: A Journal of the Environmental Humanities* 4, no. 1 (Winter 2016): 44–59.

Horsman, Reginald. *Race and Manifest Destiny: The Origins of American Racial Anglo-Saxonism*. Cambridge: Harvard University Press, 1981.

Johnson, Christopher. *This Grand and Magnificent Place: The Wilderness Heritage of the White Mountains*. Lebanon, NH: University of New Hampshire Press, 2006.

Johnson, Claudia D. *The Productive Tensions of Hawthorne's Art*. Tuscaloosa: University of Alabama Press, 1981.

Karcher, Carolyn L. *The First Woman in the Republic: A Cultural Biography of Lydia Maria Child*. Durham: Duke University Press, 1994.

Kant, Immanuel. *Critique of Pure Reason*, edited by Patricia Kitcher, translated by Werner S. Pluhar. Indianapolis: Hackett Publishing, 1996.

Kesselring, Marion Louise. *Hawthorne's Reading, 1828-1850: A Transcription and Identification of Titles Recorded in the Charge-books of the Salem Athenaeum*. New York: Haskell House, 1975.

Kevorkian, Martin. "Reading the Bloody 'Face of Nature': The Persecution of Religion in Hawthorne's *The Marble Faun*." *Contagion: Journal of Violence, Mimesis, and Culture* 13 (2006): 133–45.

Kopley, Richard. *The Threads of the Scarlet Letter: A Study of Hawthorne's Transformative Art*. Newark: University of Delaware Press, 2003.

Kroeber, Karl. *Ecological Literary Criticism: Romantic Imagining and the Biology of Mind*. New York: Columbia University Press, 1994.

Lathrop, Rose Hawthorne. *Memories of Hawthorne*. Boston: Houghton Mifflin, 1897.

Levine, Robert. "American Studies in an Age of Extinction." *States of Emergency: The Object of American Studies*, edited by Russ Castronovo and Susan Gillman, 161–82. Chapel Hill: University of North Carolina Press, 2009.

———. "Genealogical Fictions: Race in *The House of the Seven Gables* and *Pierre*." In *Hawthorne and Melville: Writing a Relationship*, edited by Jana L. Argersinger and Leland S. Person, 227–47. Athens: University of Georgia Press, 2008.

Lewis, R.W.B. *The American Adam: Innocence, Tragedy and Tradition in the Nineteenth Century*. Chicago: University of Chicago Press, 1971.

Lindholdt, Paul. *Explorations in Ecocriticism: Advocacy, Bioregionalism, and Visual Design*. Lanham, MD: Lexington Books, 2015.

"Literature Related to Native Americans and the Scarlet Letter." *Hawthorne in Salem*. www.hawthorneinsalem.org/page/11445.

Locke, John. *An Essay Concerning Human Understanding*, edited by. Roger Woolhouse. New York: Penguin, 1997.

Longfellow, Henry Wadsworth. "Nature." *Poetry Foundation*. www.poetryfoundation.org/poems/44641/nature-56d223cf7262b.

Lundblad, Jane. *Nathaniel Hawthorne and the Tradition of Gothic Romance*. New York: Haskell House, 1964.

McGann, Jerome J. *The Romantic Ideology: A Critical Investigation*. Chicago: The University of Chicago Press, 1983.

McIntosh, James. "Nature and Frontier in 'Roger Malvin's Burial.'" *American Literature* 60, no. 2 (1988): 188–204.

Mann, Horace. *Speech of Mr. Horace Mann, of Mass., on the Subject of Slavery in the Territories, and the Consequences of the Threatened Dissolution of the Union*. Washington, DC: Gideon, 1850.

Marshall, Ian. "Reading the Willey Disaster: An Evolutionary Approach to Environmental Aesthetics in Cole's *Notch of the White Mountains* and Hawthorne's 'The Ambitious Guest,'" *The Journal of Ecocriticism: A New Journal of Nature, Society and Literature* 3, no. 2 (2011): 1–15.

Martin, Robert K. "Haunted by Jim Crow: Gothic Fictions by Hawthorne and Faulkner." In *American Gothic: New Interventions in a National Narrative*, edited by Robert K. Martin & Eric Savoy, 129–42. Iowa City: University of Iowa Press, 2009.

Marx, Leo. *The Machine in the Garden: Technology and the Pastoral Ideal in America*. 1964. New York: Oxford University Press, 2000.

Mason, Jennifer. *Civilized Creatures: Urban Animals, Sentimental Culture, and American Literature, 1850-1900*. Baltimore: Johns Hopkins University Press, 2005.

Mather, Cotton. *The Christian Philosopher,* edited by Winton U. Solberg. Urbana: University of Illinois Press, 1994.

———. *Magnalia Christi Americana; Or, The Ecclesiastical History of New-England, from Its First Planting, in the Year 1620, Unto the Year of Our Lord 1698,* vol. 2. Hartford: Silas Andrus & Sons, 1853.

Matterson, Stephen. *Melville: Fashioning in Modernity.* New York: Bloomsbury Publishing, 2014.

Matthiessen, F.O. *American Renaissance: Art and Expression in the Age of Emerson and Whitman.* 1941. New York: Oxford University Press, 1968.

Maule, Thomas. "Truth Held Forth and Maintained: According to the Testimony of the Holy Prophets, Christ and His Apostles Recorded in the Holy Scriptures." 1695. In *Better That 100 Witches Should Live: The 1696 Acquittal of Thomas Maule of Salem, Massachusetts, on Charges of Seditious Libel and Its Impact on the Development of First Amendment Freedoms,* edited by James Edward Maule. Villanova, PA: Jembook Publishing, 1995.

Melville, Herman. "Hawthorne and His Mosses." Review of *Mosses from an Old Manse,* by Nathaniel Hawthorne. In *Nathaniel Hawthorne: The Contemporary Reviews,* edited by John L. Idol, Jr. and Buford Jones. New York: Cambridge University Press, 1994.

Merchant, Carolyn. *The Death of Nature: Women, Ecology and the Scientific Revolution.* New York: Harper Collins, 1980.

Michaels, Walter Benn. "Romance and Real Estate." In *The American Renaissance Reconsidered,* edited by Donald Pease. Baltimore: Johns Hopkins University Press, 1985.

Miller, Edward Haviland. *Salem Is My Dwelling Place: A Life of Nathaniel Hawthorne.* Iowa City: University of Iowa Press, 1992.

Morrison, Toni. *Playing in the Dark: Whiteness and the Literary Imagination.* Cambridge, MA: Harvard University Press, 1992.

Mudie, Robert. *A Popular Guide to the Observation of Nature, Or, Hints of Inducement to the Study of Natural Productions and Appearances, in Their Connexions and Relations.* New York: Harper, 1833. *Google Books.*

Outka, Paul. *Race and Nature: From Transcendentalism to the Harlem Renaissance.* New York: Palgrave Macmillan, 2008.

Panofsky, Erwin. *Meaning in the Visual Arts: Papers in and on Art History.* Garden City, NY: Doubleday Anchor, 1955.

Paris, John Ayrton and J.S.M. Fonblanque, *Medical Jurisprudence,* vol. 3, London: W. Phillips, 1823. *Google Books.*

"pastoral, n. and adj." *OED Online.* March 2018. Oxford University Press.

Pennant, Thomas. *British Zoology,* vol. 1, 4th ed. Warrington: Benjamin White, 1776, *Google Books.*

Petersheim, Steven. "Celebrating the 'Great, Round, Solid Self' of Earth in Hawthorne's Short Fiction." In *Writing the Environment in Nineteenth-Century American Literature: The Ecological Awareness of Early Scribes of Nature,* edited by Steven Petersheim and Madison P. Jones IV, 33–55. Lanham, MD: Lexington Books, 2015.

———. "Hawthorne and Natural Landscapes." In *Nathaniel Hawthorne in Context,* edited by Monika Elbert, 376–85. New York: Cambridge University Press, 2018.

Poe, Edgar Allan. "The Philosophy of Composition." In *Poe: Essays and Reviews,* edited by Gary Richard Thompson, 13–25. New York: The Library of America, 1984.

———. "Review of *Twice-Told Tales* and *Mosses from an Old Manse* (1847)." In *Poe: Essays and Reviews,* edited by Gary Richard Thompson, 577–89. New York: The Library of America, 1984.

Pratt, Julius W. "The Origin of 'Manifest Destiny.'" *The American Historical Review* 32, no. 4 (1927): 795–98.

"race, n.6." *OED Online.* March 2018. Oxford University Press.

Review of "Principles of Geology," from *Monthly Review.* In *The Museum of Foreign Literature and Science* 20 (June 1832).

Reynolds, Larry J. *Devils and Rebels: The Making of Hawthorne's Damned Politics.* Ann Arbor: University of Michigan Press, 2008.

"romance, n. and adj." *OED Online.* March 2018. Oxford University Press.

Ronda, Bruce A. *Elizabeth Palmer Peabody: A Reformer on Her Own Terms.* Cambridge, MA: Harvard University Press, 1999.

Rosenberg, Liz. "'The Best That Earth Could Offer': 'The Birthmark,' A Newly-Wed's Story." *Studies in Short Fiction* 30, no. 2 (1993): 145–51.

Ryskamp, Charles. "The New England Sources of *The Scarlet Letter.*" *American Literature* 31, no. 3 (1959): 257–72.

Scott, Sir Walter. "Essay on Romance." In *The Miscellaneous Prose Works of Sir Walter Scott,* vol. 6. Edinburgh: Robert Cadell, 1834.

———. *Letters on Demonology and Witchcraft, Addressed to J. G. Lockhart, Esq.* London: John Murray, 1830.

Sears, John. "Hawthorne's 'The Ambitious Guest' and the Significance of the Willey Disaster," *American Literature* 54, no. 3 (1982): 354–67.

Shakespeare, William. *The Winter's Tale,* edited by Stephen Orgel. New York: Oxford University Press, 2008.

Sigourney, Lydia. "Indian Names." *Poetry Foundation.* www.poetryfoundation.org/poems/52037/indian-names.

Smith, Shawn Michelle. *American Archives: Gender, Race, and Class in Visual Culture.* Princeton: Princeton University Press, 1999.

Snow, Caleb Hopkins. *A History of Boston, the Metropolis of Massachusetts, from Its Origin to the Present, with Some Account of the Environs.* Boston: A. Bowen, 1825.

Sprague, Charles. *An Ode: Pronounced Before the Inhabitants of Boston, September the Seventeenth, 1830, at the Bicentennial Celebration of the Settlement of the City.* Boston: John Eastburn, 1830.

Stewart, Dugald. *Philosophical Essays,* 2nd ed. Edinburgh: George Ramsay and Company, 1816. *Google Books.*

Stewart, Randall "Recollections of Hawthorne by His Sister Elizabeth," *American Literature* 16, no. 4 (1945): 316–31.

Swann, Charles *Nathaniel Hawthorne: Tradition and Revolution.* New York: Cambridge University Press, 1991.

Tanner, Tony. Introduction. *The Blithedale Romance.* New York: Oxford University Press, 1999.

Tellefsen, Blythe Ann. "'The Case with My Dear Native Land': Nathaniel Hawthorne's Vision of America in *The Marble Faun*." *Nineteenth-Century Literature* 54, no. 4 (March 2000): 455–79.

Theis, Jeffrey S. *Writing the Forest in Early Modern England: A Sylvan Pastoral Nation*. Pittsburgh, PA: Duquesne University Press, 2009.

Thoreau, Henry David. *Walden*. Princeton: Princeton University Press, 2004.

Turner, Arlin. *Nathaniel Hawthorne: A Biography*. New York: Oxford University Press, 1980.

Van Leer, David. "Hester's Labyrinth: Transcendental Rhetoric in Puritan Boston." In *New Essays on The Scarlet Letter*, edited by Michael Colacurcio, 57–100. New York: Cambridge University Press, 1985.

Van Wyhe, John. "The History of Phrenology on the Web." www.historyofphrenology.org.uk/constindex.html.

Voller, Jack G. *The Supernatural Sublime: The Metaphysics of Terror in Anglo-American Romanticism*. DeKalb: Northern Illinois University Press, 1994.

Waggoner, Hyatt Howe. *Hawthorne: A Critical Study*. Cambridge: Harvard University Press, 1963.

Waples, Dorothy. "Suggestions for Interpreting *The Marble Faun*." *American Literature* 13, no. 3 (November 1941): 224–39.

Warren, Karen J. "Ecological Feminist Philosophies: An Overview of the Issues." In *Ecological Feminist Philosophies,* edited by Karen J. Warren, ix–xxvi. Bloomington: Indiana University Press, 1996.

Washizu, Hiroko. "Celestial Hieroglyphics." *Hawthorne in Salem*. www.hawthorneinsalem.org/ScholarsForum/MMD2683.html.

Weber, Alfred, Beth L. Lueck, and Dennis Berthold. *Hawthorne's American Travel Sketches*. Hanover: University Press of New England, 1989.

Weinland, D.F. "Some Principles of Animal Psychology." January 1859, 1. In Benjamin Silliman et al., *The American Journal of Science and the Arts* 27 (May 1859). www.biodiversitylibrary.org/bibliography/44570#/summary.

Weinstein, Cindy. Introduction. *The Scarlet Letter*, by Nathaniel Hawthorne, edited by Brian Harding, ix–xxxii. New York: Oxford University Press, 2007.

"The Wife and Children of Nathaniel Hawthorne." *Hawthorne in Salem*. http://www.hawthorneinsalem.org/page/10064.

Williams, Raymond. *The Country and the City*. New York: Oxford University Press, 1973.

Wilson, Christine. "Haunted Habitability: Wilderness and American Haunted House Narratives." In *Popular Ghosts: The Haunted Spaces of Everyday Culture,* edited by María del Pilar Blanco and Esther Peeren, 200–212. New York: Continuum, 2010.

Wilson, Eric. *Romantic Turbulence: Chaos, Ecology, and American Space*. New York: St. Martin's Press, 2000.

Wineapple, Brenda. *Hawthorne: A Life*. New York: Random House, 2004.

Winthrop, John. *The Journal of John Winthrop, 1630-1649,* edited by Richard S. Dunn, James Savage, and Laetitia Yeandle. Cambridge: Harvard University Press, 1996.

———. "A Modell of Christian Charity." In *Collections of the Massachusetts Historical Society,* vol. 7. Boston: Little and Brown, 1838.

Index

abolition, 86, 103, 129–30, 168–70, 174n97
adaptation. *See* environmental adaptation; literary adaptation; physical adaptation
aesthetic, xviii–xix, xxii, 32. *See also* beauty
African American, xxix, 90, 101, 103, 112, 158, 169–71, 179–80
agrarian, 24, 132, 144
agriculture, 8, 130–32, 144, 146n53. *See also* agrarian
air, 2, 57, 128, 150, 152, 161, 164–65, 171. *See also* atmosphere
allegory, xii, xxv–xxvi, 23–24, 30–31, 48–53, 56, 62, 66, 70, 75–77, 78n17, 138, 146n53
ambiguity, xxii, xxv, xxvi, xxxi, 4–5, 45, 57, 70, 75, 84–85, 170
American Civil War, xxix–xxxi, 1, 93, 142, 168, 178–82
American Indian, ix, xxvi–xxix, xxxin2, 21, 25–29, 50, 53, 56–62, 67, 69, 73, 83–84, 87–88, 90–112, 115n62, 128, 130, 178–80. *See also* Indian deeds; Indian removals
American landscape, xiv, xix, xxiii, xxvi, 1–3, 9, 11, 17–30, 52–57, 97–105, 156, 181. *See also* landscape painting

American Renaissance, x–xi, xiii
American Revolution, 24, 25, 95, 179
anatomy, 88, 165
ancestral, xxvii, 22–23, 60–62, 83, 85–89, 90–91, 94, 97, 105, 109, 155, 163–64, 168
ancient. *See* antiquity
angels, 5, 46, 53, 61–63, 66, 68, 72, 84, 92
Anglo-Saxon, 84, 99, 105, 112,
animals, ix, xii–xvi, xxiv–xxviii, 11–14, 28, 37, 50, 57–60, 72–73, 86, 88, 91–93, 97, 105, 110, 126, 133–35, 149–59, 164–67, 171, 178. *See also* creatures
antagonism, xx, 26, 31–32, 41, 52, 66, 77, 87–89. *See also* enemy
anthropocentric, 13, 23, 35
antiquity, ix, xvi, xxix, 9–10, 92, 100, 102, 106–7, 133, 151, 159, 163–64, 168
apocalypse, 21, 32–33, 171
apoplexy, 87–89, 102, 110
appearance, xi, xxiii, xxiv, 22, 45–48, 54, 63, 90, 124, 141, 162
Arcadia, xvi, xxi, 27, 119, 122, 139–41, 154, 161, 163
architecture, 10, 34, 98
aristocratic class, xxvii, xxx, 30, 72, 86, 108

195

art and nature, xx, xxv, xxviii, 33–35, 51, 150–51, 169
artificial, xviii, 10, 33, 77, 123–24, 129, 143
artist, xx, xxiii, 1, 12, 21, 46, 74, 120, 134, 169, 182
artistic technique, xix–xxi, xxv–xxvi, xxxivn59, 14, 19, 41, 62, 95, 115n62, 127, 152, 169, 181. *See also* composing practices
atmosphere, xxvii, 14, 98, 126, 151, 158–63, 168–71
atoms, 83, 85, 105, 165
attitudes toward nature, ix, xi–xiv, xix–xx, xxv–xxvi, xxx, 5–9, 13, 19–27, 29, 31–32, 38–42, 50–61, 74–77, 93, 99, 105–11, 123–26, 132, 136, 168–69
authority, 25, 54, 77, 84, 105, 166. *See also* sources

Bakhtin, Mikhail, xxiv–xxx, xxxiv–xxxvn81
beauty, vii, xxix, xxxin1, 1, 5, 8–9, 12–14, 21, 27, 30, 35–38, 50–51, 59, 62–64, 73–74, 90, 97, 102, 104, 111, 119, 124, 127, 135–38, 144n2, 149, 154, 159–162, 168
beliefs about nature, xii, xxi, xxv, 17–18, 25, 46–49, 66, 69–70, 84–86, 108, 158, 164, 167–68, 183
Berkshires, xvi, xxiii, 1, 31, 156
Bible, xvi, xxx, 24, 51, 56, 62, 92–93
biology, xxiv, xxx, 19, 33, 35, 49, 68–69, 72, 76–77, 83–86, 97, 133–36, 157, 163, 178, 182
biosphere, xiii, 9, 11, 14, 123, 151, 163. *See also* ecosphere
birds, xvi, 5, 7, 11, 57, 59, 97, 102, 108, 123, 150, 152, 164, 165, 171
blithe, xx, 120, 122, 138, 141, 183
Blithedale Farm, 119–24, 127–35, 139, 143–44
blood, xxvii, 13, 83–93, 105, 106, 111, 114n40, 135, 151, 158, 168, 179

blossom, 7, 29, 51, 69, 73, 124, 135
body. *See* human body
book of nature, xxvi–xxvii, 55–58
Boston, ix, 1, 24, 29, 53–54, 59, 76, 105, 129
Bowdoin College, xvi, xviii, xxiii, xxix, 1, 2, 18, 22, 28, 156, 181
brain, 88, 91–92, 133, 136, 180
breeds, 84, 86, 89–91. *See also* blood; races
Bridge, Horatio, xxix, 2
British nature poets, xxii, 11–12
British Renaissance, xvi, xix–xxi, xxv–xxvi, 50
Brook Farm, ix, xxviii, 8, 128–31
Bryant, William Cullen, ix, xiv, xxxin1

Calvinism, xi, 56
canals, 1, 2, 10, 34
cathedral. *See* church
cats, 88, 133, 150, 156
cautionary, xv, 9, 11, 21, 35, 70, 107, 151–52, 169
Cervantes, Miguel de, xvi, xxi
chemistry, xxiii, 38, 39, 71
chickens, 87, 89, 92, 102
Child, Lydia Maria, ix, xxxin3, 95, 115n62
Christ, 51, 63, 160–61
church, xxx, 10, 11, 24, 48, 53–54, 150
city, xv, xix, 1, 5, 10, 24, 30, 33–35, 52, 68, 125, 129–32, 136, 143, 150, 157, 160–63, 168. *See also* city and country
city and country, xv–xviii, xx, xxv, 1–2, 5, 9–10, 24, 33, 35, 57, 68, 129, 132, 143, 150, 160, 163
class (social), xviii, xxx, 18, 39–40, 57, 66, 83–86, 89–92, 101, 106, 144, 154, 158, 161–64, 182
classical literature, xvi, xix, xxxiiin38, 163. *See also* mythology
clergyman, 24, 48–49, 54, 64, 68, 70, 72, 89. *See also* sermons
climate, 132–33, 162, 170

Index

civilization, xiv, xvii, xx, xxv, 4, 8–11, 18, 28–29, 34, 50–52, 56–57, 60, 71, 73, 100, 103, 123, 143, 150, 181
civil war. *See* American Civil War, xxix–xxxi, 1, 93, 142, 168, 178–82
Cole, Thomas, xiv, xxiii, 21–22
Coleridge, Samuel Taylor, xvi, 51, 125–26, 130
colonialism, 20, 25, 28, 52, 54–55, 83, 94, 97, 100, 103, 105, 170
Combe, George, 91–92, 114n45
comedy, xx, 85, 111, 141
communication, xxiv, 35, 40–41, 48, 92, 112, 156, 165–66
communion with nature, 63, 163–68, 178
community, ix, x, xiv, 5, 17–19, 24–28, 33, 54–58, 60–61, 66, 69, 71–76, 100, 120–32, 138, 143–44, 152, 158–59, 179–80. *See also* utopia
companionship with nature, xi, 23–26, 40
companion species, xii–xiii, 11, 150, 156
competition, 54–55, 83, 86, 105, 111, 129
composing practices, xvi, xix–xxi, xxvi–xxxi, xxxivn59, 1–3, 13–14, 51, 98, 119. *See also* dialogic; novel; romance
Concord, Massachusetts, xiv, xxvii, 1–8, 19, 31–32, 35, 40, 128, 150, 156, 180, 182
conscience, 28, 53–54, 112–13
contemplation, xvi, xxx, 3–10, 14, 46, 56, 60
continent (North American), ix, xiv, 4, 18, 101, 112
control of nature, 11, 23, 28, 35–40, 56, 66, 99, 106, 111
conventions, xviii, 5, 35, 85, 122, 134, 179
Cooper, James Fenimore, xiv, 57, 95
correspondence, 66, 77, 124–25, 127, 141, 165

cottage, 22–23, 30, 58, 71, 76, 87, 101, 131–32
countryside, x, xviii, 1, 2, 18, 22, 96
court of law, 84–85, 88, 105–8
cows, 2, 101, 122, 154
Cranch, Christopher, 120–21, 124–25
creation, xix, xxiv, 6, 32, 34, 56, 62, 146n53, 178. *See also* creatures
creatures, xxiv, 19, 32, 41, 56, 74, 135–36, 144, 149–59, 164–65, 167, 169–71, 178, 182–83
crime, 87, 102–3, 108, 134, 142, 151–52, 166–67, 170
cultivation, 18, 102–3, 109–11, 129, 163
cultural criticism, xviii, 36, 45, 95, 97, 112–13
cultural inheritance, xxv, 122, 171, 178
cultural landscape, xiii–xv, xx, 18–23, 32, 36, 41, 45, 84, 95
culture and nature. *See* nature and culture
custom, xv, 73, 102, 104, 134
Custom House, xxvii, 65
Cuvier, George, 69, 155, 157, 167

dark nature, xi, xii, xvi, xx, xxx, 27, 57, 59, 62, 73, 111–12
darkness, x, 8, 19, 24, 35, 41, 51, 61, 66, 85, 87, 107, 163
Darwin, Charles, xxiv, 71, 91, 133, 157
death, xxviii, 7, 27, 29, 31, 35, 53, 55, 58, 64–65, 84, 87–92, 102, 110, 113, 119, 123–25, 127, 136–41, 144, 144n2, 159–63, 165, 179–81, 183
decay, 19, 34, 73, 108, 137, 154, 159, 161–63
De Cervantes, Miguel, xvi, xxi
Declaration of Independence, xiv, 50
Defoe, Daniel, xvi, 63
degeneration, 86, 91, 123, 160, 163
delusion, xv–xvi, 5, 90–91, 147n79
democracy, ix, xiv, xxx, 107
descendants, 86–89, 91–92, 100, 111, 133, 151, 171, 178–79

descriptions, x, xiii, xv, xxiii, xxvi–xxviii, 2, 5–6, 8–13, 19–21, 29–31, 38–39, 41, 46–48, 50, 55, 58–63, 66–68, 72–77, 90–91, 98–100, 106, 108, 120, 125, 135–37, 150, 155–58, 161, 164–65
desert, ix, xxxin1, 62, 76. *See also* wilderness
destiny, 22, 50, 55, 89, 92, 94, 106, 111–12, 143
devil, 13, 25–26, 33, 50, 52–53, 56, 59–61, 67, 70, 77, 89, 93, 109
dichotomies, xx, xxv, 27, 35, 57, 123
Dickinson, Emily, xxx, xxxvn82
discernment, xxi, xxvi, 24, 51, 76, 119, 128
disease, 13, 38, 46–47, 59, 88, 91, 102, 110–12, 124, 130, 132, 142, 151, 160–62, 171, 180
displacement, xxii, xxvii, 3, 11, 13, 99, 101, 105–6, 110, 126, 170
disputes. *See* property disputes
divine, xii, 6, 21, 26, 50–52, 56, 61–64, 75, 77, 143, 165
domestic, 6, 100, 110, 122, 134, 144, 158
Douglass, Frederick, 170
dreams, xxvi, xxviii, 3, 5, 22, 25–26, 29, 32, 37, 41, 55, 60–61, 86, 98, 127–28, 138, 144, 179–80
dwelling, 8, 10, 28, 56, 58, 71, 87, 97, 99, 100–103, 108, 111, 154, 165. *See also* cottage
dynamism of nature, 5–6, 25, 30, 58–59, 74

Early Modern Literature. *See* British Renaissance
earth, xi–xiii, xix, xxiv, 2, 7, 11, 17–21, 24, 28, 32–39, 50, 57, 59, 63, 65, 70, 75–77, 87, 101–2, 109, 111, 119–28, 132, 138, 144, 151–52, 159, 163–67, 171, 183
East, 1, 92, 94–95, 105–9, 112
ecocriticism, xi–xiii, xix, xxii–xxvi, 36, 40, 97, 100, 132, 177. *See also* ecology

ecology, xiii, 25, 34, 38, 140. *See also* ecocriticism; ecosphere
economy, 54, 103, 108, 129–32. *See also* economy of life
economy of life, 7, 21, 131–32, 144
ecosphere, xi–xiii, xxii, 33–35, 40–41. *See also* biosphere
ecosystem. *See* ecosphere
elements of nature, 9, 26, 34, 45–46, 69, 74, 123, 137, 160, 165
elixir, 178–81, 183
Emerson, Ralph Waldo, ix, xvi, xxi, 31, 40, 124–30, 141–142, 168, 183; *Nature* (essay), xxvi, 3–5, 17, 33–34, 104, 120, 127
enemy, 28, 68, 89, 141, 166. *See also* antagonism
England, xiv, xix, xxviii–xxix, 1, 3, 10–13, 27, 63, 68, 72, 131, 180
English landscape, xx, xxii, xxix, 3, 9–12, 16n33
English Renaissance. *See* British Renaissance
English scenery. *See* English landscape
Enlightenment, 121–22, 124, 132, 141
environment, reality of, 23–24, 30, 39–42, 62
environmental adaptation, xxviii, 10–11, 29–31, 71, 74, 96, 167–68, 178. *See also* physical adaptation
environmental consciousness, x–xv, xix–xxii, xxvi–xxx, 1–8, 18–19, 21–25, 27–32, 35, 39–41, 46, 52, 66, 85, 128, 143–44, 178
environmental crisis, xi, xxii, 9–10, 35, 149, 159–60, 163–64, 171, 181
environmental criticism. *See* ecocriticism
environmental destruction, 9, 11, 30–31, 35, 103, 106, 149, 151–52
environmental ethos. *See* ethics
environmentality, xiv, xv, xxxiin17
environmental justice, 162–63, 181
environmental literature, xi–xiii, xv–xvii, xix, xxii, xxvi, xxxiin17, 4, 6, 12, 18, 20, 30, 41, 133

environmental sensibility. *See* environmental consciousness

environmental writing. *See* environmental literature; nature writing

environment as teacher, 13–14, 21, 24

equality, xxix, 4, 91–92, 130, 178–79, 182

escape, 11, 20, 57–58, 72, 159–60, 167, 170

essay (form), xiv, xxiii–xxiv, 3–5, 7, 22, 31–36, 70, 97, 104, 120, 130, 158, 181

estrangement, xvii, 6, 96, 141, 151, 166, 171

ethics, xxx, 31–32, 57

European, ix–x, xiv, xvi–xvii, xxiii–xxiv, 2, 4, 18, 52, 58, 69, 71, 73, 76, 84, 90, 95, 99–101, 103–4, 106–7, 179–80

evil, 12, 25, 50, 56–57, 59, 74, 85, 111–12, 152, 154, 158, 162, 169, 182

evolution, xxiv, 34, 71, 133, 155–57. *See also* Darwin, Charles; physical adaptation; transmutation

existence, xiii, xxiv, 4–7, 11–14, 19, 32–35, 49, 73, 76, 92, 102–3, 123–26, 149, 151–52, 156, 159–62, 165–71, 182–83

expansionism, xxiii, 84, 107, 112

experience, x, xiv, xxiii–xxviii, 3–4, 7, 12–14, 18, 20–21, 23–25, 32, 39, 41, 48, 54–55, 61, 66, 77, 84, 109, 127–29, 132, 142, 158, 165, 169, 171, 177

experiment, xxii, xxv, xxxi, 4, 8, 23, 33–34, 38, 112, 119, 122, 129–30, 134, 139, 143, 144, 147n79

exploitation, 32, 107–8, 132, 169

external reality, xv, xx, 10, 25, 27, 46, 40–41, 91, 100–101, 119, 127–29, 155, 163

extinction, 35, 89–91, 151, 155, 157, 159, 171, 183

eyes, xxix, 4, 5, 12, 60, 64, 74–75, 87, 98, 109, 120–21, 135–37, 141. *See also* sight

fable, x, xxi, 21–23, 163, 183

factories, 9–10, 30–31, 122

Faerie Queene, xix, xxxiii, 51

fairyland, xvi, xxi, xxvi–xxviii. *See also* *Faerie Queene*

falsification, xvii–xix, xx, 12, 71–73, 103, 111–12, 122–23

family, xix, xxvii, 3, 18, 20–21, 24, 28–30, 38, 54, 60, 85–86, 88–90, 92, 96, 99, 104, 110–11, 131, 155–58, 160, 171

farms, 10, 18, 20, 24, 28. *See also* Blithedale Farm; Brook Farm

faun, xxviii, 149–59, 163–64, 167, 169, 171, 182

fear, xvi, 19, 24–27, 30, 49–50, 54, 64, 66–67, 89, 170, 178

feminist, ix, xi, 36–39, 61–64, 66, 69, 72–74, 136–39, 144n2, 158, 179–80. *See also* gender

fertility, 18, 102, 106, 138, 183

fiction, xii–xvi, xxi–xxx, xxxiin17, 1–2, 14, 17–42, 45, 95, 97, 122, 127, 129, 131, 159, 179. *See also* stories

fields, xv, xx, xxxin1, 2, 4, 9, 33, 67, 104, 122, 124, 129, 134, 154

figurative language, 20, 30, 46, 54, 56, 65, 70–71, 76, 86, 98–100, 122, 134–35, 151, 177. *See also* personification

fire, 2, 5, 30–32, 59, 93, 123, 128, 143

fish, 4, 14, 28, 31, 102

Florence, Italy, 50, 161, 163–64

flowers, 7, 10, 12, 18, 29, 34, 51, 66, 69, 75, 87, 97, 102, 122, 150, 154, 164–65

forest, ix, xii, xxxin1, 1–2, 10, 20, 22–23, 25–27, 29, 49, 50, 53, 56–62, 64–65, 67, 71, 73, 76, 94, 102, 106, 164–65, 180–81

Fortunate Fall, 152, 159, 165, 169, 171

Fourierism, 130–31, 134, 146n53

freedom, xxix, 28, 52–55, 96, 112, 134, 139, 159–60, 170, 182

frontiersmen. *See* settlers

fruits, 2, 5–7, 13, 18, 29, 35, 85, 87, 102, 161

Fugitive Slave Act, xxvii, 83, 86, 105, 158
Fuller, Margaret, ix, xi, 4, 36, 40, 130, 139

gardening, 3, 6, 7, 8, 13, 28, 31, 36, 38, 129
Garden of Eden, xvi, 3, 6, 18, 29, 50, 53, 54, 66–68, 111, 125, 128, 140, 151, 156, 161, 178
gems, xxiii, 19, 21–23
gender, 7, 36–40, 72, 110–12, 119, 124, 134–36, 144, 146n53, 166; *See also* feminist
generation, 4, 7, 59, 69, 85–86, 89, 104, 109–10, 132, 161, 177; *See also* degeneration; regeneration
genre, xvii, xxi–xxiii, xxxiin17, xxxiv–xxxvn81, 41, 50, 98
geography, xx, xxiii, 87, 92, 178
geology, xxiii–xxiv, xxx, 133, 178, 182
germs, 69, 85–86, 161, 170, 177, 182
God. *See* theology
Golden age, xvi, xxi, 106, 163, 171
Gothic, xvi, xx, xxv, 86–88, 98–102, 108–12, 178
government, xiv, 26–28, 46, 72, 87, 91, 96, 98, 112, 122
grace, xx, 27, 36, 68, 89, 152
grass, 9–10, 33–34, 45, 67, 101–2, 137, 154, 165, 181
graves, 27, 35, 37, 52, 91, 93, 95, 137–41. *See also* death
greed, 33, 60, 83, 85, 87, 95, 99–110, 129–30
Greek literature. *See* classical literature
grotesque, 92, 99, 101, 104, 137
growth, ix, 3, 6–7, 9–10, 18, 33–34, 58, 69, 75–76, 85, 101–2, 132, 135, 157, 163–64, 181–82
guilt, xi, 58, 66, 72, 93, 99, 105, 109, 141, 149, 164–69. *See also* sin

habit, xv, 40, 123, 135
habitation. *See* dwelling

happiness, 8, 35, 37, 52, 59, 63, 131, 136, 138, 143, 154, 157, 171
harmony with nature, ix–x, xvi, xx, 4–7, 10–13, 22, 26, 40, 50, 52, 57, 70–71, 74–76, 119–20, 128–30, 134, 141–44, 150–52, 156, 163–64, 168–69, 183
haunted houses, 90, 99–100, 104, 110
Hawthorne, Nathaniel: "The Ambitious Guest," 19–21; "The Birthmark," 36–40; *The Blithedale Romance,* xv, xix, xxi, xxviii, 41, 119–44; "Earth's Holocaust," 32–34; "Endicott and the Red Cross," 27–28, 36, 56; "Ethan Brand," 30–31; "The Great Carbuncle," 21–23; "The Hall of Fantasy," 17, 31–32; *The House of the Seven Gables,* xv, xxvii, xxix, 83–113, 141, 169; letters, x, 18, 20, 28, 40, 156, 168, 180; *The Marble Faun,* xxiv, xxviii, 3, 149–76; "The May-pole of Merry-Mount," 26–28, 36, 56; *Mosses from an Old Manse,* 5, 18, 31, 33, 36, 40; "My Kinsman, Major Molineux," 24–26; "The New Adam and Eve," 33–35, 68, 171; notebooks, x, xvi, xxiii–xxvi, 1–6, 9, 14, 17–18, 30–31, 35, 130, 156, 160, 172n25, 177, 182; "The Old Manse," 5–6, 18, 31; prefaces, xxii, xxvii–xxx, 2, 5, 33, 39, 65, 83, 85, 98–100, 103, 127–29, 168; "Rappaccini's Daughter," 36, 38–39; "Roger Malvin's Burial," 29–30; *The Scarlet Letter,* xii, xv, xxvi, 39, 45–77, 94, 103, 105, 112, 115n62, 128, 141, 143; *Septimius Felton* and Elixir of Life manuscripts, 178–81, 183; "Young Goodman Brown," xvi, 23–26, 41, 53, 61, 177
Hawthorne, Sophia Peabody, xxxiiin38, 3–5, 17, 31, 33, 35, 40, 130, 156, 169, 180
health, xi, 7, 13, 48, 62, 65, 71, 75–76, 88, 132, 135, 144, 155, 157, 159–64, 171, 178–80

Index

herbs, 2, 33, 38, 69, 75–76, 178, 180
hereditary, xv, 11, 70, 72, 88, 110, 135. *See also* inherited characteristics
heteroglossia, xxv, xxx, xxxiv–xxxvn81
hidden, xi, xv, xx, 12, 25, 36, 64–65, 76, 84, 94, 107, 111–12, 119–22, 125, 127–29, 157, 161, 163
history, xv, xxi, xxvi, 3, 18, 23–27, 30, 39, 50, 52–57, 61, 64, 83–86, 93–96, 99, 101, 105, 109, 150–51, 158, 163, 179, 182. *See also* natural history
horror, 30, 48–49, 66, 87, 97, 119, 137–38, 141
human activity, 10–11, 18–20, 23, 30, 110–11, 123, 149, 158
human body, xxiv–xxvii, 31, 34–39, 45–49, 62, 64–74, 77–78, 124, 133–38, 150–57, 160, 165, 183
human development, xxiv, 5, 49, 58, 65–66, 68–69, 76, 91, 131–39, 154–55, 157, 163, 167–70
human failure, xxviii, 21, 23, 37, 39, 48, 65, 71, 97, 119, 123–24, 142–44
human flourishing, 9, 57, 70–71, 182
human nature, xiii, xviii, xxv–xxvi, 1–2, 6–7, 11, 17, 19, 38–40, 50, 53, 57, 65, 68–70, 74–77, 85, 119, 124, 132, 142, 144, 157–59, 164, 167–69, 180–81
humans as members of natural world, xiii, xviii, 7, 11, 14, 33, 40–41, 138, 161, 182

idealism, xi, xiv–xvii, xx, xxi, xxvi, xxviii, 19, 27–29, 34–37, 52, 55, 89, 120–21, 126–31, 136–41, 183
identity, xxvi, 33, 36, 68–69, 84, 94, 111–13, 169, 171, 179, 181
idyllic, xvi, xix, xxv, 30–31, 137
imagery, xxvii, xxix, 3, 11–12, 18, 35, 51, 62, 69, 120, 135, 137–38, 152, 161, 168
imagination, xii, xvi–xxix, 3, 7, 12–14, 18, 20, 23, 29, 31, 38–41, 62, 65, 67, 77, 98–100, 120, 128–29, 134, 164, 166, 171, 177, 180

immortality. *See* mortality
impositions, 53–55, 64, 77, 100–101, 106, 110, 123, 142
imprisonment, 51–52, 61, 72, 94, 96–97, 102, 110, 134, 141, 152, 159, 170–71
Indian deeds, xxix, 87, 92, 94, 102, 105–7, 111
Indian removals, xxvii, xxix, 95–96, 105. *See also* Vanishing Indian (myth of)
individual (humans), xxvii, 21, 26, 35, 50, 60, 89–90, 92, 99, 103–5, 131–34, 169
industrialization, 6–10, 14, 31, 103, 129–32, 143
infinite, 120, 125–26, 137, 177, 182
inherited characteristics, 68–70, 87, 133, 135
innocence, 4, 24, 30, 34, 122, 152, 167, 169, 171
instinct, xvi, xxiv, 6, 66, 96, 154, 164–69
intelligence, xxiv, 34, 63, 130, 155–56, 165, 167, 170
interpretation, xxi, xxx, 4–5, 25–26, 39, 41, 45–52, 55, 65–66, 71–74, 77, 120, 139, 142, 149, 159
interracial. *See* mixed-blood
intuition, xxii, 127, 132, 154
investigation, ix, xxi, xxv–xxvi, 1, 4, 18, 33, 50–51, 66, 84–85, 87–88, 111, 125, 143, 150, 178–79, 183
irony, xv, xxvii–xxix, 20, 23, 120, 126, 162, 168, 179, 181
Irving, Washington, xiv
isolation, x, xxx, 21, 29–30, 38
Italian landscape, xxix, 3, 150, 156–57, 160, 163
Italian Renaissance, 38, 139, 150–51
Italy, xxiv, xxviii–xxix, 1, 3, 13–14, 38, 149–51, 159–71

judgment, 46–49, 55, 63, 92–94, 100, 113, 137, 182
justice, xix, xxiv, xxvii, 55, 84, 87–96, 101–13, 130, 152, 162, 166–67

labor, 6–8, 122–24, 129
laboratory, xxiii, xxvi, 17, 23, 37
Lamarck, Jean-Baptiste, 69, 133, 157
land as gift, 107, 110–11, 178
land claims, 83, 85–87, 89, 94–99, 104–13. *See also* Indian deeds
land inheritance, 85, 99, 102, 105, 109–13
landownership, 83, 85, 87, 95–113
landscape. *See* American landscape; English landscape; Italian landscape; landscape painting
landscape painting, xiv, xxiii, 21, 139–41. *See also* painting
land squatting, 87, 99, 101, 108–11
language use, xiii, xviii, 29, 39–41, 54, 68, 86, 90–92, 107, 109, 120, 123, 132, 154, 181–82. *See also* figurative language; speech
leaves, ix, 2, 34, 45, 58, 60, 71, 76, 162, 101–2
legends, x, 21–22, 140, 151, 163, 180
liberty. *See* freedom
lifeforms, 33, 133, 161, 178
limited perspective, xv, xxi, 12, 84, 120, 142, 154, 165
Linnaeus, Carl, 69, 154, 171
literary adaptation, xvi, xx–xxi, xxv–xxxi, 182
literature, x, xiii, xv–xvi, xx, xxix, 39, 45, 53, 86, 98, 130, 154. *See also* environmental literature
living things, xiii, 4, 7, 24, 35, 39, 67, 110, 132–33, 151, 154, 157, 163
location, xviii, xxix, 17, 46, 58, 60, 70, 73, 98, 161
Locke, John, xiv, 22, 125
loneliness, x, 24, 56, 58, 76, 96
Longfellow, Henry Wadsworth, ix–x, xxxin1, 181
Lyell, Charles, 69, 133

machine, xix, 5, 38–39, 126, 133–34, 183
magic, 49, 65, 70, 89
Maine, 1–2, 18, 28–30, 97, 105–9, 156

malaria, 151, 159–63
manifest destiny. *See* destiny
maps, xxiii, 83, 92–93, 97, 101, 105–6
marriage, 1, 3, 17, 22, 33–37, 73, 85, 91–92, 111
Marx, Leo, xviii, xix, 5–6, 30
masculine. *See* gender
mask. *See* masquerade
masquerade, xv, xxii, 26–27, 107, 119–20, 129, 182
Massachusetts, 1, 17, 28, 69, 79n51, 91, 122, 150. *See also* Boston; Concord; Salem
mastery of nature. *See* control of nature
materialism, 54, 70, 74, 106, 127, 135
material reality, xxvi, 8–9, 19, 31–32, 49, 70, 74, 90, 98, 122, 124, 132, 138, 141–42, 152, 182–83
Mather, Cotton, 55–56, 93–94
medicine, 13, 69–70, 76, 88, 178–83
meditations, x, xxvi, 7, 35, 61, 149
Melville, Herman, xi, 1, 7, 45, 51
memory, xxix, 4, 28, 72, 87, 91–92, 105, 128, 165
mesmerism, 89, 136
Milton, John, xvi, xix–xx, 63, 68
miraculous, 21, 69, 87, 134, 161
mixed-blood, 90–91, 111, 151, 158, 169, 178–81
modern, xi, xxi, 46, 125, 139, 152, 154, 164, 183
monster, xxi, 38, 112, 154, 165
mortality, xv, 20, 30, 37–39, 62, 85, 119, 123, 129, 141, 178, 183. *See also* death
mosquito, 5–6, 11, 13
Mother Nature, ix, xxxin1, 17, 30, 32, 58–59, 74, 124
mountains, ix, xx, xxiii, xxx, 2, 5, 12, 14, 30–31, 155, 161–65, 170. *See also* White Mountains
murder, 60, 109–10, 141, 152, 156, 160, 163, 165–67, 170
mystery, xv, xvii, xix, xxix, 12, 19, 21, 35, 41, 48, 60, 62, 68, 102, 119, 128–29, 135, 157, 161, 168

mythology, 52, 150–54, 163–64, 169, 171, 177, 182. *See also* classical literature; myths
myths, x, 52, 95, 102. *See also* mythology; Vanishing Indian (myth of)

narrator. *See* limited perspective; unreliable narrator
nationalism, 84–85, 93, 99, 105, 107, 112–13, 168–69, 179
Native American. *See* American Indian
natural environment, x–xi, xxii, xxx, 8, 14, 18–32, 40–41, 46, 52, 62, 128–29, 165, 171
natural history, xv, 14, 20–21, 30, 69, 92, 111, 143, 151, 163, 177
natural law, xiv, xxv, 33, 122, 124, 139, 142
natural limits, xii, xxviii, 12, 37–38, 40–41, 89, 119, 123, 126, 144, 151
natural order, 6, 60, 70–71, 133, 142–43, 151, 164, 167, 183
natural philosophy, ix, xii–xviii, 4, 6, 33, 36–37, 40, 66, 69–71, 73, 76, 96–97, 122, 125–26, 130–31, 135, 138, 141, 143
natural processes, xiii, xxviii, 6, 10–13, 18–24, 31–42, 45–46, 70–71, 127
natural rhythms. *See* rhythms of nature
natural rights, xiv, 87, 91, 95, 104–5, 110–11, 127, 178
nature and civilization. *See* nature and culture
nature and culture, xiii, xxv, xxix, 17–18, 40–42, 56, 57, 71, 77, 130
nature writing, ix, xi, xiii, xiv, xvi, xxii, xxv, xxvi, xxix, xxx
New England, x, xxvi, xxix, 1, 3, 18–23, 49, 53–55, 57, 60, 67–69, 85, 90–91, 94, 96–99, 106, 108, 135
newness, 4–5, 33, 35, 52, 124, 126, 129, 136, 144
new world, xix, xxv, 5, 27–28, 33, 50, 52, 54, 58, 69, 130, 141, 178

New York, 1, 3, 18–19
Niagara Falls, ix, 1–2, 19
nonfiction, xiii, xxiii, xxvi, xxxiin17, 1–14, 18, 19, 40–41
nonhuman, xiii–xiv, xxii, xxv–xxvi, 1–2, 6–7, 11, 13–14, 17–19, 26, 33, 40–42, 50, 68, 73–77, 102, 119, 124, 132, 144, 154–59, 164, 167–69
novel, xvi, xxi, xxvii, xxxiv–xxxvn81, 9, 16n33, 57, 63, 98–100, 156, 181

observation, ix–xii, xv, xix, xxiii–xxvi, 1, 4, 8–13, 17–22, 26, 33–37, 45, 61–69, 87, 125–29, 133–36, 142, 156, 165, 177
ocean. *See* sea
offspring, 59, 70, 85, 91, 158
optimism, 4, 52, 75, 122, 129, 142
organic, 74, 85–86, 91, 135, 161
original relation with nature, xxvi, 4, 17, 83, 85, 126, 151, 169, 171
original sin, xi, 63, 67–68, 99, 105, 107. *See also* sin
origins, xii, xxi, xxiv, 48–49, 51–53, 83–85, 91–92, 105, 133, 151, 157–58, 167, 171, 183. *See also* original sin; sources

pacifism, 29, 93–94, 159, 181
pagan, 27–28, 53, 63, 151
Paine, Thomas, xiv
painting, xi, 12, 34, 46, 78n6, 132, 139–40, 160, 166. *See also* landscape painting
pantheism. *See* pagan
paradise, xx, 7, 49–56, 68, 77, 121, 123, 127–28, 140, 143, 152, 167, 178
passion, xiii, xviii, 51, 59–62, 66, 69, 72–74, 89, 126
pastoral, ix, xii, xvi–xxii, xxv–xxix, 1–6, 28–30, 35, 50–52, 75–77, 119–22, 128–30, 138–40, 143–44, 150, 171, 178
paths, 10, 18, 20, 31, 61, 72, 101, 106, 149, 162, 164

Peabody, Sophia. *See* Sophia Peabody Hawthorne
perception, xiii, xxiv, 12, 19, 26, 41, 46–49, 60, 95, 124–25, 149, 156, 166
persecution, xxiv, 109, 149, 168
personification, 30, 41, 45, 62, 75–76
perspective, xiv, xv, 12, 26, 30, 46, 65, 84, 97, 120, 125, 177
pets, 150, 155–56, 165. *See also* companion species
philosophy. *See* natural philosophy; political philosophy
phrenology, xxiv, 91, 136
physical adaptation, xxiv, xxviii, 71–74, 119, 123, 128–38, 170, 182. *See also* environmental adaptation
physical reality, xiii–xvi, xxii–xxx, 2–3, 5, 8, 12–14, 18–23, 25–26, 30–32, 39–41, 65, 75–77, 121, 125–27, 132, 138–40, 143, 149, 177–83
pictures, xiv, xviii, xxvii, 12, 14, 34, 92–93, 100, 105–6, 123, 135, 140, 168, 182
picturesque, xii, xv, xxix, 12, 119, 128–29
pigs, 122, 129, 141
place, ix, xiv, xx–xxi, xxvi–xxvii, xxxi, xxxiin17, 1–2, 5–7, 24–25, 32, 50, 52, 56–62, 66, 71, 74–75, 84, 87, 91, 99–102, 124, 127–28, 131, 142–43, 160, 162, 169, 183. *See also* displacement; location
plants, xxvi, 7, 10, 13, 18, 20, 35, 75, 85–86, 131–35, 146n53, 158, 164–65
poetry, ix, xiii–xviii, xx, xxii, xxviii, xxx, xxxin1–2, xxxiin17, 4, 10–12, 18, 56, 96, 120–24, 130, 134, 138, 144n2, 163
poison, 13, 36–38, 49, 70, 75, 88, 160–63, 168
political philosophy, xviii, xxvii, xxix, 28, 39, 50, 52, 55, 68, 83–86, 93, 100, 107–8, 120, 131, 144, 158, 168,
pollution. *See* smoke
Praxiteles, 150, 152–55
prayer, 38, 124, 137, 152, 160

predisposition, 88–89, 97, 155, 167
prehistoric, 19, 101, 151, 163, 166, 170–71, 177
principles, 54, 69–70, 122, 133, 164, 167
prison. *See* imprisonment
property disputes, 83, 85, 87, 98, 108
property inheritance. *See* land inheritance
prophetic, 54–55, 62, 119, 132, 142, 169
Providence, 7, 21, 46, 63–64, 69–70, 112–13, 138
pseudoscience, xxiv, 70, 132, 136
psychology, x–xi, xxii–xxv, xxxivn59, 24, 46, 96, 150, 155, 164–65
public, 7, 21, 40, 62, 68, 72, 90–91, 95, 103, 132, 136, 154, 157
publication, xiv, xvi, xvii, 4–5, 18, 39, 83, 86, 157, 172n25
Puritan, xii, xvi, xxi, xxv–xxvii, 5, 19, 25–29, 41, 46–77, 83, 89, 92–97, 103–8, 111, 168, 178, 180

Quaker, xxvi, 53, 93–94, 97

race, xxiv, xxix, 17, 62, 83–86, 89–92, 96–97, 102–3, 111–13, 124, 144, 149, 154, 158–59, 163–64, 168–70, 178–82
racism, xxiv, 84, 97, 151, 168–70, 178
realism, xiv, xviii–xx, 56, 99, 120, 138
reality. *See* physical reality
redemption, 53, 63–64, 68, 74, 127, 152, 161, 169
reform, ix, 32, 72, 123–26, 129–30, 132, 134, 142–43
regeneration, 31, 35, 86
regional, xxi, 12, 21, 25, 29–30, 67, 85, 92, 97–98, 160
religion, xxx, 4, 25–29, 49–58, 70, 76–77, 86–87, 93–94, 96–97, 105, 122–23, 129, 149, 152, 160–61, 167, 171, 182
Renaissance. *See* American Renaissance; British Renaissance

representation of nature, x–xxiii, xxxiin17, 2, 6, 12, 14, 39–42, 45, 49, 64, 76–77, 96, 99, 149, 154, 159, 169
resolution, 70, 85, 110–13, 125, 157–59, 170, 183
restorative, xx, 4, 29, 76–77, 102, 110, 111, 140, 142, 151, 162, 164–65, 171
revelation, xx, 5, 8, 23, 45–46, 48, 52, 62, 67, 72, 88–89, 94, 101, 125, 129, 132, 143, 160, 170
revolution, social, xxiv, xxx, 91, 141. *See also* American Revolution; industrial revolution
Revolutionary War. *See* American Revolution
rhetoric, xviii, xxii, xxix, 36, 41, 52–53, 55, 62, 83, 91, 93, 95
rhythms of nature, ix, 24, 71, 97, 136, 144, 152, 167, 178
rivers, ix, 1–2, 10–11, 18, 20, 22, 31, 33–34, 56
rocks, xxiv, 10, 14, 20, 23, 56, 97, 131
romance, ix, xiv–xvi, xx–xxx, 3–7, 14, 18, 32, 39–40, 46, 50–51, 57–59, 74–77, 83–88, 98–100, 107, 110–12, 122–23, 128, 130, 136, 139, 142, 144, 149, 151–52, 157–58, 160, 168–71, 177–81
Romanticism, x, xiv, xxii, xxviii, xxx, 2–3, 12, 18–19, 24, 27, 29–30, 45, 59, 67, 74–75, 119, 121, 125, 127
Rome, 10, 14, 150, 151–53, 155, 159–63, 166, 168, 171, 179
Rousseau, Jean Jacques, 130, 140
ruins, 9–10, 26–27, 55, 60, 149, 159–63, 171, 180
rural. *See* countryside

Salem, xxvii, 1–3, 28–29, 54, 63, 65, 67, 69–70, 91, 93–95, 97–100, 106, 109, 133
Salem witch trials, xxvii, 93–94, 97–100. *See also* witches and witchcraft
sanctity, 31, 36, 38, 57, 61, 162
satire, xvi, xxi, xxii, xxviii, 120–21, 128, 181

scenery, xiv, xxiii, xxvi, xxix, 1, 10, 13–14, 16n33, 18, 30, 41, 150, 165, 181. *See also* descriptions; landscape
science, xi, xvii, xxiii–xxv, xxx, 23, 36–39, 49, 65–66, 69–71, 76, 89, 91, 123, 130–36, 154–57, 161, 173n53, 177–78, 182–83
scientific racism, xxiv, 84–85, 91, 151
scientist, 23, 36–39, 69, 130, 161
sculpture, xxiv, xxviii, 34–35, 146n53, 150–55
sea, xxix, 3, 23, 28, 53, 58–59, 68, 71, 76, 79n51, 95
seasons, x, xvi, 2, 7–8, 13, 20, 27–28, 58, 102, 127, 135, 160, 162, 170, 171
secrets of nature, ix, xxiv, 4, 12–13, 19, 30, 61–62, 69–70, 75, 84, 88–89, 94, 99, 107, 127, 137
Sedgwick, Catharine Maria, xiv, 1, 95
senses, xxiv–xxv, 22, 67, 124–26, 160
sensibilities, xxvi, xxx, 36, 49, 51, 53, 75, 126, 137, 142. *See also* environmental sensibility; senses
sermons, 48, 51–55, 62, 65, 79n28, 89. *See also* clergyman
settlers, xvi, 21, 23, 27, 29–30, 54, 58, 62, 65, 93, 95, 97, 101, 107–8, 130
shadows, xxvii, xxix, xxxi, 2, 10, 12–13, 20, 27–29, 34, 37, 48–51, 56, 64, 67, 71, 85–87, 94, 129, 132, 164, 166, 168
Shakespeare, William, xvi, xix, xx, xxviii, 111
sickness. *See* disease
sight, xiii, xix, 9, 12–13, 24, 26–27, 30–31, 37, 41, 48, 92, 120, 124, 126, 135, 142–43, 160. *See also* eyes
simplicity, xviii, 4, 102, 132, 165, 170, 182
sin, xi, 31, 64, 67–68, 72, 105, 134, 137, 169. *See also* guilt; original sin
skepticism, xxi, xxii, xxiv, xxviii, 5, 22, 37, 47–49, 83, 95, 107, 126, 159, 168, 183
slaveholders, 83, 106, 158, 171

slavery, xxv, xxix, 83, 86, 99, 101, 103–6, 112, 158–59, 168–71, 174n97, 181–82. *See also* Fugitive Slave Law
smoke (pollution), 10, 30, 132
soil, xxvii, 9, 28, 30–31, 52, 87, 98, 101–2, 106, 124, 130, 132, 135, 138, 159–65
solipsism. *See* subjectivity
soul, xxiv, xxx, 7, 26, 40–41, 46, 52, 59–60, 62, 65, 77, 104, 124, 135, 154, 157, 160, 170, 178
sources, xix, 40, 45–46, 63, 75–77, 84, 93, 104, 106, 126, 143–44, 178. *See also* authority; origins
space, xvii, xx, xxii, xxv, xxvi, 12, 14, 31, 34, 50, 52, 60, 100, 110, 120, 122, 125–26, 131, 143, 162–63, 165
species, xii–xiv, xxiv, 35, 71, 91–92, 133, 154, 157–58, 167, 171, 183. *See also* companion species
specimen, xxiv, 89–91, 134, 182
speculation, xxv, 13, 19, 32, 69, 103, 108, 128, 159
speech, xxx, xxxiv–xxxivn81, 28, 37, 61, 112, 149, 159
Spenser, Edmund, xii, xvi, xix–xx, xxxiiin38, 51
spirituality, xxi, xxx, 8, 32, 49, 63, 65, 70, 73, 76–77, 124, 128, 142, 144, 151, 160, 182–83
state of mind, 5, 13, 46, 124, 160–61
state of nature, 32–33, 140, 154, 156, 158, 163, 167, 169, 171
statue. *See* sculpture
stones. *See* rocks
stories, xi, xiii, xvi, xxiii, xxiv, xxvi–xxx, 2, 5, 18–42, 45–51, 57–61, 67–70, 73, 77, 84–85, 88–89, 94–98, 103–5, 109–12, 120, 122, 129–32, 143, 151, 152, 155–58, 163, 169–72, 180, 183
Stowe, Harriet Beecher, 83, 86
subjectivity, xxv, xxxiin17, 12, 26, 41, 120, 127, 142
suffering, xxiv, 39, 47, 72, 90, 161, 180

sun, xvi, 7, 11, 18, 45–46, 48, 56, 60, 63, 71, 75, 77, 135, 157, 160–61, 163, 170
supernatural, xxiv, xxvii, 45–48, 63–64, 69–70, 75, 77, 87–88, 113, 120
superstition, 27, 59, 61, 93
suspicion, xii, 25–26, 29, 34, 41, 59–61, 69–71, 74–77, 84, 87–88, 92–93, 121, 126–27
sustainability, 65, 102, 129–31, 141, 143–44
symbol, xxii, 45, 49, 51, 57, 74, 93, 124–25, 146n53, 163, 182
sympathy with/of nature, xxviii, xxxin3, 7, 11, 22, 30, 36–39, 52, 59, 63–64, 69, 73–77, 149, 151, 155–56, 159, 164–67, 169, 171

territory, 60, 77, 92, 94, 97, 103–9, 112
terror. *See* horror
Theocritus, xvi
theology, ix, xxiv, xxxin1, 4–8, 25–26, 28, 35, 49–56, 64–68, 70, 76–77, 90, 93, 120, 124, 127, 137, 161. *See also* divine; Providence
theory, xiii, xxii–xxv, 38–40, 49, 63, 65, 67, 69–71, 76, 84, 123–25, 128, 132–36, 155–57, 161
Thoreau, Henry David, ix, xi, xii, 3–4, 17, 45, 128, 180
tombs. *See* graves
tragedy, xx, 57
train (railroad), 5–6, 8, 10–11, 102
tranquility of nature, 6, 11, 104, 180, 183
transcendence, xxii–xxiii, 77, 119–20, 122, 125
Transcendentalism, ix–xiv, xxi, xxv–xxvi, xxx, 1–6, 17–18, 31, 35–36, 39–41, 50, 53, 75–76, 120–31, 138–39, 142, 183
transmutation, xxiv, xxx, 60, 68–71, 76, 133–34, 157. *See also* evolution
travel writing, x, xxviii, 1–3, 9–11, 18–21, 149, 169

treatise, xvi, xxiii, 91, 157
trees, xvi, 2–3, 7, 10–12, 18, 20, 24–25, 28–31, 34–35, 56, 58–59, 71, 75, 125, 128, 131–32, 136, 150, 154, 161–65, 171, 181
truth, xv, xviii, xx, xxi, xxii, xxv, xxvii, 1, 4–5, 12, 36, 40, 51, 64, 72–74, 84–85, 93, 136, 151
Tuscany, 160–61, 163–64
types, 51, 124, 133, 135–36

ugliness, 6, 9–10, 119, 134, 137–38, 144n2, 160, 162
universe, ix, xxv, xxvi, 4, 17, 63, 125–26, 134, 143, 177
unnatural, 24, 33, 48, 51, 58, 73, 100, 122, 163
unreliable narrator, xxx, 77, 84, 120, 127, 140
urban. *See* city
utopia, xxviii, 27, 41, 52, 128, 130, 141, 144

Vanishing Indian (myth of), 90–91, 95–96, 102
vegetables, 6–7, 13–14, 18, 129, 133–34
violence, 11, 40, 86–87, 93–94, 97, 102–4, 108–10, 149–52, 155, 158–59, 164, 167, 169, 178, 180
Virgil, xvi, xix
visibility, 49, 101, 105, 119, 125, 128, 131, 161–62
visionary, xx, xxiii, 4, 27, 31, 36, 40–41, 52–55, 63–64, 68, 98, 105, 123, 133–34, 143–44, 152, 169, 181

vitality, xvii, 19, 23, 25, 41, 52, 59, 132, 135, 142, 160, 171

Walden, xxvii, 4–5, 8, 11, 17, 128
Water, 11, 77, 101, 102, 154, 164, 171
wealth, 85, 87, 89, 100, 106–8
weather, xvi, xix, 7–8, 18–21, 27, 60, 75, 102, 123, 127–28, 132, 135, 143, 157, 160–63, 170–71
weeds, 9, 10, 13, 69, 75, 138
westward expansion, xxiii, 83, 91, 107
White Mountains, xxiii, 1–2, 19–23
white supremacy, 58, 62, 84, 90, 93–95, 170
wilderness, 21, 25, 27–31, 49–62, 64, 76, 100, 110, 163, 177–78
Williams, Raymond, xvii, xviii, xix
wind. *See* air
Winthrop, John, 5, 46–47, 52–56
witches and witchcraft, xxvi, 1, 3, 25, 50, 52–53, 57, 59–61, 87–90, 109, 179. *See also* Salem witch trials
woods, ix, xv, xx, xxvii, 2–5, 17–18, 24, 28–29, 31, 56, 59–60, 62, 67, 76, 102, 104, 123, 130, 136, 154–55, 163–66, 179, 181
Wordsworth, William, xvi, 12
wrongdoing, xxvii, xxix, 69–73, 83–113, 152, 163–64, 166, 168–69, 178. *See also* sin

youth, 1, 18, 22–25, 28–29, 38, 61, 64, 68, 72–73, 111–12, 135–38, 140, 162

About the Author

Steven Petersheim is a professor English living with his family north of Boston. He is co-editor of *Writing the Environment in Nineteenth-Century American Literature: The Ecological Awareness of Early Scribes of Nature* and has published numerous articles and book chapters on Hawthorne and nature. His most recent work engages ecotheology, poetics, and ethnic literature.

www.ingramcontent.com/pod-product-compliance
Lightning Source LLC
Chambersburg PA
CBHW070828300426
44111CB00014B/2488